When Will the Joy Come?

Telling the Story True

ABENA AMPOFOA ASARE,
ROBIN PHYLISIA CHAPDELAINE, AND
MICHELLE DIONNE THOMPSON

The seed for this collection was planted within a writing group for Black women historians. We met sporadically over the years and tried to support one another through the turbulence of academic life. When we started having these group conversations, most of us were on the tenure track, one of us was an adjunct professor. As we worked to achieve our academic goals, we celebrated our successes and shared the challenges in moving toward promotion. Ours were not idle complaints that the process was hard. We expected our academic journeys to be rigorous. These were conversations about the profound challenges we faced in our personal and professional lives as we moved forward.

As mothers, educators, and scholars, we needed support from our academic institutions. We grappled with jobs that failed to meaningfully support our parenting journeys as service was heaped on us. There was no room to refuse any of it. There was no letting up on teaching loads and the support we provided students (even as an adjunct). Each of us are mothers of Black males ranging from age seven (currently) to adulthood. We all grappled with school systems that did not respect our children's minds, bodies, and souls.

There were not enough hours in the day to be fully with our young people and do the jobs we were "lucky to have" in the ways we wanted to. We worked for institutions that often lacked the resources to fully support our scholarly work. Nevertheless, we continued to teach, we continued to write. Some of us changed jobs, some of us hopscotched around the country, others stayed put. Some of us started businesses, others had more children, others got divorced. Some of us faced health crises, most of us contemplated leaving academia, a few of us lost parents, some of us earned tenure. Throughout it all, we came together to focus on our writing. What should I include in my tenure packet? How do I press forward with this book or that article despite the circumstances? What are the best ways to approach that grant proposal? Always, our question was: How do we keep writing through, despite, and regardless of our experiences? Then came COVID-19.

Ten months into a global pandemic we gathered again. When we met virtually in January 2021, the virus that had taken over 79,000 lives in the United States in that month had changed much about our lives, our labor, and our sense of these. In a society profoundly shifted on its axes, much had also stayed the same. George Floyd's public murder spurred a wave of protest and a flood of press releases and public rhetoric that the U.S. media insisted, oddly, was the substance of a racial reckoning. The COVID vaccine, it was clear, would become another commodity to be haggled over and hoarded in the global marketplace. Each crisis that predated COVID-19—climate destruction, the rise of global fascism, the yawning U.S. wealth gap, American racial terror—remained with us. The unfolding tragedies were not new, but our vantage point had been altered, as it had for many around the country. Now we were thrust, precipitously, nearer to the "wreckage of a train that has been careening down the track for years."[1] When we began our writing group meeting, our usually brief introductory check-ins became an outpouring. We had always been so concerned with our writing, but now we could talk only about our living. Amid the joy of our reconnection, there was a palpable fear: Black academic women were dying young before the global pandemic.[2] How would we fare now? Each of us spoke about the dangers facing our communities and how these were settling into our bodies, spirits, and minds. Now, there was no talk of strategies, no techniques offered, no how-to books recommended. The succor that we could offer was to bear witness to one another's experiences, to watch the doubts, losses, and sorrows roll out with the tears. The best that we could do was to look into one another's faces without flinching and with tenderness. If the pandemic is a portal, as Arundhati Roy prophesied, we glimpsed that the doorway to Black academic women's survival would begin with this single act: telling the story true.

Together in this moment, we decided to take space to confront the emotive processes that accompany Black women's journeys through academia.

Building on Black feminist theory's commitment to locating "alternative epistemologies," we invited sister scholars to consider the question of our joy—specifically, when and if it might come—so as to push open the door to the place where we safekeep our affective and emotive experiences of academia.[3] Black scholars have long been documenting sexism, racial microaggression, classism, and other types of identity-based exclusion in academic settings. A recent #BlackInTheIvoryTower Twitter thread created a new public space to gather Black scholars' stories of struggle and words of collective encouragement. Over the past thirty years, an assortment of texts about Black academic women's labor have been published. Monographs and edited collections in this vein can be placed in three main categories: Black women's experiences in faculty, administrative, and leadership positions where sexism, microaggressions, and overt racism prevail; Black women's experiences in specific disciplines, such as women's studies, education, sociology, and history; and works that expose institutional and pedagogical challenges facing Black women educators and offer potential avenues for transformation.

Black women have fought to have a place in U.S. higher education institutions, as Stephanie Y. Evans shows in her comprehensive *Black Women in the Ivory Tower, 1850–1954: An Intellectual History*. Throughout the nineteenth and twentieth centuries, our foremothers accessed college and university education at great cost, in order to pursue our human potential and to equip our communities with the power and resources necessary for survival and thriving.[4] Having walked through those doors, Black women scholars find themselves on no easy road. *Presumed Incompetent: The Intersections of Race and Class for Women in Academia* (2012), a pathbreaking work that explores the contradictions plaguing U.S. higher education, displays the power of personal narratives to "bridge the epistemological gap[s]" shrouding women of color's experiences within academia's "byzantine patterns of race, gender, and class hierarchy."[5] Adding to this growing literature and aligned with popular and scholarly currents, this volume tarries with the question of Black academic women's joy. We pursue stories of joy lost, sought, discovered, and imagined to "foreground a flourishing relation of the self to the self."[6] We know now that our pleasure, delight, and rejoicing are neither incidental nor irrelevant to the political and institutional transformations that we seek. After all, the ivory tower is yet another institution that Black women were not meant to survive. Ironically, today, we are portrayed as "change agents" whose labor should be directed toward undoing the entrenched exclusions of these same institutions.[7] "What is it like to be a black woman professor in a white university?" literary scholar Nellie Y. McKay asked in her 1983 article "Black Women Professor—White University." "I sometimes like to think that I contribute in some small way to a better understanding of a shared humanity."[8] The contributions of Black women are clear, but what is the cost?

In "The Double-Edged Sword: Coping and Resiliency Strategies of African American Women Enrolled in Doctoral Programs at Predominately White Institutions" (2014), Marjorie C. Shavers and James L. Moore III use the metaphor of the "double-edged sword" to name the high price that Black women pay for their resiliency and progress within toxic academic institutions. Finding a way through, as Prisca Anuforo, Elizabeth Locke, Myra Robinson, and Christine Thorpe explain in chapter 13 of this volume, may leave you with a "back of steel." However, affixing this new, impenetrable hardware to the tender parts of the spine may not be entirely painless or benign. "Black women," Shavers and Moore muse, "are faced with the dichotomy of choosing to persist academically at the expense of their overall well-being."[9] There is no doubt that Black academic women are resilient, but what about our joy?

Shanna Greene Benjamin's breathtaking biography of Nellie Y. McKay reveals the sacrifice and maneuvering that lay beneath this academic ancestor's determined assertion: "Black women professors like it here [in the university]. We aim to stay." After her death, Nellie McKay's dissemblance was discovered by the colleagues she left behind. This Black woman professor completely "rewrote her past to pursue her ambition," keeping the existence of a daughter, a son, a divorce, and even her true age, hidden. For McKay, narrating an "academic persona" was a survival strategy, a way to evade the strictures of racism, classism, and sexism that pervade academia and threatened to bind her wings before she could even catch air. But as one eulogist noted at her funeral, "Perhaps it left her feeling quite alone."[10] We do not know the emotional consequences of McKay's choice to keep "half her life in shadow," even from her closest colleagues. A wordsmith by profession, she did not write about this. Shaped by the silences of McKay and many others, this volume publicly attends to the emotional and psychological complexity accompanying Black women's journey through the academy. *Telling the story true*, we suggest, matters, both for ourselves and the institutions we support, lead, invest in, and inhabit.

This collection is part of the tradition of "Black women . . . located within, around, and against the academy" coming together to reflect on the same. In 1994, revolutionary abolitionist scholar Angela Davis identified celebration of self, recognition of foremothers, and collective self-defense as the goals drawing Black academic women together to reflect and analyze. By centering Black women's pursuit of joy within the academy/despite the academy/in tension with the academy, this collection suggests one additional lens through which to view our sojourn through the halls of the ivory tower. In this book, joy is a semantic placeholder; it is a way to approach the alchemic admixture of well-being, pleasure, alignment, and purpose that, in our experiences and observation, can be elusive for ourselves and other sister scholars. Amid "all our wonderful, complicated, and sometimes frustrating diversity," Black academic women must consider where, when, and if joy enters our livelihoods; in this way, we bend our bodies and spirits toward our full humanity.[11] Without attending to joy, our capacity to locate, experience, and create pleasure alongside our labor, Black women's journey through the academy may appear as yet another site in which we are, in the words of Zora Neale Hurston's character Janie Crawford, "de mules uh de world."[12] It is our birthright to carefully consider the consequences of our labor *on ourselves*. Meditating on our joy is tactical; it is a strategic foregrounding of Black women's "struggle . . . to escape the new forms of servitude awaiting them, and to live as if they were free."[13] Black women will not be reduced, we insist, to their productive or reproductive capacity.

If, as foundational Black feminist theorist Patricia Hill Collins writes, "most African-American women have grasped this connection between what one does and how one thinks," Black women's particular labor in the academy shapes both body and mind.[14] There is scholarship documenting the obstacles, microaggressions, differential workloads, student skepticism, and lack of collegiality that Black women professors face and our coping strategies in institutions that are often "hostile and unwelcoming."[15] However, publicly dwelling on the psychological and emotional consequences of our experiences is risky. *Telling Histories: Black Women Historians in the Ivory Tower* (2008) shares the stories of eighteen Black women historians and their significance to African American history. Editor Deborah Gray White describes the volume's contributors as doubly brave; they are "brave to be among the first large cohort of black female American historians and brave to share with readers some of their experiences in the profession."[16] Assigning someone the badge of bravery is always a recognition of risk; *telling the story true* is not without reprisals and hazard. "To be heard as making a tiresome complaint," Sara Ahmed writes, "is to be heard as being tiresome, as distracting somebody from doing '*important work elsewhere.*'"[17] Black women exist, as Ahmed recognizes, within particular historical narratives that make it likely that our testimonies about institutional violence are heard as redundant, unimportant, or tiresome. We had to consider this history and what we were exposing sister scholars to when we invited women to contribute to this collection. Ungrateful. Mentally ill. Socially difficult. Complicated. Impolitic. Indiscrete. Failure. Complainer. Each of these, all of these (indeed, there are more), are labels that Black academic women court when they choose to tell the story true. We weighed the risk of being called openly the names we are already called in secret. Then we considered the reality of our living and dying and decided to open the door for those who would step through.

We are, after all, in one another's good company. Audre Lorde's 1981 masterpiece, "The Uses of Anger: Women Responding to Racism," describes the social and psychic alienation that accompanies Black academic women as they go about their work. "I speak out of direct and particular anger at an academic conference, and a white woman says, 'Tell me how you feel but don't say it too harshly or I cannot hear you.' But is it my manner that keeps her from hearing, or the message that her life may change?" Not for nothing, when Lorde gives this talk, she is the keynote speaker at the annual National Women's Studies Association Annual Conference. Just picture Sister Audre at the podium in Storrs, Connecticut, laying it out for the people, some nodding vigorously, others shifting uncomfortably in their seats! Her treatise on anger's righteousness and utility includes a snippet of poetry.

> Everything can be used except what is wasteful (you will need to remember this when you are accused of destruction).[18]

This, for us, is the talisman and keepsake.

More than three decades later, Claudia Rankine's *Citizen: An American Lyric* is chosen for the National Book Critics Circle Award for poetry. Among its many triumphs, *Citizen* describes the harrowing emotional harm facing Black women in academia, because they are Black women in academia.

> You are in the dark, in the car, watching the black-tarred street being swallowed by speed; he tells you his dean is making him hire a person of color when there are so many great writers out there.
>
> You think maybe this is an experiment and you are being tested or retroactively insulted or you have done something that communicates this is an okay conversation to be having.
>
> Why do you feel okay saying this to me? You wish the light would turn red or a police siren would go off so you could slam on the brakes, slam into the car ahead of you, be propelled forward so quickly both your faces would suddenly be exposed to the wind.[19]

In this poem, the acts of interpersonal violence blighting a Black academic woman's everyday life keep the subject trapped in a defensive state. Is it valuable, then, for the target to speak out about the "commonplace daily verbal, behavioral, and environmental indignities, whether intentional or unintentional, that communicate hostile, derogatory, or negative racial slights and insults to the target"? Does it help our communities when these stories emerge in the public eye? Is change possible within these academic institutions, and might Black women's journeys through—in practice or in the subsequent telling—catalyze this change? And what does this impulse to value Black women's testimonies only if these stories help to "fix" institutions say about just how little Black women are loved? In contrast to microaggression scholarship's focus on "coping mechanisms" and "resiliency,"[20] Claudia Rankine exposes the violence and how it eats at our peace. Ancestor Audre Lorde reclaims the "well-stocked arsenal of anger" that is "potentially useful against those oppressions, personal and institutional, which brought that anger into being."[21] Telling our stories may be a road to our own survival or a means of destroying the world; perhaps these are one and the same.

Even as we focus on Black women's journeys through academia, we are aware that this collection does not encompass the totality of what Black women face as they labor within higher educational institutions. We use the term *women* as a point of inclusion; we include all who identify themselves as such, regardless of and in conversation with other facets of identity. The first point of narrowing is the nation-state: most chapters are rooted in the United States context. Apart from this volume's third section—Annette Kappert's meditation in chapter 12 inspired by Britain's academic milieu, Cécile Accilien's visitation with the histories of Caribbean marronage in chapter 15, an anonymous contribution by four Black German women in chapter 16, and Abena Ampofoa Asare's transnational survey of Black academic women's writing in chapter 17—these reflections emerge from the twenty-first-century neoliberal U.S. academy. In addition, most of the contributors write about their experiences in predominantly white institutions (PWIs). Although some of the contributors studied at or have worked in historically Black colleges and universities (HBCUs), most of the chapters reflect the specific milieu of the PWI.

Another point of narrowing is the collection's focus on scholars—researchers, teachers, students, administrators. "Why, in fact, is it considered more important to defend the name of the assistant professor who is refused tenure than the secretary who is kept in a dead-end job? Or the woman of color janitor who is not allowed to unionize?" Angela Davis asked in 1994.[22] The same question could be posed today. Teachers, students, and administrators are not the only Black women laboring in our universities—far from it. Black women change and are changed by academia as they work in the janitorial staff, as administrative assistants, event planners, childcare workers, and in myriad other positions. Our hope is that by critically listening to the scholars in this volume, we carve out space to consider the working conditions, labor, and joy of other workers located in twenty-first-century universities and colleges.

Another winnowing point to which we must attend: the various types of precarity that structure the lives of Black academic women also shape our ability to contribute to a collection such as this one. Many of these chapters speak directly to the ways universities and colleges resist seeing, acknowledging, or supporting the full lives of the Black women in their midst. Disability, illness, neurodiversity, family life—there are myriad responsibilities and rigors that shift Black women's relationship to academia's vaunted productivity standards and thus our ability to participate in a collection such as this. There were sisters in our orbit who wanted to participate in this volume but were unable to because of already massive work- and life loads. The ongoing and deepening crisis in U.S. colleges and universities, what has been called the "adjunctification of higher education," means that many scholars work under conditions in which pausing to write and reflect on the journey seems impossible. Some in our number are also no longer here. Among the many sisters whose spirits inspire this collection we remember Thea Hunter. Her story of life and death as academic contingent labor, recorded in the *Atlantic* (2019),[23] reminds us to name, as often as necessary, the violence of the neoliberal university as a "hyper producer of inequality for marginalized populations, particularly academic women of color."[24]

PART I: "CATCH WHILE YOU CLIMB"

The title of this book's first section, "Catch While You Climb," refers to three aspects of Black women's experiences in the ivory tower. The first relates to "catching up" as a process whereby Black women become attuned to the institutional processes, both formal and informal, that prevent them from achieving success in their academic positions. The second refers to "catching one's breath"—finding space to reflect, recharge, and heal—in an environment where these women are expected to work twice as hard only to get half as far with little recognition. The third aspect, "catching the hand of others," refers to the importance of mentorship and support systems, a notion that Karsonya Wise Whitehead has championed.[25] As reflected in this volume, we must note that recruiting and maintaining the presence of Black women in higher education requires that those of us with tenure and seniority be willing to serve as mentors and as a safety net to those who come after us.

This part includes personal experiences focused on the transition from graduate school to visiting assistant professorships and tenure-track employment. The diversity of experiences is reflected in the style and framework of each chapter. The authors offer critical analyses of power and identity politics at play in the ivory tower as well the physical and mental health struggles Black women often endure with little or no assistance from their respective institutions. Robin Phylisia Chapdelaine, Felice Ferguson Knight, and Ashley D. Clemons pursue an autoethnographic approach to illuminating their academic trajectories. In chapter 1, Chapdelaine shares her third-year review process and delineates the challenges of working at a predominantly white institution where there is little to no mentorship for Black women. She interrogates the prevalence of white supremacy in the ivory tower and the rage that it provokes for Black women. In chapter 2, Knight calls attention to a revelatory tradition of Black women's writing. Incorporating excerpts from her journal entries during her job search, which spanned almost six years, she analyzes the emotional tribulations accompanying her transition from graduate school to adjunct employment to a tenure-track position at an institution with a complicated legacy in her family's history. Clemons also shares her graduate school and job search journey in chapter 3, exploring the ways chronic illness, economic precarity, and social stigma shaped her pathways. Using the framework of Black music as an analytic tool, she addresses both racism and ableism. Her artful use of music lyrics to reinforce "daily mantras, affirming incantations, and guided meditations" speaks to African Americans' long history of using voice and song to heal the mind, body, and soul.

Another common theme among our authors is the alienation of working in an ivory tower that is a site of capitalist exploitation and so, routinely, lacks meaningful support systems and opportunities to create affinity among colleagues. In consideration of Black women's graduate school experiences and their climb toward earning a PhD, in chapter 4 Kristian Contreras asks the question, "What can the doctorate mean to Black women when the university relegates us *to* and keeps us firmly *at* the proverbial bottom?" In a call to reenvision the ivory tower, Contreras examines the emotional and intellectual labor Black women graduate students are expected and coerced to perform. Diversity, equity, and inclusion efforts have significantly increased in the past two years, but such efforts have not eradicated the tendency for institutions of higher education to applaud "the mere presence of Black women" and "disappear[] the racist and patriarchal practices that limit our learning."

Who belongs in academia? This is a question that Kimberly M. Stanley attempts to answer in chapter 5. Stanley maps her "invisibility/hypervisibility" in academia as she seeks out emotional, psychological, and financial support. She identifies the ivory tower as a place where "African Americans, single parents, and those differently abled, queer, LGBTQ+, or those whose presence is considered 'nontraditional'" can enter institutions of higher education only through "the cracks" and asks the question, Will the ivory tower "make ya or break ya"? As a testament to her own fortitude and determination, she outlines her personal wellness journey and its sustaining power.

PART II: POLICY AND PRACTICE

Policy and Practice reflects the challenges Black women face as our work is regularly undervalued, we often find ourselves in profoundly isolating circumstances, and we are disproportionately burdened with remedying the systemic racism that is embedded in institutions of higher education. The contributors, ranging from tenured to adjunct professors, reflect on their experiences and suggest concrete ways of navigating the ivory tower. The challenges of "performative wokeness," to quote Sayam Davis, leads Black women to create spaces for sanity and networks for advancement, particularly in predominantly white institutions. However, these institutions often undermine Black women by creating challenging requirements for promotion and tenure or by relegating undervalued diversity, equity, and inclusion work to Black women, work that competes with the scholarly output institutions require for promotion and tenure. As a result, Black women have formed and/or participated in organizations for emotional and professional support, left their institutions, and sometimes built their own businesses to remain whole people.

This section begins with Michelle Dionne Thompson's reflections on her work as a contingent faculty member in a public institution. Rarely afforded opportunities to convert her employment to full-time permanent status, she decided to build a business that supports her body, mind, and soul. As she describes in chapter 6, while not fully outside academia, no longer does Thompson contend with the stresses of thriving within the ivory tower and finds joy ensuring that she does not exploit her own labor. One tool that enabled this transition was creating a community of academic writers so that she could still publish.

Littisha A. Bates and Whitney Gaskins grapple with the challenges of doing diversity, equity, and inclusion work while on the tenure track. Indeed, this work is profoundly undervalued by the institutions: while there is lip service declaring its importance, the work is rarely well resourced, and the recommendations of Black women on these committees are often not implemented. Their chapter 7 offers a list of solutions for changing the status of this work, including incorporating it into the standards required for tenure and promotion and allowing the recommended change to happen.

Heather I. Scott and Nyasha M. GuramatunhuCooper reflect on what it means to have agency in the academic setting, particularly as they earn tenure and promotion. Exhausted from the seven-year process leading up to this remarkable achievement, Black women often face the question of whether they should stay at the institutions that granted them tenure or promotion or use it as an opportunity to move to an institution that may have the same challenges. Unable to fully celebrate and embrace their achievement, in Chapter 8 these authors discuss balancing the interests of the people they love most and the communities they value, ultimately reaching divergent conclusions.

Is it possible for scholars to find joy under these conditions? In Chapter 9 Sayam Davis suggests that even after achieving the pinnacle of tenure track, witnessing the shallow institutional commitment to diversity leaves her in a position to rethink her place within the university. There is little joy as colleagues who were seemingly supportive of her tenure contort themselves to find reasons to leave her isolated as the sole BIPOC scholar in her department. Like Scott and GuramatunhuCooper, she is left grappling with whether it makes sense to stay or leave the institution.

In Chapter 10, Paula W. White, Eva M. Gibson, and Jessica A. Fripp point to the importance of affinity groups for their ability to navigate their roles in the college and university settings. White, Gibson, and Fripp, all tenure-track professors, point to the need to create "communities of resistance," as coined by bell hooks. Performative allyship by white colleagues often creates conditions under which Black women are doing more than service, teaching, and scholarship to earn tenure, conditions that often lead to burnout and vacating the academy. Communities of resistance allow Black women to manage the organizational barriers, the institutional climate, the lack of respect from one's colleagues, the university's unwritten rules for university life, and mentoring, all essential components to ensure success with tenure and promotion.

Tiffany Monique Quash confronts similar questions of agency in a chapter about the inadequate institutional response to claims of harassment and abuse. Sharing a story about her experience as a graduate student who reported the abuse of a faculty member, in Chapter 11 Quash considers where responsibility lies when institutions fail to live up to their standards of protecting vulnerable members of the community.

PART III: THE ENIGMA OF JOY

How many of the women in this volume have faculty unions? How many of us are first-generation PhDs? How many of us carry significant amounts of debt into our employment, and how do these factors (and numerous others) shape our work and the capacity for agency and wellness? In the final section, "The Enigma of Joy," women reflect on the factors, both internal and external, that contribute to and separate us from joy as we move through academia. Considering the interplay between individual choices and historical systems, collective solidarity, creative pursuits, and the constraining violence of academia's patriarchy, racism, misogyny, classism and other exclusions, this section's authors plunge into a discussion about not only how to find joy but also what joy may be for Black woman scholars.

The section begins with Annette Kappert's lyrical meditation on the conjoined personal and institutional transformations required for Black women to set a course past the harms of imposter syndrome, self-doubt, and alienation and toward a future of well-being. In chapter 12, Kappert claims nothing less than decolonization as the foundation for Black women scholars' joy and provides a model of ways to think and feel past the neoliberal academe's colonialist language, bargaining, and stagnation.

Subsequently, Prisca Anuforo, Elizabeth Locke, Myra Robinson, and Christine Thorpe offer a sustaining typology of resilience, describing in chapter 13 how Black women leaders in academia might develop the "backs of steel" that preserve and protect them while they wade through the high waters of academe and propel themselves toward excellence.

LeAnna T. Luney and Cassandra Gonzalez consider "the quotidian life of anti-Black womanness" in chapter 14, detailing the practices and institutional norms that allow misogynoir to flourish, unchecked, even in a supposedly progressive ethnic studies department. This chapter exposes the limits of social justice rhetoric alone for creating a space where Black women can thrive and illuminates the institutional transformations required to protect Black women in academe.

In the spirit of planting seeds that point toward joy, Cécile Accilien's chapter on marronage as a survival strategy recovers the inspiration and wisdom of Caribbean social and political history as a resource for Black women scholars navigating academia. Freedom, Accilien shows clearly, is part of the process of finding and sustaining joy. Contemporary U.S. academia may not be eighteenth- or nineteenth-century chattel slavery, but as chapter 15 reveals, the lessons of those ancestors who stole themselves away as acts of resistance are evergreen sites of sustenance.

In chapter 16, four Black German women who wish to remain anonymous discuss the liminality of their positions within disciplines, nations, and universities that struggle to register their heritage, expertise, or knowledge. Writing together as an act of healing praxis, these authors highlight their diverse experiences of working and joy-seeking within academia. This contribution's power is supported by the authors' decision to claim anonymity. Choosing to reveal and disclose according to their own desire, and not one iota more, illuminates the maneuvering of many Black women scholars who daily discern how to maintain their wholeness while sharing their contributions.

Finally, in chapter 17, Abena Ampofoa Asare considers Black academic women's writing in a transnational lens to search out the geographic and political roots of the harm facing us. By asking where else Black women thinkers ought to go if they hope to thrive, Asare exposes the disturbing continuity within a neoliberal academe that crosses national borders and everywhere asks Black women to "leave some of our world-work—and thus, some of our power—behind." In this chapter, particular landed geographies and the political histories therein are simultaneously sites of oppression and sources of resistance and sustenance. Seeking out the multiple elsewheres available to us, recognizing the power of place, Asare intuits, is a road to joy.

Joy, in the conversation between these scholars, is a matter of autonomy, agency, and community. It is found in the moments of connection and reclamation that each scholar seeks, still, despite the alienating systems through which they journey. Together, these contributions refuse any facile rendering of joy, instead delving into the elusiveness of Black academic women's well-being and thriving. Still, not one of these authors wavers; the potential of joy is not something we are willing to relinquish despite the context of our lives and labor. And perhaps this assertion is the point. In this volume we invited writers to meditate not on our endurance, our resilience, or even our magic but about our joy. Approaching the matter of joy is an invitation to Black academic women to plunge into planes of meaning-making and value, to consider the sensibility that may lie beyond the rubrics of the toxic colonial and slave systems to which we, by dint of our global history, remain tethered. Now, we invite you, our readers, to hear these stories told true and dare to consider your own joy, where it lies, and how it might take shape.

NOTES

1. Roy, "Pandemic Is a Portal."
2. Benjamin, *Half in Shadow*, xiv.
3. Collins, "Social Construction of Black Feminist Thought," 746.
4. Evans, *Black Women in the Ivory Tower*, 1.
5. Gutiérrez y Muhs et al., *Presumed Incompetent*, 2.
6. Stewart, *Politics of Black Joy*, 9.
7. Patton and Haynes, "Hidden in Plain Sight," 6.
8. McKay, "Black Woman Professor," 147.
9. Shavers and Moore, "Double-Edged Sword," 23.
10. Benjamin, *Half in Shadow*, 13, 3.
11. Davis, "Black Women and the Academy," 422.
12. Hurston, *Their Eyes Were Watching God* (1978), 29.
13. Hartman, *Wayward Lives, Beautiful Experiments*, xiii.
14. Collins, "Social Construction of Black Feminist Thought," 748.
15. Ellis, "Impact of Race and Gender," 30–45; Shavers and Moore, "Double-Edged Sword," 18.
16. White, *Telling Histories*, 20.
17. Ahmed, *Complaint!*, 1.
18. Lorde, "Uses of Anger," 7, 8.
19. Rankine, *Citizen*, 11.
20. Sue et al., "Racial Microaggressions in Everyday Life," 271, 283.
21. Lorde, "Uses of Anger," 8.
22. Angela Davis, "Black Women and the Academy," 423.
23. Harris, "Death of an Adjunct."
24. Nzinga, *Lean Semesters*, 2.
25. Whitehead, "Five Women Who Influenced Me."

Part I
Catch While You Climb

CHAPTER 1

I Found My Joy

ROBIN PHYLISIA CHAPDELAINE

I am working within the system, still struggling, still fighting but bending my life a little bit every day to fit my job.

—Karsonya Wise Whitehead, "HBCU Graduates," *Afro* (May 21, 2022)

What does it mean to be or to become an acceptable Black woman in academia? Are there unsaid social and professional parameters to which one must adhere to be considered "palatable" to others in the academic profession? Can such strain on one's professional self leave room for joy in the ivory tower? These are the questions I have asked myself since I entered the halls of higher education in 2014. What I have learned is that the joy I engender is produced from my consistency and determination to push back and push forward despite adversity. In this chapter, I share my experience as a graduate student at Rutgers University as a foundational entry point where I learned to derive strength from my largely student of color cohort and Black women mentors. I also address the importance of "catching up and catching on," "taking time to catch one's breath," and "catching the hand of others" on this journey shared among Black women scholars. In doing so, I will examine my personal experiences where I endured the random application of standards that threatened my inclusion in the ivory tower, a white male colleague's unprofessional behavior, and highlight the need for mentorship among women who share similar intersectional identities. My story, my truth, will unveil why catching up and catching on, catching one's breath, and catching the hand of others is essential to finding joy in the ivory tower.

I received my PhD in women's and gender and African history from Rutgers University where I was ever so fortunate to share physical and intellectual space with strong Black women, including Drs. Carolyn A. Brown,

Deborah Gray White, Jennifer Morgan, and Kim Butler. As with myself, some of these women had young children, went through a divorce while finishing their graduate programs, and navigated the job markets nearly on their own. Additionally, I was part of a diverse cohort that relied upon each other as we navigated graduate school. I developed meaningful friendships with other Black women in graduate school who remain critical confidants to this day. They give me strength. The amazingly supportive institutional environment in which I received my graduate degree has never been replicated during my employment at various universities. I have learned that moving from an extremely supportive environment to the unknown demanded a significant amount of faith and fortitude.

Black women's survival in the ivory tower necessitates constant self-reflection and adjustment. They must "catch up" and "catch on" to what is expected of them according to formal and informal institutional processes as quickly as possible. Black women closely monitor their personal emotions, expressed attitudes, and physical actions to avoid negative responses from colleagues, thus reducing the risk of social ostracization and professional penalization. This is true even when those emotions, expressions, and actions would be considered innocuous or benign had they been exhibited by a non-Black academic. Unlike their non-Black colleagues, Black women have more to lose when their assertive behaviors are read as aggressive. "To catch one's breath" is a method, a habit, that offers a lifeline in the midst of never-ending demands—teaching, scholarship, service—that would ultimately drown the spirit and stunt the scholar. Taking into consideration all that is expected of Black women in the ivory tower, I implore my sister colleagues to catch their breath, to find time to meditate and heal. "Catching the hand of others" is an idea that prioritizes the development of mentorship initiatives between junior and senior Black women academics and administrators. I draw this idea from Karsonya Wise Whitehead's discussion where she gives credit to her academic mentor and states, "She is the hand that pulls me to the top of each academic mountain and reminds me that we are the ones that make the space for the next Black woman to get to the top."[1]

If I am to tell my truth, writing this chapter is a manifestation of my anger and a move toward producing an honest assessment of a traumatic experience—a process that inescapably makes room for joy. During my first two years in my first tenure-track job from Fall 2016 to Spring

2018, I was jointly appointed in a department and a university center. I was tasked with teaching and service responsibilities in each program. I served on a search committee, became a faculty adviser for a student group, joined a steering committee, became a member of the university Academic Integrity Appeals Committee, planned a graduate student conference, served as a research judge for undergraduate and graduate research, offered a summer seminar, served on a grant committee, participated in a student-faculty dorm night, and, perhaps most important, functioned as a safety net for students of color. Students came to me for formal tutoring and informal advice. Even after they finished my course, they would return for the purpose of receiving intellectual and emotional support. As Kristian Contreras notes in chapter 4, "Black women are expected to provide care work within their departments, without question, supporting their counterparts in their academic pursuits as well as the labor that traditionally falls under the domestic sphere." This service "in the margins" is precisely what is rarely valued or formally acknowledged in the ivory tower. Nevertheless, I did all this while maintaining high student evaluation scores and focusing on my scholarship. At the time of pre-tenure review, which occurred at the beginning of my third year, I had one chapter published in an edited volume, three articles under review, and was making significant process revising my book manuscript.

Reflecting on the amount of service I took on during my first two years of employment, I began to catch on. I realize that my tendency to say yes to numerous service requests was in direct correlation to my fear that saying no would negatively impact my pre-tenure review and, in time, tenure review. I now know I could have benefited from having a mentor who previously followed a similar academic trajectory and unburdened me of the idea that working harder and faster would ensure a positive outcome. Rashida Harrison has underscored "the importance of having representation in the midst of the hierarchical muddle that characterizes the ivory tower," where women of color are in a "constant state of negotiation, grappling with issues of race, gender, and scholarship."[2] However, even when mentors are available, I agree with Heidi Safia Mirza, who asserts that sometimes expectations are just higher and that retribution can occur when we, as women of color, do not exceed the standard.[3] In my experience, this has proven to be true.

In March 2019, the dean of the college called to inform me that I had not passed pre-tenure review. I was, of course, disappointed. After receiving the decision, I immediately requested a summation of the votes. I found out that the votes were unanimously in my favor at the department- and college-level committees and from the dean and head of the center with which I was affiliated. Conversely, when the University Promotion and Tenure Committee (UPTC) received my file, they voted unanimously against my continued employment. *They were pushing and I was bending.*

I learned secondhand that as the UPTC reviewed my file, one faculty member expressed frustration with the opinion pieces I published with *Huffington Post.* I had neither listed my public writings on my curriculum vitae nor detailed them in any form in my pre-tenure review application because they were not related to my academic research. But, *who was I* to spend time on public-facing publications? This experience prompted me to think about Mirza's work in which she accurately explains the phenomenon where "there is the 'burden of invisibility' or hypersurveillance: you are viewed suspiciously and any mistakes are picked up and seen as a sign of misplaced authority."[4] It is evident that the faculty member in question searched for information by engaging in her/his/their independent sleuthing, enacting a form of hypersurveillance I had not anticipated. Even so, I did not foresee that my public pieces would be viewed as problematic, as *suspicious.* My work addressed the importance of women's bodily autonomy and the power of the Black vote.[5] Was the critique about the desire to silence my voice? I also wondered, Was the reflex to vote no on my file born from the "contradictory culture of academia" that presumes women of color as inherently "incompetent"?[6] I can only make educated assumptions based on the global scholarship that addresses these issues, but I was determined to have my voice heard. I decided to file a grievance in April 2019 that would request a reconsideration of my pre-tenure file, which ultimately happened during Summer 2019.

Teaching, tending to service commitments, and maintaining a pleasant demeanor on campus was difficult during this time, but I continued to do what was expected of me without fault. As I waited for the grievance process to run its course, a white male faculty member in my college took it upon himself to tell a graduate student, whose thesis I was chairing, that I had not passed pre-tenure review owing to "subpar scholarship." When the student shared the news with me, I was profoundly astonished. No. I was angry with a rage that I had never experienced in an academic setting. *Why would he? How could he?* Soraya Chemaly suggests that women "experience anger as the result of power imbalances" and that they/we "rarely" get to express anger . . . from a position of actual institutional power."[7] I and the other faculty member were both untenured, but his actions were suggestive of the prevalence of power dynamics at play in the ivory tower. He was a white man with little or no concern about the ramifications of his violent actions, something a Black woman could never ignore. *He was pushing and I was bending.*

If our celebrated sister Audre Lorde's claim that "EVERY BLACK WOMAN in America lives her life somewhere along a wide curve of ancient and unexpressed angers" is true, we must interrogate how this anger is sheltered, exposed, and exploited in the ivory tower.[8] Would I accept this act of violence and marginalization? Did I have any power to remedy the damage that had been done? LeAnna T. Luney and Cassandra Gonzalez theorize in chapter 14 that "misogynoir demands the undermining of Black women and femmes to uphold white supremacist and patriarchal thought that is inherently antagonistic to the well-being and flourishing potential of Black women and femmes because it demands their submission to and acceptance of the violence and marginalization that is done to them." I decided to have a brief stern (without yelling or cursing, but yes—I was filled with rage) conversation with him the same day I received the news from the student. I then wrote him a letter several weeks later that read, in part:

> The harm that you have caused is irreversible. I was/am waiting for a decision to be made about my appeal before I made a determination about whether or not to share *any* information with students. I could have departed [redacted] with my professional reputation intact. Unfortunately, you, not me, have determined that our graduate student body is now privy to my current precarious employment status. Even if the decision about my third year review is reversed, I will have to work in an environment wherein the graduate students have likely lost faith in me as an educator and scholar. Furthermore, in addition to the stress brought on by the denial, I now have to contend with the fact that you thought so little of my input and autonomy, or worse that you didn't think about it at all. You inserted yourself into a non-emergency situation. Your actions were completely unnecessary and ultimately professionally damaging.[9]

My predicament brings to mind Chavella Pittman's claim that "while understanding institutional racial oppression is important, one must also attend to interpersonal racial oppression."[10] One could argue that failing pre-tenure review or the subsequent professional assault by a colleague was not an instance of overt racial oppression at the institutional or personal level. However, considering that colleagues in my department had passed pre-tenure review with achievements similar to mine and that it was unlikely that my white male colleague would have sabotaged another white male colleague in the same way, I had to consider potential embedded biases on both accounts. I began to feel justified fighting on my own behalf by filing a grievance, addressing my concern with my colleague, and not giving up even though I lacked institutional power. *I was now pushing back and getting stronger—closer to achieving my joy.*

Four months after receiving the denial, I received a letter from the university president stating that even though the UPTC had once again voted unanimously to end my employment contract, he decided to overturn the decision, explaining that he was giving me "the benefit of the doubt." In the aftermath of this unlikely outcome, it is worth considering the demographic makeup of the committees that are established for the purpose of pre-tenure and tenure review and how that influences overall outcomes. As with other universities, teaching, scholarship, and service are the formal categories by which promotion is denied or awarded at my institution. Although often unsaid, it is undeniable that interpersonal relationships, the ability to fit in, and exhibiting restraint from rocking the institutional boat is of upmost importance when pre-tenure or tenure files are considered. Achieving success in these areas is difficult when inclusion or exclusion may be subconsciously determined by race, class, and gender, intersectional identities over which Black women have little control.

At the time that I began writing this chapter, my tenure file was under review, moving from the department-level to the college-level committee, both of which lacked significant diversity. The university is a predominantly white private institution where the faculty is 85.8 percent white; 3.9 percent Asian/Pacific Islander; 0.0 percent Native American/Alaska Native; 3.1 percent Black/African American; 1.6 percent Latina/o/x; 2.4 percent other race/ethnicity; and 3.1 percent two or more races/ethnicities. There are 54.3 percent self-identified women and 45.7 percent men/trans men among the faculty.[11] I have very few colleagues who share my racial and ethnic background. I am the only woman of color in my department and one of two Black women in my college. Limited access to women with whom I might identify, create affinity, and receive mentorship is one of the more disenfranchising aspects of my appointment. Whereas most non-Black academics at my university have numerous avenues to find and benefit from mentorship, this has not been my experience. However, even when there are substantial administrative efforts to increase diverse faculty, such endeavors do not always result in equity or inclusion.

To fully understand the challenges Black women face in higher education, it is essential that their experiences, *our* experiences, are considered within a framework that uses race, class, and gender as categories of analysis.[12] Kimberlé Crenshaw has shown that "because the intersectional experience is greater than the sum of racism and sexism, any analysis that does not take intersectionality into account cannot sufficiently address the particular manner in which Black women are subordinated."[13] In response to Mirza's call that Black feminists "ask questions about what shapes these worlds and how we are implicated in racist and sexist discourses through our inclusion, exclusion, choice, and participation," I offer my story as an intellectual site where answers might be found.[14]

Accessible and equitable mentorship is a key factor in faculty success and should be a priority for universities, especially those with few Black faculty. It is well known that "in addition to institutionalized sexism and the 'chilly climate' for women in the academy, the studies have also documented that there is a lack of mentorship and networking opportunities for women because there are so few women at the highest rungs of the academic ladder."[15] In chapter 5, Kimberly Stanley adeptly assesses that the ivory tower tends to render Black women "silent, invisible, and dissembled" and that this phenomenon should be a concern, not just to women of color but also to those who publicly proclaim that diversity, equity, and inclusions efforts should stand at the forefront of university goals. Moreover, at the heart of every institutional mission statement is the importance and value of student learning and student-educator relationships. How can students learn from diverse faculty when those faculty members are relegated to the margins if not outright eliminated? Some scholars suggest that one viable method is to institute reverse mentoring, a method whereby underrepresented students mentor underrepresented faculty, which would "reduce the isolation that minority faculty experience at predominantly white" universities.[16] Although reverse mentorship may have positive outcomes, the problem with this approach is that the burden is carried by people of color and not the institution itself. Equitable mentorship is essential to achieving tenure.

Scholarship on how tenure is awarded has shown that even within the same university, there is no standard that is applied evenly among faculty who are under review. Sarita Echavez See goes as far as to claim that "the standards for evaluating faculty are pretty much just as random as any kind of fraternity or sorority."[17] Throughout this edited collection, readers are privy to numerous examples of women who have been charged to provide extraordinary service, including emotional, physical, and intellectual work that exceeds that of their non-Black colleagues, but have shown that this type of invisible service is often unrewarded. Service, as important as it is, continues to create a risk for faculty of color because they are rarely rewarded in concrete ways.[18] Such is not uncommon for Black women scholars. As others have noted, "The negative repercussions of declining invitations to participate in service activities may be intensified for those who are already marginalized from the academy."[19] I can attest to such experiences where my colleagues seek out my participation in various forms of service precisely because of my intersectional identity. And though this work is important and integral to building community and kinship on campus, it can be exhausting and professionally detrimental.

Over the last few years, I have caught my breath and reflected on my journey on the tenure track, especially the period between pre-tenure denial, grievance filing, and subsequent outcome. I began writing this chapter in that liminal state where scholars stand after they have submitted a summary of all their efforts in scholarship, teaching, and service at the time of tenure review. In the time spanning three to five years of service, I have enjoyed a significant amount of success in my peer-reviewed scholarly endeavors. I have published one book, four articles, and two chapters and have this edited volume, two coauthored chapters, and one article forthcoming. I was invited to write a commentary on the history of children and childhood for the premier academic journal in history, have published a pedagogical journal article, and have several other projects in the making. It is with great pride that I note my book, *The Persistence of Slavery: An Economic History of Child Trafficking in Nigeria* (2021), made the top-forty list (at number 17) of bestselling African history academic books within nine months of publication.[20]

Even though the UPTC did not value the work I had done, presumed me to be incompetent, and did not acknowledge my worth and potential as a rising Black woman scholar, I find it useful to think about the larger academic community that values and seeks out my scholarship. This experience has led me to think critically about the history of white supremacy in the ivory tower and about the way white dominance and nonwhite subordination manifests itself in interpersonal relationships as well as in institutional processes. My journey is worth sharing not because it is unique but because other Black women often suffer similar injustices and sharing our frustrations is a path to joy.

I have to consider that anger is necessary and that I should not be afraid to express myself when my circumstances are such that provoke the emotion. Was it not Lorde who proclaimed, "My response to racism is anger. I have lived with that anger, ignoring it, feeding upon it, learning to use it before it laid my visions to waste, for most of my life. Once I did it in silence, afraid of the weight. My fear of anger taught me nothing."[21] She admonishes her readers that their fear of anger, *my fear of anger*, is not something to bury. She also asserts that "there is an intellectual rigor that comes along with the attempt to refuse to participate in the aspirational search for respectability and social mobility in academia—the attempt to not be safe."[22] This coedited volume is a collective intellectual effort to *not be safe* because the search for respectability in the ivory tower does not promise to deliver the same—that is, safety—for Black women academics.

In March 2022 I received news that I had earned tenure and promotion to associate professor. This journey has demanded that I catch up and catch on to institutional practices that would subordinate me and my work. I practiced catching my breath through the process of writing about my experience, which has allowed me to meditate and heal. Finally, it is clearer now more than ever that I need to offer a hand to catch others as they move through similar processes to ensure that those who need mentoring receive it. In doing so, my hope is that Black women and students of color in the ivory tower will find space to thrive and find joy. *I found my joy.*

NOTES

1. Whitehead, "5 Women Who Influenced Me."
2. Harrison, "Building a Canon, Creating Dialogue," 49–50.
3. Mirza, "Postcolonial Subjects, Black Feminism," 242.
4. Mirza, 242.
5. Chapdelaine, "Celebrating Breast Cancer Awareness Month" and "Black Votes Matter."
6. Harris and González, introduction to *Presumed Incompetent*, 1.
7. Chemaly, *Rage Becomes Her*, 284.
8. Lorde, "Eye to Eye," 145.
9. Robin P. Chapdelaine, email to unnamed colleague, April 4, 2019.
10. Pittman, "Racial Microaggressions," 82.
11. Duquesne University: HERI Faculty Survey 2019–2020 Results: Full-Time Undergraduate Teaching Faculty, 6. In author's possession.
12. Walkington, "How Far Have We Really Come?," 51.
13. Crenshaw, "Demarginalizing the Intersection of Race and Sex," 140.
14. Mirza, "Postcolonial Subjects, Black Feminism," 234.
15. Social Sciences Feminist Network Research Interest Group, "Burden of Invisible Work," 230.
16. Campbell et al., "Reverse Mentoring," 185–86.
17. See, "Talking Tenure," 157.
18. Stanley, "Coloring the Academic Landscape," 718–19.
19. Social Sciences Feminist Network Research Interest Group, "Burden of Invisible Work," 232.
20. Library Journal Reviews, "Literary Afrofuturism."
21. Lorde, "Use of Anger," 22.
22. See, "Talking Tenure," 152.

CHAPTER 2

No Easy Road

My Journey from PhD to Tenure-Track
Employment

FELICE FERGUSON KNIGHT

INTRODUCTION

During graduate school, I often reflected on the scripture, "Weeping may endure for a night, but joy *comes* in the morning."[1] I wondered whether joy, which I equated with successful completion of my dissertation and acceptance of a tenure-track job, would ever come for me. I completed my dissertation in 2013 but did not obtain tenure-track employment until 2019. Many factors contributed to this delay, including a decision to take an adjunct job after graduation to gain teaching experience, complications with the health of one of my children, a two-year hiatus from work while I helped her recover, and a subsequent, two-year search for tenure-track employment.

In telling my story, this essay provides an autoethnographic account of my emotional and mental state during my six-year journey to tenure-track employment. I experienced numerous events during the journey that should have brought me joy, but troubling circumstances related to each experience dampened my joy and led to feelings of shame, anxiety, and fear. I realize that being this transparent about my feelings and thoughts risks others (mis)labeling me as weak, unstable, or even incompetent.[2] However, I have deliberately chosen an autoethnographic lens through which to frame my story because it explicitly recognizes the subjective aspects of one's identity, the "stories rather than theories," and those of us who are "self-consciously value-centered rather than pretending to be value free."[3]

I further take solace in knowing that I follow in the footsteps of a long line of Black women who have chosen to write about deeply personal aspects of their lives to highlight the struggles that Black women face, even when others dismiss their negative experiences as self-victimization or exaggeration. For example, Harriet Jacobs, an African American woman who escaped from slavery in 1842, offered this explanation of her decision to tell the unvarnished truth about her experiences in slavery: "Reader, be assured this narrative is no fiction. I am aware that some of my adventures may seem incredible; but they are, nevertheless, strictly true . . . I have not written my experiences in order to attract attention to myself; on the contrary, it would have been more pleasant to me to have been silent about my own history. But . . . I want to add my testimony to that of abler pens to convince the people of the Free States what Slavery really is." Like Jacobs, it would have been "more pleasant to me to have been silent about my own history," but I desire to add my testimony to that of other Black women—past and present—whose experiences reveal uncomfortable, yet important truths.[4]

My journey to tenure-track employment was not easy, and I often thought I would not make it. But I emerged from the journey stronger and more resilient. I learned how to have hope. The following recollections lay bare my thoughts and feelings as I traveled that long, lonely road.

OFF TO A ROCKY START, AUGUST 2013

In August 2013, as I sat waiting for my graduation ceremony to begin, I decided to take a selfie. I stared at the camera—doctoral hood, tam, and robe in place—but I did not smile. On what should have been one of the happiest days of my life, the day I earned a PhD in African American history, I felt disappointed and ashamed. I felt disappointed because I had expected to graduate within five years of starting my program. I had come in with an MA, so I did not expect to take as much time as the typical doctoral student. When it ended up taking me seven years to finish my degree, I felt like a failure. Similarly, I felt ashamed because I had not written the kind of dissertation that my dissertation adviser or I had expected me to write. Although my adviser called my topic "brilliant," she found my dissertation manuscript to be less analytically developed than she (or I) had imagined. We both knew I should revise it before I graduated, but we also knew that I wanted—and needed (I could not sustain another student loan)—to graduate. She graciously allowed me to submit it with minimal revisions. I should have been happy, but I was not. I knew I had accomplished something significant and had experienced tremendous favor. Yet, I felt insignificant and unaccomplished.

My feelings of shame led to doubts about whether I would be successful on the job market. The market was tight that year anyhow. In my field, the ratio of applicants to jobs was 2:1, so I forewent applications for tenure-track employment and instead sought adjunct positions in the town where I completed my PhD.[5] I thought I would spend some time getting teaching experience and then get on the job market in a year or two. I landed an adjunct position rather quickly at a local community college and found that I really enjoyed teaching. The light-bulb moments that students experienced as they learned about African American history brought me great joy. Yet my position as an adjunct instructor brought little else of benefit. It came with no health care provisions, no job security, and very little pay.[6] I knew I could not remain in adjunct employment for long. Especially because my spouse and I wanted to start a family.

DETOURS AND DELAYS, OCTOBER 2014–JUNE 2017

My husband and I had always wanted to have children but had chosen to delay until I completed graduate school. Now that I was done, we began to try. To our overwhelming delight, in October 2014, we found out we were pregnant. Moreover, by the end of the year, we learned that we were going to have not one but *two* bundles of joy. I was pregnant with fraternal twins. We could not contain our excitement, and beginning in January 2015, when we learned that our twins were both girls, we eagerly began picking out cute little baby girl clothes.

In February 2015, however, we received deeply troubling news: one of our baby girls' amniotic sacs had ruptured. It was a tiny tear, but enough to raise alarm because if it ruptured further, I could go into labor at any time. My doctor promptly admitted me to the hospital, and as my employers at the community college scrambled to find someone to cover my classes, I hoped and prayed that my children would stay in utero as long as possible.

Two months later, my baby girls were born. I rejoiced at their birth, but I knew that additional struggles lay ahead. Doctors had informed us that the baby whose amniotic sac had ruptured would likely have under-developed lungs, and they were right. This precious little girl could not even muster a cry after she was born, because she was struggling so hard to breathe. Doctors immediately whisked her off to the neonatal inten-sive care unit (NICU). She ended up staying there six months, during which time she had various surgeries to help her breathe and eventually had a G-tube placed because her tiny body could not muster the strength to both breathe and suckle. We were devastated. It hurt that our precious baby girl had to go through so much at such a young age.

Meanwhile, her twin sister fared better. She came home after only one month in the NICU. She was still tiny—only five pounds—but she was robust and made sure everyone knew when she wanted or needed some-thing by issuing a hearty cry. We loved having our baby girl at home but found it extremely hard to adjust to life with one child at home and one in the hospital. To add to our troubles, mounting bills and the cost of formu-la compelled me to go back to work at the community college in August 2015. We hired a nanny to take care of the child who was home and prayed that the child in the hospital would come home soon.

The answer to our prayers came in September 2015, when doctors released our baby girl from the hospital. But there was still a long road ahead. She came home with the feeding tube and oxygen. We hired a nurse to take care of her and continued to employ a nanny for her twin sister. By November, I became so overwhelmed by the process of having to get up early to prepare for work and having to stay up late at night to take care of the twins that I knew I would have to make a very difficult decision. I would have to quit work. In December 2015, after fall semester classes ended, I informed my employers that I would not be returning the next semester. I also told them that I was not sure when—or if—I would be back. My children needed my undivided attention, and I was going to stay at home until both of them were (prayerfully) in good health.

Miraculously, our child with the medical disabilities started turning a corner shortly after I made the decision to stay at home. She came off oxygen in early 2016 and started working with an occupational therapist to learn how to eat without the assistance of the feeding tube. It ended up taking another year for her to wean from the G-tube, but she made it. When doctors declared her no longer medically disabled in the summer of 2017, my husband and I were overjoyed. We now had *two* healthy children. I contemplated what to do next. I was not sure whether I should go back to work or stay at home with the kids. I treasured every moment I spent with my kids but also missed teaching. Moreover, my family needed additional income. With this in mind, I went back to work at the community college, but I knew I would not stay for long. I simultaneously began to apply for tenure-track jobs for the upcoming academic year.

JOB MARKET ANXIETIES, SEPTEMBER–DECEMBER 2017

In the fall of 2017, as I began to apply for tenure-track jobs, many questions flooded my mind. Was I still marketable? Would the fact that I had prioritized my family over my career make me look like I was not a serious scholar? How could I compete with newly minted PhDs whose research reflected the latest trends in scholarship and methodology? If my bid for employment was successful, where would I end up? Would we have to move to a new city and build a new network of support for our family? Our friends at the church we attended had been vital during the trials we went through with the children. Should we risk losing it all for me to take a new job?

These questions reflect the high level of anxiety I felt as I got on the job market in late 2017. The following excerpts from my journal reveal additional thoughts and fears:

September 27, 2017
Areas in my life in which I currently feel stuck:
-Stuck in fears about the future
-Stuck in regrets about not getting a job as a history professor at a four-year university
-Stuck in worries about what other people think about me for not doing "what I was supposed to do with my degree"

December 27, 2017
-I'm scared my writing sample will not be looked upon favorably by the hiring committees
-I wonder if they'll think my ideas are legitimate
-I worry that they will critique my writing harshly and conclude that I am not a serious scholar

As I reflect on these entries today, I think about how much power I mistakenly gave to others to define who I was and what my potential was. As Brené Brown writes, I was stuck in a web of shame composed of "layered, conflicting and competing social-community expectations."[7] The "social-community expectations" that entrapped me in this web originated in graduate school. Throughout my doctoral program, faculty, colleagues, and advisers upheld tenure-track employment as the epitome of success after completion of the PhD. Research confirms that "most ranking graduate programs still consider any PhD who doesn't land a tenure track job a failure or an aberration."[8] Likewise, the "publish or perish" mantra had been drilled into my head since I started the program. How could I publish my book within the six-year period required of most tenure-track professors when I had not worked on my dissertation for several years?

Yet, the truth was, if I gained tenure-track employment I would have plenty of time to revise my dissertation. I just needed to stay focused on the task ahead. I began reading self-help books to build my confidence as I applied for jobs. The books helped. As I awaited the results of my applications, I settled into what I hoped would be my last academic year as an adjunct instructor.

OPPORTUNITIES MISSED AND GAINED,
JANUARY–JULY 2018

Just in case the applications I sent out were unsuccessful, I decided to apply for a few "late season" jobs in January 2018. Such jobs appeared the same year that job would start, thus applying for such was risky. Prospective employers usually notified first-round picks for these jobs in the summer, which barely gave the successful candidate enough time to pack, move, and settle in before the start of the new academic year. Nevertheless, I decided to take my chances—and good thing I did. One of my late-season applications resulted in an interview.

The interview took place by videoconferencing, and I thought it went very well. I felt confident that I would get a call back for an on-campus interview. However, when one month went by and the call did not come, I began to worry. I had not gotten interview requests from any other schools, so I felt like everything was riding on this chance. Finally, when another month rolled around and the call still did not come, I contacted the school's human resources department to find out the status of my application. I discovered what I had suspected: the search had officially closed, and the committee had offered the position to another candidate. I was heartbroken. Since none of my other applications had been successful, I began to think that perhaps it really was too late for me. Who would hire a five-year postdoc like me?

Then, an unexpected opportunity came my way. In late May 2018, I learned of an opening for a visiting assistant professorship at a four-year college in my hometown. The position was for only a year, but it could transition into tenure-track employment if one's application for a soon-to-open tenure line was successful. I was elated. I had always wanted to move back home. My parents lived there and all of my favorite stomping grounds were there too. I decided to apply.

The application process moved swiftly. I submitted my application in May, did a videoconference interview in June, and received an offer for the position in July. I was stunned. I had no idea my fortunes could change so quickly. Within a few months of not getting a job at one institution, I landed a job at another. Moreover, this job was in my hometown. I could barely contain my joy. A few weeks after I received the news, I wrote the following in my journal:

> *July 18, 2018*
> *Can you believe it? God has done exceedingly abundantly above all we can ask or think according to the power that is at work within us! On Friday, July 6, I was offered a full-time Visiting Assistant Professor position . . . guess where? Our hometown! Wowzers! God did it!*

In the weeks that followed, my husband and I packed with frenzied excitement. This was going to be one of the biggest moves we had ever made, and it was going to happen fast. My new position started in August. We decided to move in stages. The kids and I moved first and stayed with my parents while my husband packed up our remaining things and prepared our home for sale. At first, we thought he would have to look for a new job when he arrived, but, shortly after I accepted my position, my husband found out that his employer had an opening at a site in the same city. He applied and got it. We marveled at God's blessings upon us. Everything seemed to be lining up.

Yet anxiety began to creep in as I considered the gravity of what I was about to do. Not only was I going to start a new job, but my family had a unique historical relationship to the institution at which I would be working—a relationship that was not entirely pleasant.

THE JUXTAPOSITION OF TIME AND PLACE: MY FATHER'S EXPERIENCES AT A PREDOMINANTLY WHITE INSTITUTION AND MINE, 1969–1995 AND AUGUST–DECEMBER 2018

The institution at which I had been hired was located in the South. It had been founded as an all-white, all-male college in the 1840s. It desegregated in the late-1960s and began to admit women in the 1990s. Ironically, my father experienced both of these transitions. In 1969, three years after the school admitted its first Black student, he enrolled as a freshman. He faced several forms of discrimination while at the school. For example, during his freshman year, he joined the band, only to find that he would have to play "Dixie" at football games. Fearing repercussions as an underclassman, he played the song. But, in his sophomore year now that he was an upperclassman, he refused. The president of the institution summoned him to a meeting and threatened to remove his academic scholarship if he did not either play the song or put his instrument to his mouth and pretend to play it. My father's parents came to the school and informed the president that they would take legal action if he rescinded my father's scholarship. In the end, the president allowed my father to keep his scholarship, but ordered him expelled from the band. My father was disappointed—he had been first chair clarinetist in high school and had looked forward to continuing to hone his skills as a member of the college band. Despite experiencing this overt case of racial discrimination, my father remained committed to seeing changes on campus concerning race. That same academic year, he and another African American student founded a club called the Afro-American Society. It was open to all students with the mission of facilitating dialogue among Black and white students. Shortly thereafter, he became a victim of hazing and contemplated leaving the school. Family and friends encouraged him to stay, knowing that he was making history not only by being there but also by standing up for what was right.[9]

Ironically, sixteen years after graduating, my father found himself seated across the table from school administrators again. Except this time, they were commissioning him as a newly appointed member of the board. In a move inspired by state legislation to promote racial diversification of the boards of public colleges, his alma mater had begun recruiting minority board members. They turned to my father because, in the years since he had graduated, he had begun giving talks on behalf of the Black alumni association to prospective African American students. Though he told the unvarnished truth about his experiences, he used his story as an example of how to turn one's problems into solutions and one's pain into purpose. The board learned of his work and asked him to help lead the school's efforts to increase the number of African American students.[10]

Shortly after my dad got on the board, a prospective student who, unbeknownst to administrators, was female, gained admission to the school. She had failed to specify her gender in her application and possessed a unisex name. Upon discovering her gender, the school rescinded her admission. She took legal action. As the school found itself enmeshed in a legal battle over single-gender education, the board was faced with a decision. Should they change admissions policies or keep them the same? Many board members wanted to keep things the same, but my dad did not. He supported women's right to enroll. He told fellow board members that just as the school had admitted Black men like himself in a previous era it should admit women in this era. The snide comments that followed his remarks gave him considerable pause. A court mandate forced the school to enroll the female applicant in 1995. My dad's term on the board ended the same year, and for the next decade or so, he did not return to the school—not to visit and not to attend any events. Years later, when asked about his hiatus, he remarked, "My mind was going back to a time when I knew the same board was having the same argument about why Black people shouldn't be there, and so I walked away."[11]

The juxtaposition between my dad's decision to walk away from his alma mater and my decision to "walk toward" it when I accepted a job there in 2018 weighed heavily on my mind. I knew, to borrow a phrase from Melissa Harris-Perry, that I was about to enter a *crooked room* where stereotypes and false tropes about Black people, in general, and about Black women in particular, had historically been the norm.[12] I wondered whether I would fit in, in this "space never meant for me."[13] Still, I knew I had to give the institution a try. It had been nearly fifty years since my dad had enrolled there and twenty or so years since he had served on the board. Surely, it had changed. I soon found out that in some ways it had. In other ways, it had not.

In August 2018, as I settled into my first semester as a visiting assistant professor, I encountered a number of situations that made me feel like the institution would not be a good fit for me. First, in addition to being a predominantly white and predominantly male institution, it was a military institution. The students and certain faculty and staff were required to wear uniforms. As a visiting professor, I was not. I noticed a difference in the way students treated me and the way they treated faculty who were in uniform. In the hallways, students greeted uniformed faculty with a nod of the head and a "Good morning, sir" or "Good morning, ma'am." Students said nothing to me.

Certainly, one reason for this treatment was that I was not in uniform, but I also believe race played a role. I was the only full-time Black faculty member in my department, and when I attended campus-wide faculty meetings, I could count the number of other Black faculty on one hand. By contrast, nearly all of the custodial workers and a significant number of staff members were Black. Studies have shown that at institutions with few Black faculty, students assume that Black personnel are custodial workers or administrative staff. They then subject Black faculty to mistreatment and microaggressions.[14] I believe this is what was happening to me.

Moreover, once I entered the classroom, I encountered other micro-aggressions. First, though I introduced myself as "Dr. Knight," students addressed me as "Mrs. Knight" or "Ms. Knight." Even after correction, some persisted. Additionally, other students displayed passive-aggressive behavior. For example, in a class I taught on slavery, memory, and historical monuments, a handful of white male students sat at the back of the class, with arms by their sides or hands in their laps. They did not take notes. Furthermore, one or two of them made comments in class or in papers that reflected neo-Confederate and Alt-Right leanings.

Research has shown that in classes taught by female faculty of color, white males have a propensity to challenge the instructor's authority—especially through the use of passive-aggressive behavior; [15] thus, I believe my race and gender played a role in these students' actions. I also suppose that other factors—related to the institution's troubled racial history—played a role as well. During the Civil War, numerous students, administrators, and faculty of this institution fought on the side of the Confederacy. For nearly a century after the war, school administrators sought to venerate the actions of these alumni by naming buildings and awards and commissioning murals and memorials in their honor. These buildings, awards, murals, and memorials remain on campus today and—whether intentionally or not—send a message to students with neo-Confederate or Alt-Right perspectives that this is a safe space for their viewpoints. I believe the students who displayed passive-aggressive behavior in my class did so because the subject matter I taught challenged their views of history.

My experiences in the classroom indicated that some things had not changed since my dad's time at the institution. Racism and sexism were still problems. I began to think that I might not apply for the tenure-track position after all. Then, I learned of a research initiative that showed a different side of the school than I had experienced in the classroom. The research project, which had the full support of the dean of the school of humanities and of the provost, aimed to document the historical connection between slavery and the founding of the institution. It had resulted, in 2017, in the formation of a research committee that joined a national consortium of colleges and universities doing similar work. I was intrigued and surprised. If administrative support existed for a project of this nature, then maybe there was room for someone like me at this school. Additionally, I realized that if I joined this committee, I could encounter new avenues for my own research, which focused on slaveholding by municipalities and other government entities. I began to attend committee meetings and decided to apply for the tenure-track position. Of course, I also applied for jobs at other institutions. But now I had an incentive for getting this job. As fall turned into winter, I awaited the results of my applications.

JOY COMES IN THE MORNING, FEBRUARY 2019

I remember where I was when I heard the news. I was at work, at my desk, checking emails in February 2019. That is where I was when my department chair walked into my office and told me I had gotten the job. I cried. Not tears of sadness, but tears of joy. I had made it. I had finally made it. I finally had a tenure-track job. It had been a long road to get this point. My doubts about my success on the job market after graduation, the unexpected premature birth of my twins, and the recurrent adjunct positions I had held made this accomplishment especially sweet.

Yet, as I sat in my chair overwhelmed by the joy of the moment, I knew that additional trials lay ahead. The difficulties I had faced in the classroom provided important insights into the challenges I would face. Though I took solace in knowing that, at the senior leadership level, there was support for research into racial disparities, I knew there was still much work to do. As I pondered the road ahead, the scripture that had given me pause after graduate school came to mind again. I knew that nights of weeping likely lay ahead, but this time, I had hope that joy would come in the morning.

NOTES

1. Psalm 30:5, *The New King James Version of the Bible* (Nashville, TN: Thomas Nelson Bibles, 1982), https://www.biblegateway.com/passage/?search=Psalm%20 30:4-6&version=NKJV.
2. Niemann, Gutiérrez y Muhs, and González, *Presumed Incompetent II*.
3. Ellis, Adams, and Bochner, "Autoethnography," 274.
4. Jacobs, *Life of a Slave Girl*, 2–3.
5. Mikaelian, "The 2013 Jobs Report."
6. Flaherty, "Barely Getting By."
7. Brown, *I Thought It Was Just Me*, 17–18.
8. Kelsky, *The Professor Is In*, 11.
9. Much of this information derives from personal recollections of my father's stories. However, on occasion, he shared some of these stories with scholars and journalists. Excerpts can be found in the following published works: Macaulay, *Marching in Step*, and Wallace, "From Foster to the Future."
10. Wallace, "From Foster to the Future."
11. Larry Ferguson, phone call with author, January 12, 2023; Jordan, "Citadel Ordered to Admit Woman"; Mike Clary, "Faulkner Takes Her Place"; Wallace, "From Foster to the Future."
12. Harris-Perry, *Sister Citizen*, 29–30.
13. Davis, "Tokenization in the Era of Performative Wokeness," in chapter 9 of this volume.
14. Pittman, "Racial Microaggressions," 88.
15. Pittman, "Race and Gender Oppression," 187–88.

CHAPTER 3

"Now I'm choosing life, yo"

Finding Joy in Neo-Soul Music and Poetry While
Navigating Graduate School and the Academic
Job Market

ASHLEY D. CLEMONS

INTRODUCTION

My search for joy spanned a turbulent, decade-plus-long graduate school journey. Initially, I entered my graduate studies knowing little about navigating institutional barriers and politics. Soon, I discovered what too many underresourced and underrepresented Black women graduate students faced. There is a shared reality, as if a rite of passage, in which the ivory tower sustains systems, such as funding, curricula, and programming, that perpetually foster micro-/macroaggression, isolation, oppression, and debt. Simply put, academia and its gatekeepers are not designed to provide a space for the marginalized to succeed. As a first-generation Black college and graduate student living with sickle cell disease (SCD), I faced additional barriers that made joy even more elusive as I pursued my degree. Given my experiences, I take an autoethnographic approach to the joy-centered discourse in this chapter. My background and experiences related to physical, social, and mental wellness are inextricably connected to my search for joy. Broadly, I draw from Black feminist and disability justice scholars to understand Black artistic production as praxis to search for joy in the ivory tower. Specifically, I examine how Black music and poetry offer critical tools to navigate racism and ableism in graduate school and the academic job search. I discuss joy in conversation with mental health first, followed by physical struggles. I disclose my often-stigmatized medical diagnosis as an account that demonstrates how I reached beyond fear, pain, and anxiety to accomplish goals I had never witnessed anyone in my family or community achieve. Attaining and maintaining joy was critical to my overall mental and physical health throughout my graduate studies. At its core, this chapter is a joy work in progress.

Collectively, many of my colleagues in this section call on Audre Lorde's Black feminist oeuvre, *Sister Outsider* (1984), to capture their individual stories about joy. Our shared summoning of Lorde's text points to a history in which Black, Indigenous, and people of color (BIPOC) sought unconventional tools and experienced peripheral positionalities within the ivory tower. Profoundly, Lorde's "Master's Tools" addresses a predominately white audience at New York University Institute for the Humanities to underscore the importance of alternative approaches for BIPOC success and survival. Lorde emphasizes that "*survival is not an academic skill*."[1] In other words, Black women must navigate countless "isms" embedded within academic infrastructures to accomplish their goals. To this end, I knew that to excel in my graduate school journey, I would have to create and maintain skill sets beyond my academic training. When I was accepted into graduate school, I was overwhelmed by what I thought I did not know. Initially, I struggled with imposter syndrome and often questioned my worthiness. One way I overcame the matter was by seeking welcoming and inclusive spaces where I could build my village. However, I needed to find unconventional support to survive, undermine, and resist the ageist, racist, classist, and homophobic systems that prevailed in academic spaces.

Primarily, focusing on my mental health improved my capacity for joy. At the predominantly white institution (PWI) that I attended for grad school, access to Black or LGBTQIA+ therapists and therapy groups was limited and challenging to join given the overwhelming demand. In recent years, discussions have centered on Black women professionals' pursuit of mental, physical, and financial wellness while simultaneously addressing national, political, and social climates that not only devalue Black women's labor and worth but also ignore their humanity. Notably, Black athletes have increasingly spoken publicly about mental health issues, struggles within their respective sports, and misrepresentations of those struggles and health issues in the news media. For instance, Naomi Osaka and Simone Biles refused professional accomplishments to prioritize their mental health. Moreover, both women bravely opted to make unpopular decisions to withdraw from significant sporting competitions. In 2021, Naomi Osaka, four-time Grand Slam champion, withdrew from the French Open, news/

media press conferences/interviews, and several Women's Tennis Association tournaments. Similarly, Simon Biles, one of the most successful gymnasts in U.S. history and the youngest recipient of the Presidential Medal of Freedom, departed from the individual all-around competition at the 2021 Tokyo Olympic Games despite being favored to win. She navigated mental wellness needs while also enduring a widely covered sexual assault trial in which she, among countless other gymnasts, was a victim. Although both women faced broad scrutiny and criticism, they prioritized their health over the profession. Osaka's and Biles' individual stories offer a blueprint for Black women in other industries and professions, particularly ones that are merit and production based.

Furthermore, throughout my graduate studies, my mental health impacted how I experienced joy. Often, I missed the joy of milestones owing to my feelings of depression, isolation, and anxiety. Given the overwhelming challenges I faced in the middle of my journey, I took temporary leave during my final semesters of coursework. When I returned, I was in my thirties and faced additional challenges. To find such support systems I used music and poetry. Since the beginning of my PhD journey, these tools have been my access to joy in the ivory tower.

REFUSAL AND NEO-SOUL MUSIC

Considering the power of music to the mind, I used neo-soul music and connections I found in the music to grapple with the subjugation of Black labor that I experienced and witnessed in other graduate students' experiences. Countless PWIs in the United States and many Ivy League institutions were founded during or soon after the antebellum period. Many universities continue to operate in a Sharpe-esque slavery afterlife and develop under unjust economic infrastructures.[2] Despite the flaws in these infrastructures, they empower the gatekeepers of the ivory tower to keep certain people out while propagating false illusions of diversity, equity, and inclusion.

Interestingly, neo-soul music and many other Black music traditions capture a pain, struggle, growth, and joy that I often did not know how to verbalize as a student. For example, Ms. Lauryn Hill strategically describes this labor as "slaving."[3] Tionne "T-Boz" Watkins's poem "i wanna be free" accuses the music business of enslaving her.[4] Watkins's constant use of the lowercase *i* replaces the specific individual with a collective. Even the icon Prince used his art to express the maltreatment and control that his label Warner Bros. had over his creations and name. He changed his name to a symbol and often performed with the word "slave" marked on his face to break his contractual chains. Each artist refused the industry's claim to their bodies and identities. Although I do not liken the position of Black women in graduate school to the incomparable enslavement of Black people, I offer this reading of the word as it captures institutionalized subjugation, manipulation, and mistreatment of Black labor.

To begin reaching for joy, especially amid difficulties, I repurposed many music lyrics and poetry as daily mantras, affirming incantations, and guided meditations. As a result, my alternative support positioned neo-soul and R&B music as "pedagogical spaces" and praxes.[5] Neo-soul music walked me to every class. Blaring from my headphones in the sweltering southern days and late rainy evenings was neo-soul and then-contemporary/socially conscious R&B. A music disciple, I had specific albums on rotation, such as Jill Scott's *Who is Jill Scott?: Words and Sounds* (2000), Lalah Hathaway's *Outrun the Sky* (2004) and *Self Portrait* (2008), Erykah Badu's *Mama's Gun* (2000), Maxwell's *BLACKsummers'night* (2009), India.Arie's *Songversation* (2013) and *Songversation: Medicine* (2017), and D'Angelo's *Black Messiah* (2014). An exemplar, Ms. Lauryn Hill refused the industry's and fans' high expectations in sales and musicality. Amid mass popularity and international success, Hill put her personal needs first. As she shows, refusal offers an important boundary for BIPOC graduate students, especially students who must also teach and work additional jobs during their studies. Additionally, refusal paves the way toward joy. Cécile Accilien explains "that we say yes so much, we spend so much time trying to prove ourselves, that either we end up not having time and energy to write, or we get burned out."[6] Considering these consequences, I would say no to daily racist tasks expected of BIPOC grad students, such as performing or code-switching to ease the minds of white counterparts.

Anti-Black rhetoric permeates too many college towns, no matter the geographic location. I attended a northern PWI for my bachelor's degree and migrated to the South to attend another PWI for my doctorate. Although many commonalities were present in both the North and the South, north central Florida was inflamed long before the murders of Trayvon Martin and Jordan Davis (which occurred at a gas station that

I unknowingly frequented), which most definitely existed well after the media coverage faded. Too many local citizens shared the views that were reflected in university policies and school-sponsored events, leaving Black students with the complex task of navigating racism while excelling academically. As a result, teaching in the classroom took on a new challenge. I remember teaching a class during the semester of increased protests and discussions related to police brutality, race, and Confederate monuments. Also, during this time, the literary world gained an ancestor in the death of Toni Morrison. I led a class reading and discussion based on her Nobel Prize lecture to honor her. As students began sharing thoughts, one student became very aggressive and visibly hostile. After de-escalating the situation, I soon learned that the student did not want to hear about a Black woman whom he considered a nationalist. At the end of the semester, the student expressed his anger and dissatisfaction in my evaluations. Often, Black women graduate instructors must not only perform for their department but also for racist students who do not want to learn from a BIPOC instructor. In these moments, I refuse to allow evaluations completed by some people who delight in Black women's destruction to become how I measure my success or improvement as an educator.

I held my learning spaces as sacred, inviolate of racist dominance and violence, which meant I rebuffed the "micro" in microaggressions. I called them exactly for what they were: violence and aggression. Black graduate students across the nation experience microaggressions. For instance, faculty might constantly confuse the names of the few Black women in the department. Religious extremists may threaten to burn the Koran and protest at the funerals of LGBTQIA+ individuals. Rallies glorify white supremacy and local Confederate statues. There may be incidents in which white fraternities host blackface parties for mere entertainment. And for so many recently, gubernatorial and other campaigns might be allowed to spread racist ideals within the academic setting. Often, I wondered, How did Black women graduate students deal with loneliness? With the isolation? With the grief and loss that seems to be inevitable in working in academia? How can we survive and excel in a field, in a nation, or, as Sayam Davis puts it, "in a world addicted to white supremacy"?[7] To borrow from the racially biased 1980s antidrug slogan, "Just Say No."

In her song "I Get Out," produced by Bob Marley's son Ziggy Marley, Ms. Lauryn Hill talks about escape for the sake of her soul's joy. Hill is perhaps the music industry's most notable practitioner of refusal for joy. She refused dominant standards and its control over her peace and agency. She demonstrates this through her second album and quasi-retirement. *Unplugged*, a twenty-two-track double album, grapples with the Black woman's positionality within racist infrastructures.[8] Her widely misunderstood and highly criticized performance during the concert was full of sudden pauses, unexplained giggles, conversations with voices in Hill's mind, off-key guitar playing, and raspy vocals. These aspects, which many critics used as fuel for poor reviews, created an important space for me. Conversely, this album sparked much discussion about the state of Lauryn Hill's personal life, particularly her mental health. "I Get Out" refuses subjugation. Despite industry standards, Hill's commitment to amplifying her individuality and agency offered a revolutionary approach. In one verse, Hill sings, "Your stinkin' resolution is no type of solution," which could also hold true for diversity initiatives that universities continue to use to avoid having their racism exposed. However, Black women continue to be underresourced and underrepresented in every level of higher education.[9] By the end of the song, Hill intensifies her declaration into a lamenting directive: "Just get out."[10] Here, Hill exposes the degree of labor that Black women are often subjected to, without a fraction of the compensation they deserve. She repeats this phrase as lamenting or incantation, which I embraced throughout my intensely difficult moments in graduate school as motivation to reach the end of my labors. Whenever I was overwhelmed, these lines empowered and reminded me that the end was near and underscored the fact that my voice mattered as the end seemed unattainable. Lauryn Hill's music teaches joy through her therapeutic, intricate, truth-evoking musicality. Both Hill and Watkins strip their music of much traditional hip-hop and R&B beats and vibrato in exchange for the acoustic guitar and raw vocals. They create an intimacy that calls for a look at "relationship" and "work" on different levels beyond physical romance. Hill's work resisted popular demand for the persona and music of her past. Her search for joy generated debate and a glimpse into the power that could be obtained in standing firm on individual boundaries. Even more than "I Get Out," Watkins's "Unpretty" completely relinquishes undervalued labor for joy.

Since my childhood, I accessed joy vis-à-vis reading, writing, and listening to poetry, which proved to be vital to achieve joy while dealing with pain in a PhD program. In the preface to *Care Work: Dreaming Disability Justice* (2018), Leah Lakshmi Piepzna-Samarasinha dives into disability justice and speaks to my physical health experiences throughout graduate school. In chapter 3, Piepzna-Samarasinha notes that "making space accessible is a form of love."[11] She discusses how people can make spaces accessible in ways that show love for people who experience pain daily. Poetry contains a distinct power to liberate. Black women poetry writers and speakers create spaces where healing happens, particularly helpful for moments of emotional, spiritual, and physical fatigue, which can cause burnout. For instance, Watkins's "Unpretty" provided backstory and meaning to the lack of joy that accompanied my struggles. Her work resonated, especially after having a pain crisis or hospitalization.[12] "Unpretty," the first poem that Watkins ever wrote, was published in her volume of poetry, essays, and prose titled *Thoughts*. Each version of "Unpretty" functions as therapy in several ways. My introduction to yoga and nonwesternized meditation came from the "Unpretty" video, which centers on a Black woman and two group members, Chilli and Left Eye, who struggle with eating disorders, racist bullies, and body dysmorphia. A floating projector displays videos of each women's story in what appears to be a futuristic sacred space. As they view the projections, each member of TLC poses cross-legged, eyes closed, and meditates. Left Eye signs American Sign Language as the song continues, adding another level of inclusion. The artists critique the oppression while taking space in their advanced technologies and consciousnesses. Both Watkins's and Hill's work pointed to a new route rather than the detours I previously took toward achieving joy.

In addition to mental health, physical struggles and financial insecurities troubled my search for joy. By the time I returned to my graduate program, I realized that financial resources would not meet my basic needs. The responsibility to fund my education often impacted the way I took care of my body. For instance, I worried about covering miscellaneous tuition fees, which influenced whether I could also afford medical copayments and expenses not covered by my insurance. As a result, many procedures and treatments vital to my quality of life were placed on hold. Even though I did not have the funding, I also did not have the time to sacrifice from graduate school obligations. In *Lean Semesters*, Nzinga points out that "for all too many students, the *joy* of being accepted into a doctoral program is soon replaced with the angst of securing funding."[13]

During my tenure as a graduate student, I worked as a research assistant, teaching assistant, and tutor. In my mind, I had no time to be sick because I had bills to pay. However, what I didn't realize is that my labor exasperated my illness.

Sickle cell disease, a genetic blood disorder, causes chronic conditions such as pain, fatigue, retinopathy, aseptic necrosis of the hips and/or shoulders, and other physical and mental illnesses.[14] Among these issues, one of the most common is what many with SCD call a "pain crisis." Pain crises are unpredictable (and typically unpreventable) episodes of debilitating pain and fatigue that can last from days to weeks, potentially leading to restricted mobility, hospitalization, or even more serious issues including organ failure or death. Two significant causes of pain crises are stress and dehydration. There are various types of SCD and still insufficient research and resources nationally. Because of the lack of resources, countless adults with SCD suffer financially, emotionally, and physically.

Moreover, my SCD was exacerbated during my graduate studies and caused struggles in several areas. Frequently, I struggled to fund the expenses that come with starting a career in academia and those basic expenses associated with SCD. For example, much of academia operates through reimbursed funding rather than directly paying or prepaying hotels, car rentals, conference registrations, professional organization memberships, and the like. These expenses became a burden as I also had to also cover my deductible and copayments for medicine, specialist appointments, and emergency room/urgent care visits. In addition to the financial dilemma, I continued to grapple with symptoms involving SCD. Daily tasks such as walking around campus, standing to teach for one to two hours, and sitting in three four-hour courses were daunting and exasperated my disease. By the time I was done working and walking on campus, I often had little energy to devote to basic needs like cooking, cleaning, and self-care. Because stress is one of the main triggers for pain crises, my hospitalizations often occurred during the most inconvenient times of high stress, for instance, midterms and finals weeks, which were incredibly difficult because I had heavy teaching and research obligations with much sleep deprivation and a terrible eating routine. I had a perfect storm every semester for health problems.

SEARCHING FOR JOY IN A VIRTUAL ACADEMIC
JOB MARKET WHILE IN PAIN

In addition to my quest for joy to survive graduate school, I needed joy to thrive during the academic job search, which favors the able-bodied. For many Black women with chronic illnesses, navigating the market can be a daunting task because of factors not traditionally discussed in much job preparation literature and workshops. As I approached the end of my grad career, outside perspectives related to my body prevented me from leaning into the joy of wrapping up my greatest accomplishment to date. Actually, one of my worst fears in preparing for the job market was that people who did not know of or fully understand my health condition would simply think I looked sickly or like other SCD stereotypes. I was afraid to be identified as "that sick girl," which caused me to worry over my exterior. In terms of physical appearance, both Sayam Davis, in in "Tokenization in the Era of Performative Wokeness," chapter 9 in this volume, and Cécile Accilien, in "Marronage in the Ivory Tower," chapter 15, address barriers, particularly by grappling with hair politics. Performance and beauty standards speak to a larger issue between the academy, Black bodies, and opportunities. Personally, my arms bruised from routine blood draws and IVs, while SCD medication sped up tooth decay (with no dental insurance in grad school, I relied on annual visits and could not afford to fund critical dental work). Although humorous at times, my rolling backpack had become famous for the loud noises it made every time I was in the building. I once again turned to music to work through setbacks regarding my medical condition. Long hours balancing dissertation writing and job material preparation exhausts those not disabled but can be a struggle for graduate students with chronic pain. For example, I frequently had to decide between working in pain or working for shorter periods under the grogginess of opioids and other medication for some pain relief. I would often draw from the song "Unpretty," because it captured my struggle with appearance. Although the university offered support, the resources were not necessarily amendable for the lifestyles of students with chronic pain. The free rideshare service, for instance, requires twenty-four-hours' notice, which is unhelpful for someone who's condition comes with unpredictable limitations with mobility. Sometimes I wondered if I would always be running this academia race from last place. I often wrote poetry during these times to avoid being depressed.

Even more important than accessing joy amid my journey was access-ing joy at the end. Specifically, during my first time on the job market, like many colleagues, I was searching for a job in the middle of a global health crisis. Since all my interviews were virtual, my face and hair were front and center. I removed my facial piercing, added extra makeup to conceal the holes, and manicured hair into a conservative style. I had to *relax* my look, despite my discomfort.

Most important, I did not want to look "sickly" or not sober, a fear growing up and frequenting the hospital. To maintain joy, I wrote poetry in bed. I read poetry despite nodding off from the medication and having to reread. Moreover, the current global pandemic, at its beginning, caused many anxieties for the nondisabled that those with disabilities experience daily, which increased the difficulty in accessing resources for many peo-ple of color with illnesses. Not at anyone's fault (I believe), I had little time to receive clearance to teach off campus. Growing talk that graduate assis-tants with university accommodations were turned down en masse in the United States only amplified my concern.

Fortunately, my hematologist and medical team worked diligently to provide support amid their "frontline" crises. The ADA approved my request. Teaching, writing a dissertation, and searching for an academic position while relocating to another home in the middle of this pandemic proved daunting. The end of my first time on the academic job market proved beneficial in some ways. However, back-to-back virtual campus visits exasperated my battle with fatigue and body soreness due to sitting in front of a computer screen for hours with minimum respite in between meetings and presentations.

"OBLIGATED TO A SYSTEM GETTING LESS THAN YOU'RE DESERVING": NEGOTIATING AND DECISION-MAKING AT THE END OF THE JOB SEARCH

Finally, maintaining joy provides significant balance and clarity at the point where decisions must be made regarding job negotiations, place-ment, and overall next steps. Making such a life-changing choice to begin early career years can be overwhelming. During my first experience, I felt a mixture of anxiety, excitement, and nervousness. For those preparing for this time-sensitive and emotional phase, I suggest relying on inner joy, especially before the job offer letters arrive. I titled this section after a line from Ms. Lauryn Hill's "Get Out" to underscore the importance of choices in the early career years. Racism and ableism play significant roles in this phase. Pay disparities stealthily arise among negotiations, often with much difference between those made to Black women PhDs and those to others. One reason stems from the gratitude and misplaced external joy accompanying receiving an initial job offer.[15]

However, inner joy is fundamental when Black women receive their first opportunities for contingent and tenure-track positions. Many unexpected and underdiscussed factors frequently come into play. That rare yet highly anticipated search committee chair's phone call solidifies the elusive and marks the transition to unchartered territories. Choosing a new institution requires much research, faith, and self-awareness, which can be particularly challenging for a graduate student preparing for a dissertation defense or a postdoc balancing teaching/research obligations along with the job market. Some people may not understand how much goes into these next steps, especially those who have not been on the market within the past decade and following a global pandemic. Some critical components include family, location, prestige, and salary. Perhaps, particularly for first-generation PhDs, several elements of this phase go overlooked and taken for granted by search committees, administrators, and even writers of job prep materials. Early career decisions have a significant impact on family and future pay. Many must decide between contingent positions and the coveted tenure-track position. In these scenarios, Black women are essentially deciding between the opportunity to pursue their research interest at reduced course loads and job security that includes extensive teaching or service obligations.

Some training or knowledge about negotiation skills can make a significant difference in the outcomes of the job search and subsequent negotiations. Wise advice can come from mentors, other academics, and experts who write about these strategies. Regarding signing a contract within academia, some questions may linger, such as: What am I willing to sacrifice? Can I live off this salary? The *real* questions should be: Are they paying me my worth? Will this position bring joy? Although these answers might be clear, they, too, are unnerving. Suppose the answer is a simple "yes," wonderful. There might be a problem if the answer is "no" to any of these questions. At this point, it's not just about having a "seat at the table." I know what I bring to the table. Everyone wants to eat. After practicing talking points, consider a "What would Dr. Karen or Dr. Ken ask for? Demand?" approach. What if the offer is less than what the graduate student knows they are worth? What if the university is unwilling to negotiate any aspect of the offer letter? These remain important questions to consider.

I was so immured by the moving components and uncertainties that I overlooked the joy of achieving tenure-track job opportunities in a declining market. I was incredibly stressed out about the job choice until I went beyond knowing my worth to exercising my worth. Once I returned to my inner joy, I felt a sense of agency in navigating the final aspect of the job search. Despite the difficulties of the pandemic job market, I secured multiple interviews, virtual campus visits, and multiple tenure-track job offers. Despite the ivory tower's exclusionary climate, having accessed moments of joy provided me with the necessary tools to succeed through one of the most arduous steps in the climb up.

JOY COMES IN THE MOURNING

Essentially, in my search for joy, I discovered that inner joy existed and awaited an invitation to reside permanently in the ebbs and flows of life and work. Though not without obstacles, my daily efforts saved me consistently from burnout and breakdowns throughout graduate studies. Most profound, poetry and music offered a paradigmatic shift in my approach to finding joy in the ivory tower. Fortunately, the work that I put in during graduate school manifests as joy in my life even more today. Joy is evidence of the improvements I achieved mentally, physically, financially, and spiritually despite countless barriers and challenges.

On the one hand, I faced several health emergencies over the course of writing this chapter. On the other hand, writing this chapter healed some emotional and mental wounds I endured during my graduate school experiences. Throughout writing this chapter, I survived several pain crises that required hospital visits and a long recovery from COVID. I had to balance creating and treating my mind and body. I had to access the joy. Ultimately, the Black women's artwork expresses and responds to

Black women's struggles in predominately white spaces. Music and poetry produce joy work through the tool of refusal. Refusal for the benefit of my mind, body, and spirit did not come without its setbacks and fears. In many ways, I grieved *missing out* and *holding out* to maintain my joy. Despite what I mourned as losses, I found internal and eternal joy in return. It is with this joy that I climbed up to "get out."

NOTES

1. Lorde, "Master's Tools," 112.
2. Sharpe, *In the Wake*. Sharpe unfolds the "wake" in multiple ways, particularly in terms of anti-Black violence, contemporary resistance, and institutional oppression. She explores this violence in slavery's "afterlife," the generations following the transatlantic slave trade and U.S. antebellum period.
3. Ms. Lauryn Hill, "Interlude 5," *MTV Unplugged No. 2.0.*
4. Watkins, "i wanna be free," *Thoughts*, 135. Considering the figurative slave, Watkins expresses:

   > this business has made
   > a slave of me.

5. Love and Abdelaziz, "We Got a Lot," 174.
6. Accilien. "Marronage in the Ivory Tower," chapter 6 in this volume. Accilien refers to her Caribbean ancestry and the history of marronage as another tool for Black woman's survival during and after graduate school. By recalling experiences on job search communities, she exposes neutrality and casual racism guised as allyship. I look at Accilien's use of marronage as refusal.
7. Sayam Davis, "Tokenization in the Era of Performative Wokeness," chapter 9 in this volume. Davis widens the look at racism in the job search from another significant perspective, the selection committee and tenure track, especially in terms of "diversity" in predominantly white departments. Her experiences powerfully capture the microaggressions that persist despite academic position.
8. The former member of The Fugees performed "I Get Out" (2002) on *MTV Unplugged: Lauryn Hill* (2002), following her Grammy Award–winning and Diamond-certified album, *The Miseducation of Lauryn Hill* (1998). Her interludes engage storytelling and meditation. Most profound, "Interlude 5," "Interlude 6," and "Interlude 7" talk about her emotional and mental health in conversation with the dominant.
9. Nzinga. *Lean Semesters*, 22.
10. Hill, "Interlude 5."
11. Piepzna-Samarasinha, *Care Work*; Piepzna-Samarasinha, "Making Space Accessible Is an Act of Love for Our Communities," chap. 3 in *Care Work*, 48.

12. She published the book on the first anniversary of her grandmother's death, to whom she also dedicated the book. The poem would eventually bring joy to her legendary 1990s trio TLC, which was also titled Unpretty. In its musical version (and music video, for that matter), the words contribute to this understanding of progress during art creation.

13. Nzinga, *Lean Semesters*, 31–32.

14. Craighead and Nemeroff, *Concise Corsini Encyclopedia of Psychology.*

15. Võ, "Navigating the Academic Terrain," 95.

CHAPTER 4

Notes from the Bottom

Black Women Doctoral Students as Academic Mules,
Mammies, and Maids in American Academia

KRISTIAN CONTRERAS

I am daydreaming beyond binaries. In the all-too-frequent
moments I feel lost, I allow myself to dream—to indulge
in questions hidden in promises of diversity and inclusion and unravel my
worries in the comfort of my feminist imagination. Here, I wonder who
I am beneath the weight of this "presumed incompetence."[1] What would
happen if we dared to choose ourselves over the respectability offered
by the institution? What (broken) promises lay at the end of this climb
up to the doctorate? How can I live a feminist life when I am learning
it is far easier to theorize about it? What will happen if I tell this truth?
You've heard this story before, perhaps, and are familiar with the warmth
of achieving the impossible on a well-lit graduation stage. It is one of grit
and triumph—of being the first and sometimes the only—and a testament
to "higher education's stated mission of creating a democratizing society."[2] Yet I, like many Black women academicians, know a different story
lies beneath our decorated mortarboards and framed degrees. To tell this
truth, I unwind the binds of gratitude and imposter syndrome from my
throat to shed the limits of a too-narrow lexicon.

Here I exchange "rigor," "excellence," and "preparedness" for "exploitation," "silencing," and "dispossession." Doing so names and exposes the
shroud of hyper-in/visibility that Black women and femmes navigate as
learners and laborers in doctoral training. What can the doctorate mean
to Black women when the university relegates us *to* and keeps us firmly *at*
the proverbial bottom? How can we move beyond the either/or when the
systematic exploitation of Black women is inherent to the operations of
American higher education? When will the joy come if the achievement
itself reopens an aching colonial wound?

The climb up from preschool nursery rhymes to graduate seminars on epistemological orientations rubbed my hands raw. I learned a quiet assimilation that felt as axiomatic as each inhale and exhale. I collected syllabi with bolded words like *decolonization, feminist,* and *transformative* while my body curved inward, buckling under the pressure to prioritize the needs of my peers in lieu of my own. Instead of engaging in my own ideas or interpretations of canonical texts, I explained them in breakout discussions after it became clear no one else did the reading, became the translator of Black and Brown writers' scholarship, and interrupted the problematic monologues (that were comments rather than questions) when my professors' silence felt too painful. I passed tissue boxes across our desks when tears overflowed after classmates were held accountable and quelled my frustration after being told I was brave for speaking up during class breaks. The growing expectation to take care of the emotional needs of my department reconfigured the doctoral journey from one of intellectual pursuit into a game of servitude. One faculty member asked me to assist first-year doctoral students in our program by helping them plan out their courses. She went on to explain that because I am so personable, organized, and advanced by comparison with my peers, talking to me instead of hard-to-reach and nonresponsive faculty advisers would be much easier and faster for new student. I practiced my tone after evaluations described me as aggressive while teaching mostly white students in a course on diversity in education. With tired eyes, I wrote letters in response to the constant violence against Black people in America, curated resources to address the rise of anti-Asian hate crimes, and reminded our department that the same racist exploitative issues raised during undergraduate-led protests were also happening in our classrooms after our faculty's continued silence. I carried the posters and markers while my white peers submitted coauthored proposals with our professors. For six semesters I was a stand-in adviser, tutor, other mother, administrative aide, financial aid guru, and big sister; in all that time, I rarely felt like an emerging scholar sharpening her voice in a community more focused on what I could *do* for them instead of how they could empower me. Unsure if this was the norm, I told myself that I was lifting as I climbed—that all this work supporting other people along their journeys would benefit me, hopefully, one day.

This pressure to make oneself small in classroom discussions, ignore deficit-informed microaggressions and blatant exclusions, embrace the role of amiable racial or gendered token, and collect surface-level compliments like "You'll be fine" and "We're not worried about you" from faculty instead of meaningful support is deeply documented in an expanse of critical scholarship. I highlighted, underlined, and dog-eared passages describing the pain of constructing a conciliatory affect to make it through each seminar, office hour visit, and study group; I held my secondhand copy of *Black Feminist Thought* to my chest and wept because I saw myself so painfully in the controlling images Patricia Hill Collins described. My calloused fingers traced citations and footnotes back to the colonial trope of the mollifying Mammy; I felt the contours of misogynoir-fueled assumptions that I, and other Black women in my courses, would smile and be of service. And so, this work explores the lineation of what this service entails in relation to our climb to the graduation stage and to the recalibration of what joy may look like along the way.

IN THE TEETH OF COLONIALITY: LEARNER OR LABORER?

From practicing our ABCs to deconstructing theory, we learn that education is integral to success and can be a pathway to improving not only personal quality of life but also that of our larger society. With my mother's lilting Caribbean voice whispering "Nobody can tek yuh education," I looked to my doctoral program as an exciting place of possibility. I knew that hard work and a 4.0 would "dodge the buildup of erasure" from centuries-long systematic marginalization.[3] Doctoral students complete an array of coursework and training as we are "socialized into academic futures" where having "Dr." ahead of my name would seemingly offer protection from dismissal in meetings, being underpaid, and garner respect in my field.[4] Black women, in particular, know that our futures "*without* higher education are even more limited."[5] After all, education would be the great equalizer, and remaining committed to the climb toward graduation would make reading lists without scholars of color, the same two articles on critical race theory, and a bevy of microaggressions worth it.

Graduate students hold a duality of positions as learners and workers. Both roles are measured by their relationship to producing for our university's benefit. Ranging from assisting with research, working as teaching assistants, serving on institutional committees, and administrative tasks to publishing original scholarship, this work appears to be a normative component of our graduate education. Yet it is the belief that diligent work, coupled with diversity and inclusion rhetoric, obscures "the racialized politics of exclusion" that makes this positioning tenuous for Black women.[6] While valued as symbolic tokens of progressive inclusion, Black women are also expected to engage in bodily work that is often gendered and distinctly shaped by racism. This duality connects to an expansive conceptualization of *work*, which includes immaterial labor that is simultaneously physical, cultural, technological, and psychological in addition to the material goods produced under capitalism.[7] It is the labor that lives in and moves through our bodies.

Black women's bodies have always been a cultural site where racialized and gendered power play out.[8] As graduate students, Black women embody the paradox of "being on the periphery" while "supposedly being on the inside" and often carry this duality into their careers after graduation.[9] I liken this to the well-known metaphor of being invited to have a seat at the table, but your chair is missing and you're forced to kneel.

For Black women, "there can be no meaningful theorization of power that is not felt first" as we are constantly forced to moderate ourselves so as to belong in our worlds.[10] The affective work expected of Black women graduate students remains rooted in the colonial construction of the palatable Mammy trope and the Strong Black Woman archetype—where given our "inordinate strength" and tacit acquiescence, there is nothing we cannot endure.[11] Yet neither of these stereotypes afford true access to the promised respectability higher education institutions advertise in their mission statements. Throughout my time as a doctoral student and now candidate, the archetype of the Mammy feels like the only tool of assessment afforded to me. My peers describe(d) me as strong, brilliant, and caring while simultaneously expecting me to review their papers, confessing feeling intimidated by me in group projects, and remaining silent during problematic issues because they knew *I* would speak up. My affective, emotional, and intellectual labor were celebrated behind closed doors: a professor thanked me for helping a classmate rewrite a paper, cohort members wept privately in gratitude for getting them through a difficult class after I listened to them parrot my own ideas in their final presentations, and a number of faculty were ecstatic to have me in class because they knew I'd carry the discussions.

As tokens of representation, Black women like me are integral to the financial operations of higher education; it cannot produce if Black women do not care for and buttress the needs of their institutions. We are the living encyclopedia on all things diversity and inclusion in our departments. We explain microaggressions in the midst of experiencing them while our professors remain silent. We quell a rational rage to avoid being labeled angry, difficult, or aggressive when our scholarship is deemed too personal. We are expected to juggle "other duties as assigned" like mentoring new students of color or joining diversity committees while teaching ourselves how to publish our work. Our arms ache from holding space for everyone else's comfort instead of putting ourselves first. Black women graduate students do this work as a condition of membership in academia—work that makes achievement possible for our classmates and faculty while we remain stuck in servile roles. We remain at the figurative bottom as our institution's mules and maids.

COLLAPSING PAST AND PRESENT: LABORING ON THE ACADEMIC PLANTATION AND NEOLIBERAL LIMITS

The capitalist exploitation we feel along lines of race and gender are inextricably tied to patterns of class formation that operate in shifting sociohistorical contexts. As enslaved persons, Black women served as invisible caretakers, as silent field-workers, and in other dehumanizing positions in the interior lives of the ruling/owning class of whites. Here the hegemonic discourse surrounding Black women focused on their subhuman status— among the negative and dehumanizing stereotypes that plague Black women, the Mammy archetype remains the "normative yardstick used to evaluate" Black women's affect and respectability.[12]

The Mammy is a role initially derived from plantation economies that demanded the enslaved woman's willing subordination and acceptance of her role on the periphery of white life.[13] She exists to care and facilitate "a feeling of ease, well-being, satisfaction, excitement or passion" for others so that she appears to happily participate in this veiled exploitation.[14] As Black women have been expected to engage in this immaterial work, regardless of their position or role in the world, coercive care work infiltrates all elements of life. To *happily* mammy others, Black women and femmes construct the affect of an eager willingness to please and placate in order to mitigate rampant misogynoir. There is no separation of work in the private and public sphere as our affective labor continues to be commodified; a historical materialist analysis of this pattern makes clear that Black women have learned to be in servitude long before matriculating in academic institutions. Black women, in these settings, learn to accept and rationalize being in service to others as part of graduate training. When our curricula, socialization, and departmental culture expects/demands this positioning, one must consider how such norms quell the fervent curiosity and resilient agency deftly illustrated in our admissions essays. Our palatability feels like the price of admission.

Neoliberalism continues to obscure these exploitative norms as students and faculty alike are "motivated by what will benefit [them] personally"; this is both encouraged and rewarded through the norms of American schooling, much in the same way "the power of the slaveholding planter class [constructed] reality in a fashion that justified their every action."[15] As a service industry, postsecondary institutions stratify their population into a hierarchy where racialized and gendered conceptions of work/labor remain the barometer of wage value that keeps Black women firmly on "the bottom rung."[16] The work we do in moderating our bodies, affects, and needs goes unpaid and often takes priority over advancing our own scholarship. As all members of an academic plantation (sub)consciously accept Black women at the bottom of the social caste system, these colonial relations ultimately rationalize the subjugation of Black women as acceptable. Black women are expected to provide care work within their departments, without question, supporting their counterparts in their academic pursuits as well as the labor that traditionally falls under the domestic sphere. This looks like being an other mother or big sister, my exceptionalism as a learner mislabeled as an exemption from support or mentorship, and pacifying classmates who felt intimidated by my intellect as well as the personal experiences I brought to our discussions. Serving in the margins feels paramount to my coursework, research, and academic training. Professors would tell me how smart I was and that they were not worried about me finishing the degree; yet I found myself encouraged to support more advanced graduate students by sharing how I completed our department's forms and paperwork or assisting with recruitment open houses instead of strengthening my research. Such unwaged care work has *always* been performed by Black women, and it is expected in higher education as a "precondition" to the intellectual work that is required to complete our degrees,[17] which holds exchange value whereas affectual work does not; it is quite easy to "[forget] Mammy had a brain" when students and faculty alike expect Black women "to always be chuckling and nurturing no matter what" intellectual prowess we have to offer.[18] In this context Black women learn to participate in academia as affective workers while our counterparts learn to normalize the expectation that we *will* perform it for them as well as our faculty. What joy can be fashioned from life on the periphery of the intellectual community we have been promised membership to?

This struggle in the academy cannot be easily divorced from the plantation politics that inform the social rhetoric of Black womanhood in and outside academia. Appearing grateful, nonthreatening, and willing to work hard can, perhaps, negate any potential of being called unruly, troublesome, and out of place in these high-achieving academic settings, but at what cost? So long as Black women function without complaint, we may experience the social mobility advanced credentials are advertised to offer. Perhaps, then, education *can* be the great equalizer. Although serving as departmental surrogate mother figures may not seem as grueling or dehumanizing as labor outside of academia, it still functions in service to a neocolonial master. Neoliberal politics provides "just enough leeway for Black people to breathe and have a sense of humanity," but I cannot ignore that "what has changed are the modes of production, not the oppression."[19] In many ways, these lessons in graduate training encourage us to be forgiving of such exploitation. For my immigrant family, the PhD will be a symbol of an oft-romanticized American dream. It will be proof of my elite membership in a unique class of academics. My family's sacrifices will be worth it. The ivory tower celebrates identity representation where the mere presence of Black women disappears the racist and patriarchal practices that limit our learning. Yet throughout the process I wondered if I really had a seat at the proverbial table or if I was merely ornamental wallpaper in the room.

When I clutched my worn copy of *Black Feminist Thought* and considered my relationship to the colonial Mammy,[20] I questioned what could be different if I were no longer willing to be complicit in my own erasure. What if I no longer accepted check marks and smiley faces in my feedback and directly asked for more substantive guidance on my assignments? Would I lose anything of worth if I pointed out that every single student funded for a particular academic conference was a white woman? Am I truly lifting as I climb if my complacency further cements my position in the margins of the academic world? Answering these questions pushed me to reframe the terrain of contemporary higher education institutions as academic plantations and guided a deeper interrogation of these superstructures that thrive through this distinct exploitation.[21] Reconceptualizing the university as exploitative rather than empowering remains necessary in divorcing my value from this expected racialized and gendered labor. I needed to delve into my feminist imagination to use those memorized citations as a blueprint for *living* a liberatory life.

TENDING TO MY JOY: THE RISK AND REWARD OF FEMINIST POSSIBILITY

When Black women graduate students name and address this misogynoir, we are dehumanized through the "assignment of negative monikers like 'angry,' 'difficult,' 'ungrateful,' and 'lazy.'"[22] Perhaps, we wonder, am I not strong enough, as brilliant as we thought, or even worthy enough to endure this lesson on what it takes to be an academic? Yet Black women are rarely afforded the luxury of mobility between/through systems of oppression.[23] Waiting for joy to come once I cross the graduation stage makes it impossible to *be* in the present—to measure my worth by how much I can endure instead of how much I can truly *live*. Reworking the roadmap of the PhD pushes me to seek affirmation outside my grade point average and publications on my curriculum vitae.

This process feels like a debridement of a colonial wound—a cleaving of the thin protection from participating in our own erasure for survival and tending to the deep scar tissue cradling the by-product of surviving misogynoir-istic exploitation. Successfully completing the degree might feel like earning one's way out of class oppression even when we know the long-desired seat at the ruling-class table "does not change the agenda."[24] Like many Black women and femmes before and alongside me in this journey, I am learning how to build my own table. I abandoned the belief that writing our truths means we must protect the institutions—and people—who taught me to prioritize obfuscation and the comfort of others. So I capitalize "Black" and choose to cite Black feminist poetry, music, and recipes in my scholarship. Joy looks like being the author of my own story, relishing the power of the journey instead of the vehicle—my doctoral training—that brings me to the final destination.

With threads spun from deficit-imbued lead turned precious metal, I know we can suture ourselves whole. As Black women carving out our path toward the doctorate and beyond, we follow breadcrumbs left by our elders; embarking on this path, illuminated by refusal and hard truths, is an act of reclamation. We begin to dream beyond binaries, to intertwine our breath with intergenerational demands for our humanity and refuse the role of academic Mammies, mules, and maids. As Ashley D. Clemons writes in chapter 3, "'Now I'm choosing life, yo,': Finding Joy in Neo-Soul Music and Poetry While Navigating Graduate School and the Academic Job Search," joy manifests in unabashed self-authorship without apology or regret. It is reveling in the completeness of "no" and the protection of the community I love beyond my campus walls. Refusal to be of service may have its consequences, but the gift of peace of mind is priceless. A rich wealth of transnational Black feminist magic provides the balm with which I cauterize this mottled wound; stitched with theories of the flesh, I know to rub lovingly, Lorde's salve of forgiveness in a requiem for Black women mired in the deficits.[25] Together with my fellow sistren, I am unraveling these colonial logics with the inky residue of refusal to write our stories as outsiders within—telling our own stories of survival, triumph, regret, courage, and desire.[26] In the times I feel most lost, I outstretch my hand and grasp the fire of my elders and feed embers of their inherited resistance nestled in my chest; I turn inward and listen to the cadence of *Words of Fire* and remember that I, me, and you are the true north of my own compass.[27] The joy comes in the act of widening the interstices where Black women can thrive as curious intellectuals instead of as laboring mules, Mammies, and maids. As I approach the end of my own climb up to the doctorate, I know that with degree in hand, I will have made it *in spite of* the constraints of this coloniality; I am no one's smiling Mammy. After all, "what we face down cannot harm us" in daydreams turned vibrant healing feminist possibilities.[28] We become more than what we can endure.

NOTES

1. Gutiérrez y Muhs et al., *Presumed Incompetent.*
2. Nzinga, *Lean Semesters*, 19.
3. Rankine, *Citizen*, 11.
4. Acker and Haque, "Struggle to Make Sense of Doctoral Study," 229.
5. Nzinga, *Lean Semesters*, 27.
6. Chatterjee and Maira, *Imperial University*, 4.
7. Elias, Gill, and Scharff, *Aesthetic Labour.*
8. Davis, "Women and Capitalism."
9. Carty, "Black Women in Academia," 33.
10. Durham, *Home with Hip Hop Feminism*, 2.
11. M. Wallace, *Black Macho*, 107.
12. Collins, *Black Feminist Thought* (1990), 71.
13. Collins, 71.
14. Hardt and Negri, *Empire*, 96.
15. Cordóva, "Knowledge and Power," 40.
16. Lomax, "Black Women's Lives Don't Matter."
17. Davis, "Women and Capitalism," 21.
18. S. Wilson, "They Forgot Mammy Had a Brain," 65–77.
19. Carby, "White Woman Listen!," 123.
20. Collins, *Black Feminist Thought*, 1990.
21. Cordóva, "Knowledge and Power"; Matias, "'I Ain't Your Doc Student,'" 59–68.
22. Squire and McCann, "Women of Color with Critical Worldviews," 411.
23. Carby, "White Woman Listen!," 110–28.
24. B. Smith, "Where's the Revolution? (1993)," 248–52.
25. Lorde, *Sister Outsider.*
26. Collins, *Black Feminist Thought* (1990).
27. Guy-Sheftall, *Words of Fire* (1995).
28. Kupenda, "Facing Down the Spooks," 27.

CHAPTER 5

Getting a PhD Will "Make Ya or Break Ya"

Surviving the "Make Ya" in the Ivory Tower

KIMBERLY M. STANLEY

I made it home. I managed, somehow, to wake, feed, and drive my six-year-old to school, navigate the drop-off line, force a smile and a "Have a good day. See you later," all while holding back waves of panic. Once home, with the thud of the door behind me, I dropped my purse, grabbed my cell phone, and instead of going to my room with its king-size bed, I entered my daughter's. I climbed into her twin bed, curled up, and pulled the covers over my head. "Is this writing anxiety?" I questioned. I had experienced writing anxiety when I was getting my master's degree, but it was never this intense. Never this debilitating. Back then I would, eventually, center myself and tap into my joy of the work. I found it exhilarating, liberating, and empowering, in fact, to create, write, and have my ideas matter. It was this precise joy that propelled me to pursue a PhD. Here I was, now, in my first year of a PhD program unable to locate, never mind activate, my power of joy. "Was this really about a five-page paper?" My mind began to race, competing with my pulsating body. Over a span of ten weeks, I had moved to the Midwest and both my grandfather and cousin had transitioned. Their deaths both shocked and stunned me, yet outwardly I tried to remain focused and unaffected—I don't think I even mentioned the loss to any of my professors for fear they would think I could not compartmentalize my personal "problems" from my academic pursuits. Still, at that time, those stressors didn't register as contributing to my panic.

Balancing, regulating, and hiding personal and family challenges sapped me. In addition to those losses, my daughter was having a hard time adjusting to her new school and our new environment. She left behind a community of friends, those "aunties" and "uncles," who had nurtured and supported her and demonstrated the value and beauty of creating bonds outside of a heteronormative family structure. She was raised and loved by a village. Minus this village, in our new town, she needed and demanded more of my emotional and physical presence. One Sunday, prior to the start of my first semester, my assigned graduate student mentor and his wife came by my apartment to introduce themselves. My daughter had "attached herself to my hip." I had read this situation as my six-year-old needing emotional reassurance. My mentor's wife, however, read it as "clingy" and a problem, asking me, "Is she always like that?" and "How will you ever finish?"

I also was having trouble adjusting. I had left a well-paying job, and my graduate stipend cut my income by more than half. I was not eligible for the Supplemental Nutrition Assistance Program (food stamps) due to how my fellowship stipend had been dispersed, and I had (erroneously) been told by financial aid that I didn't qualify for student loans. My family thought my decision to attend graduate school was both impetuous and irresponsible, although they were pleased that we were now living only a state apart. There was also the matter of my being a thirty-six-year-old, first-generation Black woman in a graduate program in which I had no previous training surrounded by white people, decades younger, who took it as sport to outdo one another when it came to eviscerating a text. I was not the only Black woman with a child in my cohort. Another woman, who had two children, seemed especially adept in class. However, she dropped out of the program within a few weeks under the allegations of plagiarism. I felt that if she couldn't handle this, then what chances do I have?

As I contemplated my lack of options, I recalled what Doris had said a few years earlier. Doris was an adjunct professor at the University of New Mexico (UNM) with her main gig working in public health. Noticing that she was the only one of my women-of-color professors without the coveted "doctor" or "professor" in front of her name, one day after class I asked why she didn't have the degree. "Girl, a PhD will make ya or break ya." I thought she was being hyperbolic or using some cliché to avoid answering a question that wasn't my business. As I lay in my daughter's bed, trembling, trying my best not to break or, at the very least, crack, her words came crashing back in waves.[1] I searched my mental Rolodex and called Minrose. She was my former professor, mentor, and friend. Minrose and her partner, Ruth, were part of a circle of white women professors at UNM who took on the role of mentoring me when my adviser passed away. When Gerry died during my first semester of my master's program, I lost the person who had confidence in me at a time when I had no confidence in myself. After class, students would gather around the lectern and just talk. Gerry would "joke" how he, a six-foot, three-inch, three-hundred-pound Black man could go from invisibility ("Sorry, I didn't see you standing there") to hypervisibility (Lady, there really isn't a need to clutch your purse). When the chair of the Africana Studies Department, a Black male professor who I hadn't *then* taken a class with, told me that I wasn't graduate school material, that I would be a burden to Gerry, and that I should just go home and be a mother to my then-infant daughter, it was Gerry who asked me, squarely and sternly, "What do *you* want?"[2] Indeed, Gerry was one of the first of many mentors to demonstrate the importance of catching the hands of others—extending to me support and mentorship and their belief that I belonged in academia. My experience with "catching the hands of others" resembles that of Barbara Ransby's, and undoubtedly countless others, who had and could depend on "supportive and respectful" mentors, not all of whom look like us. Gerry and Minrose, quite possibly rare in academia, demonstrate that "it is possible to create democratic oases within our otherwise undemocratic institutions."[3]

After Gerry passed, a few of his white women colleagues stepped up to mentor me. It was Minrose, though, a white woman from Tupelo, Mississippi, and an expert in southern literature, who knew the importance of connecting me with other African American women graduate students and professors.[4] "You need to meet so-and-so. She has a child too." At the time I thought she was facilitating friendships and networks by putting me in touch with other Black women who *just happen to* have children. Instead, she was connecting me to other Black women *with* children. Minrose, possibly knowing that my being a Black woman with a child would either render me invisible or hypervisible in the academy, facilitated me finding community that would normalize my existence and my presence within it. It was Minrose I consulted when I was considering having my then-partner and not the biological father of my daughter adopt her. "Absolutely not," she said. "You'll be trapped. What if you want to move? You'll have to get his approval to take your child out of state." And it was Minrose who encouraged me to go back to graduate school. So, I called Minrose, hoping she could normalize this feeling or at least explain it. I asked her if she ever had writer's anxiety or a fear of writing. She paused for a moment and said, "No, I don't think so." I felt a crack.

Feeling desperate, I called the only other number I had handy—the graduate secretary. I do not know what possessed me to call Alexia and what I said, I just know that my fear of breaking or having a complete breakdown was worse than my fear of exposing that I was not a strong Black woman.[5] The next day, Alexia had coordinated a crisis plan: she had contacted my adviser; she linked me to a mentor; and, after some research, she located the university's Counseling and Psychological Services. Although she had been the department's graduate secretary for years, she never once knew about the counseling resources at the health center. I do recall her saying that in the future, she'd pass this resource along to students.

I begin with this incident because it was not my only "break ya" moment. Believe me, I've had many of these "moments" as a graduate student and as I try to navigate the tenure track. I begin here, though, because it was the first definitive incident that forced me to think about the "silences" and the dichotomies of "invisibility/hypervisibility," the fear of the "make ya" and "break ya," and in retrospect, it was a moment in which, no matter how hard I tried, I could not calm myself to access my peace or joy. What does it really mean to "make it" or be accepted in academia? Was it possible to "make it" without some form of loss? Loss of family? Loss of values? Loss of joy?[6]

Joy. The (joyful) task of writing this essay had me reflecting a lot on joy and my pursuit of a career within the ivory tower. What is "joy"? I was clear that, for me, joy was distinctly different from "happy." When discussing "what is joy" with friends and family, there was a consensus that being happy or happiness relies on external stimuli. Joy, on the other hand, is internal.[7] When I think of "joy," I think of Audre Lorde's "The Uses of the Erotic: The Erotic as Power." The erotic and joy are "resource[s] within each of us," they "offer a well of replenishing and provocative force[s] to the woman who does not fear [their] revelation." They are the "measure[s] between" those spaces where possibilities are imagined. Indeed, as Lorde asserts, "once we have experienced it, we know we can aspire." The erotic and joy are revolutionary and radical, and time and time again, efforts have been made to dispossess Black women of both. As Deborah Gray White wrote in *Telling Histories: Black Women Historian the Ivory Tower*, "The ivory tower can be an exhilarating, stimulating place." "But," she also concedes "it can also be isolating, debilitating, and lonely, especially for those . . . whose very bodies stand in opposition to the conventional wisdom regarding academia."[8] As the authors of the introduction to *Presumed Incompetent: The Intersections of Race and Class for Women in Academia* made clear, the culture of academia is one that prides itself on "brilliance, rigor, seriousness, rationality [and] objectivity," all characteristics associated with masculinity.[9] Having and expressing feelings of isolation, panic, and desperation are demoralizing and shameful within the academy and are viewed as a personal and intellectual failure and a sign of weakness. Yet, as Lorde asserts, it is a "cruel" system that attempts to dispossess or "rob our work of its erotic value, its erotic power and life appeal and fulfillment . . . [that] reduces work to a travesty of necessities." Lorde posits that "as women, we need to examine the ways in which our world can be truly different."[10] This collection of essays is clearly a step toward that.

Although African Americans, single parents, and those differently abled, queer, LGBTQ+, or those whose presence is considered "nontraditional" (older and first generations) have been able to enter the ivory tower through the cracks forged by trailblazers, the institution has tried its best to maintain the status quo.[11] Scholarship written by Black women on their experiences as a "double minority" within academia rings similar with discussions of isolation and exclusion, microaggressions, tokenism, low student evaluations, and the expectation that their Black women bodies serve only the purposes of the institution. What does it mean to have the ivory tower "make" you versus having it "break" you? As a Black woman, both options sound unappealing and violent. They render me silent, invisible, and dissembled. As I reflect on this binary, it reminds me of "jumping double dutch," a strategy Black women employ (similar to dissemblance) to face the challenges of racism and sexism. Barbara J. Love and Valerie D. Jiggetts write that Black women, to escape "jumping double dutch," must "develop a liberatory consciousness." They continue: a "liberatory consciousness has enabled Back women not only to stand against the double hazards of racism and sexism but to simultaneously work toward liberatory spaces, language, and relationships."[12] The liberatory spaces or, rather, safe spaces are those liminal spaces in between the dueling ropes or the possibilities in between being "made" or "broken."

IN BETWEEN THE MAKE YA AND BREAK YA: DEALING WITH DEPRESSION AND WRITING ANXIETY

I had worked in social service in varying capacities over a decade before I moved to Indiana, and because of this, many of my friends were therapists or social workers. I had also spent years—on and off—seeing a therapist.

My professional life normalized mental health and wellness. Yoga, hikes, meditation, and taking long walks became strategies to maintain balance. Still, it was only in niche circles that I felt comfortable talking about therapy and mental health disorders. Depression and anxiety were viewed as weaknesses, and the inability to handle such was one's personal failure. When I was a child there was a saying: "Therapy is a Black man's Cadillac." Implied in this maxim is that Black folks engaged in conspicuous consumption as a form of mental wellness, and Cadillacs, like therapy, are luxuries that the average working-class person cannot afford. I can remember hearing "no one has time to be depressed," "no one cares about your problems," and "stop being so emotional." Respectability demanded that public displays of emotions be kept hidden. Crying in public was viewed as weakness; to discuss "problems" was to be thought of as a burden. So I learned from a young age to engage in dissemblance—to smile (but not too much), and not to discuss serious problems.[13] Thus, my crises always centered around interpersonal relationships, or so I thought. My attitude toward mental wellness, then, wasn't about maintaining an ongoing healthy relationship with myself or healing from past trauma but situational interventions. Therapy, like graduate school, requires some calculable risks. And just like graduate school, when it came to therapy, I didn't know how risky it was until I was knee-deep in it.

Access to mental health resources is a serious problem. The length of time that it takes to see a therapist, cost, insurance, cultural and generational attitudes regarding therapy, cultural competency, and the lack of professionals of color are impediments to receiving good mental health services. After my "break ya" moment in fall 2003 and telling the intake clinician that I was not a risk to myself, I had to wait until the beginning of spring 2004 for my first therapy appointment. My therapeutic relationship with DeeDee lasted my entire graduate school career. The work we did together was precipitated by my anxiety and depression, but she helped me deal with other deep-seeded wounds.[14] The irony, of course, is the isolation and insecurities I felt in graduate school helped unearth deeply buried traumas that continued to fuel my insecurities and pull the thin scab off never fully healed wounds. Therapy with DeeDee took me out of isolation and gave me permission to voice, without fear of judgment, the pain, shame, guilt, and inadequacies that contributed to the running scripts in my head. I began to talk to other Black women about my experiences, which, in turn, gave them permission to discuss their feelings of perceived inadequacies. These conversations over drinks or in darkened corners widened the gap between the narrow options of "making" or "breaking" and created spaces of possibilities for discourse and community.

Therapy was one resource I used to strive toward accessing my joy, mental wellness, and balance, but my problems with writing persisted. I entered my program in 2003, and I still had not completed my dissertation by 2012. Many, but not all, in my cohort had graduated, and I perceived (maybe erroneously) that my professors didn't think I'd finish. There was already a perception from white graduate students that Black graduate students were there due to "special treatment," and a few openly stated that I was just hanging around until my funding ran out. Although these reasons were untrue, I, too, began to wonder if I was going to finish.[15] I couldn't decipher if my delay in finishing had to do with my anxiety, teaching responsibilities, and being a single parent or if I truly wasn't graduate student material. Although I still had opportunities for funding, in 2012 I decided to create space for myself. I made the decision to take leave for a semester, live off of student loans, and just concentrate on my writing. If I had not made any progress by the end of the semester, I would have my answer. I gave myself permission to "write crap" and set up a writing routine. I joined a dissertation group through the counseling center where I met other graduate students—queer, white women, Latinx, and international—who were also struggling with finishing their dissertations. Within our therapeutic space, our conversations vacillated between the hope of finishing to the despair of we'll never get this done.

MAKING SPACE: THE BETWEENS THE MAKE AND THE BREAK

The first year of my PhD program was a balancing act of being a student and a parent. Single parenting, in many ways, made juggling the demands of graduate school simple. My daughter's needs always came first.[16] My daughter, who was diagnosed with epilepsy as a toddler, required medical specialists and had an Individual Educational Plan (IEP) for her schooling. Doctors' appointments and school meetings often conflicted with classes and teaching. These extra demands speak to the layers that accompany being a single parent of a child who has additional needs. I once had a professor—married white woman with an able-bodied child— tell me that I needed to reschedule my daughter's neurology appointment because it conflicted with a class. For this professor, the personal should not interfere, and most definitely not dictate, the sanctity of the professional sphere. Doctor appointments should be scheduled during the summer or around one's teaching responsibilities as to not interfere with the academic schedule. However, my values and the reality of having a special-needs child dictated otherwise. I, occasionally, would interject my child's name just to remind my professors that I was not the "average" graduate student. I wasn't asking for special treatment, just visibility and making space.

Childcare was also a balancing act. My graduate classes were held in the evening and lasted past the time childcare facilities stayed open. This meant locating "aunties" who would care for my daughter. This proved exceptionally difficult in this first year since I knew no one. And there was the matter of basic needs, such as food, paying the utilities, or the nurturing space within Black beauty salons. The university's resource page was not helpful because it didn't cater or even include information regarding childcare or subsidies, and Black student organizations didn't provide readily accessible information on how to find these resources. The latter is more surprising because of the population these organizations support. Because of my previous employment, I had the skill set to find and access resources on my own. Still, I would have appreciated recommendations and guidance from other Black students. This doesn't mean that the information wasn't shared—people often gain access to services through informal networks of information sharing. I recall informing a fellow white woman history graduate student about food stamps. I would see her in the graduate lounge eating peanut butter and jelly and an apple. She mentioned that, monthly, she needed to make the choice between food or rent. Information on and access to these subsidies and resources, especially for graduate students with families, is a necessity and makes visible that not all graduate students can or should engage with the romanticization of the graduate school struggle.

By 2005, I had met other Black, nontraditional students. We felt invisible, and thereby neglected, by traditional Black student organizations who were too focused on the social aspects of graduate school. We were looking for something different: tools and resources, professional development, activism, and an intellectual community. We named ourselves the Black Scholars Collective (BSC). Our purpose was "to specifically encourage and uplift Indiana University's graduate students of African descent . . . [by] provid[ing] useful resources, activities, and information geared toward the[ir] successful retention."[17] Our first program was Black @ IU, a mentoring session where Black faculty and senior graduate students provided insight into how to survive being a graduate student at a predominantly white institution (PWI). The following year, I spearheaded "The Collision of Two Worlds: Single-Parenting and Graduate School." The program featured professionals—both in and out of academia—who managed to get advanced degrees while being a single parent and community partners and resource providers who informed students of the resources available to them, including mental health services. Although personally pleased that I was able to put together a program that publicly acknowledged our existence, I was even more surprised by the turnout. It was well attended even by married couples and graduate students and professionals who were contemplating having a child.

In its short three years of existence, BSC hosted programs that addressed the on- and off-campus needs of Black graduate students: Brown Bags, thesis and dissertation support; financial literacy programming; and tenants' rights. We also addressed diversity and racism on campus through our own programming and collaborations with Muslim and Latinx student organizations. Within these allyships, BSC was operating in what Barbara J. Love and Valerie D. Jiggetts call a "liberatory consciousness."[18] The programs that BSC offered stemmed from the members'—mostly nontraditional African American women—despair that we were thrown into a predominantly white space without any guidance or support. We recognized what we needed, and we created that space. We were determined not to break under the pressure of exclusion.

BREAKING THE STIGMA: PARENTING A CHILD WITH MENTAL ILLNESS

Parenting a child with epilepsy, cognitive delays, and, later, behavioral issues as a graduate student presented another spectrum of challenges. As

I mentioned earlier, I deliberately made visible that I had a child with fragile health. The visibility was important to me. It disrupted who was thought of as a graduate student and who occupied these spaces. Health issues are understandable and given grace especially when it comes to one's family member or an innocent child. I felt behavioral issues, on the other hand, would further stigmatize me. I remained silent or downplayed the severity of her behavioral problems because I felt that it would limit my opportunities in academia or that people would perceive her acting out as a consequence of my parenting or my career choices. As I reflect back on graduate school, my year as an instructor at a southern research university, as a postdoc, and as a junior professor, I tried to mitigate—hide, really—that my daughter would impede my progress. Still, there is no denying that her behavioral and cognitive impairments were of great and growing concern, and at times, I felt guilty for "dragging her along" on this journey and resentful of the additional stressors. Crises and inpatient hospitalizations would disrupt writing, teaching, and time to do research. She was also treatment resistant, and finding a therapist that took my concerns seriously and didn't see her as just a rebellious teen with a controlling mother was difficult. The one time that a therapist did think she posed a risk to herself due to impulse control and poor decision-making, he dropped her as a client without a care plan and notified me as I was about to board a plane for a job talk.

In 2016, I accepted a postdoctoral fellowship at one of the leading research universities on the East Coast after spending a year as an instructor at research university in Tennessee. I was happy to get the fellowship for several reasons. For one, it was more money. As a single parent who was paying rent in Tennessee and a mortgage in Indiana, I could not make ends meet. I relied on my parents' assistance with paying bills, and my credit cards were maxed out. Most important, though, this postdoc provided the amazing opportunity to be supervised by one of the leading scholars in Black women's history. During my campus visit, she and I had lunch. Over drinks, I asked her several questions about her career and her personal life—basically, How did you do it? She referred me to a book she had edited and freely talked about some of the obstacles she encountered in being part of that small circle of women who laid the foundation for Black women's history. I cursorily mentioned some of the challenges I was experiencing with my daughter. I didn't want to divulge too much for fear that she'd think she'd made a mistake in choosing me. In return, she spoke about her own challenges raising her two daughters and her divorce. She offered me three pieces of advice: church, get a good therapist, and kick my daughter out. I nodded, which could've been interpreted as an affirmative for her advice, but in my head all I heard was the classic refrain from Meat Loaf's 1977 classic: "Now, don't be sad. 'Cause two out of three ain't bad." I remained silent in explaining that my daughter's problems, potentially, were more severe than teenage rebellion and kicking her out would not be the best intervention.[19]

The fears and the lack of knowledge about epilepsy and mental illness helped me create and maintain a culture of silence. Similar to people in academia reluctantly discussing their impostor syndrome or writing anxiety, very little dialogue exists regarding medical and psychological disabilities outside of those that have, finally, been deemed socially acceptable. It isn't uncommon to hear someone mention that they are "depressed," seeing a therapist, or taking an antidepressant. Actually, it's trendy and a marker of class respectability. Acknowledging one's emotional state and engaging in a form of self-care, as Kanika Bell states, is a rejection of the "superwoman" stereotype, and it challenges the assumptions that Black women do not suffer from mental illness.[20] Still, this acknowledgment only addresses the milder cases. Situational depression, major depressive disorder (MDD), and bipolar disorder/manic depression are different types of illnesses. My diagnosis of MDD was tinged with shame—as were the stories I heard from other women of color. The shame stemmed from feeling deficient or "not strong enough."[21] For Black women academics whose identity is so attached to their intellect, an emotional weakness or imbalance can lead to hypervisibility and further stigmatization. It was this fear of stigmatization that kept me silent regarding my daughter. I carried the shame of her illness because I believed it reflected my lack of strength and control as a parent. My child's mental health was a major influence in me returning to Bloomington. I had accepted an assistant professorship at a public university forty-five miles from the city. We had made community in Bloomington, and I believed that I could access the resources that she needed, while I also regrouped.

My first year at a state university in Indiana was stressful. I was a diversity hire in the African and African American Studies Program, which at one time was a stand-alone department but was subsumed under another department owing to budget cuts and low enrollment. Although no one in my department had told me this, I was informed that the diversity hire was a result of a movement organized by students and staff who wanted more Blacks in faculty, staff, and the administration. It is unclear if my hire was a result of the demands of that movement. A Black instructor was already a member of the faculty, and although he didn't hold a PhD, he was well liked and an institutional fixture within the program and the community. Still, no doubt my department was cognizant of the demands and the optics of not having a Black tenure-track faculty member in an African American Studies Program. Even before my arrival on campus, I was told that my office would be centrally located so students will see me as soon as they came in; the office's previous occupant had to move to a much larger, quieter, corner office. I understood the reason to want to make me visible. The institution has one of the largest African American student populations in Indiana. However, African Americans make up only 5 percent of its workforce.[22]

Adding a Black person to the faculty was a way to address the diversity issue but also a possible recruitment of Black majors and minors. I, too, wanted to teach and mentor Black students. What surprised me most, though, was how Black students reacted to me. I was not prepared for the level of microaggression, misogynoir, hostility, and disrespect that I would experience in the classroom. The experience Wanda A. Hendricks writes about in *Telling Histories* could have been mine. African American students, mostly men, challenged my knowledge of history and preferred to counter my expertise with their own social media training, web-based education of African American history. These men were part of a core group that made my semester a bit too much.[23] They expressed homophobia and sexism within my class—behaviors I would not tolerate. One student, after class, was upset with me for not reminding him, specifically, of an assignment. "I pay your salary," he fired. I shot back before I could think, "You pay for the lights. Someone else pays my salary." When I went to my chair for help, I was told to file an incident report and the assistant dean would investigate. I filed several and never heard back. I then went to the dean, who wasn't much help either, especially when he learned that the students were Black and not white. Colleagues and administrators offered suggestions, such as smile more and let them get to know you as a person; relax classroom policies, ignore the behavior; and, my favorite, have the Director of Student Conduct come to my class to review the university's policy. "He's a six-foot white guy. They are scared of him," I was told. I vetoed this immediately. It was my opinion that this was one the reasons I was experiencing the hostility in the first place. Students don't see women—especially Black women—as the authority in the classroom. The professor is always assumed to be white. My colleagues, though, didn't understand. They mentioned their own encounters with disruptive students and the tactics they used to maintain an educational milieu. My white women colleagues often recruited (white) male faculty or their husbands to accompany them to class to deter disruptions. When I asked about policies or what rights I had to safety, there were none in the handbook. No solutions offered positioned or supported me as the authority in the classroom.

My high drop/fail rate and my teaching evaluations reflected my difficult year. I felt as if students and colleagues constantly criticized my pedagogy, preferring that I lower my standards. I constantly adjusted my syllabus, tried new activities, but nothing worked. In desperation, or maybe confirmation, I reached out to the Black woman who had held this position prior to me. Her response was conciliatory. She didn't disparage or blame students, the institution, or any particular individual. She did state that some staff tried to help her adjust and handle the stress of the classroom. Mostly, though, she blamed the lack of resources available to underprepared African American students attending a PWI. What I found most interesting about her reply was what she didn't write. She never mentioned how she felt supported by faculty mentoring her or how she felt like she was valued and that her appointment was more than just tokenism. As Sayam Davis writes in chapter 9 of this book, the hiring of Black faculty without making substantive change to diversity, equity, and inclusion is just "performative wokeness" and further contributes to a hostile work environment. Although the university may have had good intentions in hiring a Black person, at that time there was little to no effort in examining and changing the structure that made it impossible to maintain Black faculty.

YOUR FACE IS LEAKING: IN BETWEEN THE "MAKE" AND THE "BREAK"

When I was a graduate student, I had biweekly appointments at "the shop." I didn't have much money, but getting my hair done and my face waxed and communing with other Black women was, for me, some modicum of self-care. The Black beauty shop, especially in a PWI college town, is the liberatory safe space that simultaneously exists because of and yet beyond the dictates of the ivory tower. It was in the shop—actually a room, a "hidden space" within a barbershop—that Black woman, some associated with the university, many not, would "transcend the confines of intersecting oppressions."[24] There we were, kee-keeing, confessing, witnessing, spilling (tea), crying, swearing, defying, and healing while someone laid back and rested her neck on the shampoo bowl as Jeanelle engaged in the ritual of Black hair care. Hair washed, scalp scratched, as the water rid her hair free of not just shampoo but the weight of the last few weeks. One by one, each of us took our turn underneath the water, transitioned to the heat of the dryer, and then, finally, moved to the comfort (zone) of the chair. Although not a "formal" site for Black feminist mental health therapy, the shop, as an informal space, allows a Black feminist perspective to emerge. It is through these "serious conversations and humor" that Black women "affirm one another's humanity, specialness, and right to exist." In *Black Feminist Thought*, Patricia Hill Collins reminds us that the women who occupy these spaces are often strangers but recognize the "need to value Black womanhood."[25] Thus the shop is transformed and a transformative space where Black women are—I am—made visible and seen. It's this space of community and belonging; of cultural sights, sounds, and smells and where the vernacular is not policed; where signifying and specifying is met with raucous laughter and where code-switching is not required. It was also my space for social support. Although I saw my therapist as routinely as I went to the shop, it was in these Black women spaces that I sought out "culturally competent" advice and found a support system. The shop was my space of marronage. As Cécile Accilien writes in chapter 15 of this volume, a strategy of marronage is to find your people, build community, and create new strategies of resistance.

After I received my PhD, leaving graduate school also meant leaving my community. The temporary appointments that I had had as an instructor and a postdoc didn't leave me time to build community outside the university. The downside of this, of course, is I didn't know where to go to escape the microaggressions or rejuvenate myself spiritually, psychically, mentally, or emotionally in a culturally responsive way. Moving twice in two years, trying to manage my daughter's mental health needs and behavioral outbursts, not attending to my own depression, and just trying to keep it together so that I wouldn't break left me exhausted—too exhausted to even engage in the routine maintenance of self-care. But I also knew that not maintaining this ritual was an outward manifestation of how I was feeling inside. So, absent of any recommendations, I ventured into the first waxing salon I saw in my neighborhood. I walked to the back room and lay on the massage table, letting my back press into the padding. I closed my eyes, took a deep inhale, and I was still. I was aware of my stillness, and it felt foreign, like I hadn't been still in a long time. I rested in the stillness and the quiet as I anticipated what was going to come next. I was not sure what caused it, though. Maybe it was my stillness or maybe her gentleness or the softness of the towel as she wiped my face of the oil and dirt in preparation for my eyebrow wax, or it could have been the welcomed shock of the warmth of the wax on my face. At first it was just one solitary tear. Then another. Soon, there was a slow and steady stream of hot tears flowing from my eyes, pass my ears, to the nape of my neck. I was still. Although my eyes were closed, I could feel her looking down at me. As she wiped my tears, she said in her broken English, "Your face is leaking. Why is your face leaking?" I smiled.

I shook my head signaling that it was nothing and let out a deep exhale. The innocence of her comment was a perfect observation of the consequences of how I had allowed myself to become dispossessed of my joy. It was in this passive stillness of self-care that I reconnected with my body and my joy.

NOTES

1. Doris would eventually receive her doctorate in international communication competence. Leslie Brown recalls asking the lone Black person she knew with a PhD what it would take to earn the degree. The woman replied, "You need to be crazy." See Brown, "History Tracked Me Down," 263.

2. Elsa Barkley Brown tells of when her admission and fellowship to a graduate school program was rescinded once the committee learned she was pregnant. See her "Bodies of History," 220.

3. Ransby, "Dancing on the Edges of History," 242.

4. Deirdre M. Bowen writes that "the mentoring women of color receive is severely lacking, even though we know support is essential to a student's continued success in academia." Part of this lack is the scarcity of Black women and women-of-color faculty. See Bowen, "Visibly Invisible," 117.

5. See Walker-Barnes "When the Bough Breaks," 43–55, esp. 47, 50–51.

6. L. Brown, "History Tracked Me Down," 262.

7. Jody Antal Nicks, text message to author, August 4, 2022; Coach Donna Jean, text message to author, August 5, 2022.

8. Lorde, "Uses of the Erotic," 87, 88; D. White, "Introduction," 21–22.

9. Harris and González, introduction, 5.

10. Lorde, "Uses of the Erotic," 89.

11. "Not until the decades following the Second World War did social movements, federal legislation, judicial decisions, and presidential decrees pry open the doors of the nation's universities to a large number of women, people of color, and the working class." Harris and González, introduction, 7.

12. Love and Jiggetts, "Foreword," xiii.

13. See Walker-Barnes, "When the Bough Breaks," 47.

14. My use of "seeded" here is intentional.

15. White writes that "jealousy and lack of support from male and female colleagues, overwhelming familial responsibilities . . . have plagued black women academics in every field, seemingly from time immemorial." See White, "Introduction," 15.

16. Barbara Ransby discusses "juggling parental responsibilities and graduate-school demands." See "Dancing on the Edge of History," 244. The concept of family first does not apply only to children. In her essay, Ula Taylor also applied the family-first ethos in being the caretaker of her dying father and sister. See her "Death of Dry Tears," 176.

17. Black Scholars Collective, "Constitution." I would be remiss not to acknowledge Stephanie Singleton, whose steady and focused leadership and vision is one of the reasons the collective lasted as long as it did.

18. Love and Jiggetts, "Foreword," xvi.

19. Meat Loaf, "Two Out of Three Ain't Bad."

20. K. Bell, "Sisters on Sisters," 25.

21. Bell, "Sisters on Sisters."

22. In 2020, Indiana State University's Black or African American student population was 16 percent. Indiana University–Bloomington Black or African American student population has consistently hovered between 5 and 6 percent. See "President's Council on Inclusive Excellence 12th Annual Report."

23. Hendricks, "On the Margins," 154.

24. Collins, *Black Feminist Thought* (2000), 103.

25. Collins, 113.

Part II
Policy and Practice

CHAPTER 6

A View from the Margins of Academia

Michelle Dionne Thompson

I must be the bridge to nowhere
But my true self

Donna Rushin, "The Bridge Poem"

When, at thirty-two years old, I finally took the leap into academia, I envisioned a particular path, the one all of us see when we start on this journey, because I knew no other way. I would earn my master's degree, start the doctoral program taking my comps, do the research, write my dissertation, and be hired into that fabulous job in the ivory tower that would provide the benefits needed to pay for my son's college tuition. My primary field was the African diaspora, my secondary field colonial Latin America and the Caribbean, and if one could complete the program in five years or less, you were likely to reap the benefits of a plum job in these rapidly expanding fields.

This was the vision before the 2008 economic meltdown that robbed people (mostly Black, Indigenous, and people of color [BIPOC]) of jobs, homes, livelihoods, and life as they knew it.[1] Institutions of higher learning were (and still are) quick to pivot in corporate ways. We must cut jobs. We must stop the searches—we cannot afford these new professors. We must focus on revenue-generating activity.[2] By the time I graduated, the jobs were gone. I started my postdoctoral academic career as an adjunct professor in a state school system.

This chapter reflects both my grim history and hopeful joy that I have taken as both an adjunct professor squarely within academic institutions and a business owner doing work adjacent to the same institutions. The view is often grim for Black women in academia. Academia, an industry within an advanced capitalist system, one built on the historical legacy of the transatlantic slave trade where Black women were relegated to particular roles, replicates these roles. If we are fortunate enough to obtain a well-earned tenure-track position, we are pulled between trying to fix a broken industry with few resources and meeting the demands of a tenure-track job without sacrificing our physical and mental health.[3] However, most of us are consigned to a contingent faculty system that values the "customers" we serve over the scholarship we have created in doctoral programs and beyond, because our work does not bring sufficient income to the programs within these institutions and/or close enough to the corporate industries that underwrite their endowments and research dollars. "Underrepresented racial and ethnic faculty members hired as contingent, as opposed to tenure-track, are not only marginalized in their academic appointment at the institution but also [in] the scope of their contributions."[4]

Heather Scott and Nyasha GuramatunhuCooper argue that resistance and prioritization are what bring agency.[5] I chose to prioritize building my own institution that would allow me the space to be adjacent to academia while creating the flexibility and income advancement that would allow me to live a full life as a mother, scholar, spouse, community member, and another soul on this planet. Concurrently, the work I do in my business with women BIPOC scholars directly resists what academia demands of Black women—I support my clients to meet the expectations for tenure and promotion, ensuring that they do not sacrifice themselves at the altar of productivity, respect, and income growth. Academia does not suggest that this is possible; the women I work with demonstrate that it is. This is where I find my joy.

Black women are profoundly *underrepresented* in the ranks of the U.S. professoriate. By fall 2016, Black women held less than 14 percent of the full-time faculty positions held by women. These numbers do not reflect whether we held adjunct positions, postdoctoral fellowships, or tenure-track, associate, or full professor jobs, while full-time, often Black women are hired into lecturer and/or instructor positions and other forms of contingent status.[6] This was the milieu in which I found myself.

I was scared to graduate in 2012 because I knew that the income supports existing while in my program would evaporate. Although my program was fully funded, I became a mother. If I were going to have success in writing anything, I would need to pay, out of pocket, for all related childcare. I borrowed money not only to cover these costs but also to conduct field research over my summers so I could write my dissertation. Both my credit card and student loan debt climbed to astronomical levels.

Suffice it to say that the income I made as an adjunct professor did not cover the bills that inevitably came due. I lived in Manhattan, New York City, New York, but worked in Staten Island and in New Jersey. The commute time for both places was the same—over one hour *each way*. I taught five different courses at three different institutions. The income was pathetic. As a result, I faced some of my hardest mental health challenges. I seriously considered suicide. If I could not even pay my bills, what point was there in this. I had no faith that I would get a tenure-track job, so initially, I did not even try going on the job market. I was useless in my current state.

And yet, my eight-year-old son was by my side. He would accompany me when he was out of school and watch me lecture. He sat in my classroom rapt with what would come out of my mouth. He wanted to learn about the Haitian Revolution. He would one day write poetry about Jamaica's Maroons, the subject of my research. I did not realize he was paying attention. How could I leave this child with the legacy of a mother who died by suicide?

Because I am stubborn, determined, and disciplined, I started on nonlinear paths of finding a way out of my conundrum. I loved journalism and thought I could easily pivot to this industry. I enjoyed an internship at a prominent show on NPR. I did a fellowship at a journalism program in the City University of New York (CUNY) system. It was clear to me that I would have to earn a master's degree in journalism to earn a living doing that work. I earned a BA, JD, MA (in history), and PhD, and they wanted me to get *another* degree. No thank you. Besides, journalism, as an industry, was in the same financial free fall in which academia found itself.

I swallowed my pride and applied for tenure-track and visiting professor positions. I formulated my research in ways that would make sense on the market. I reworked one of my dissertation chapters and started submitting it for publication to journals. I had an interview at a college and was one of the finalists but did not get the job. Searching for a job was exhausting because I was also still working as an adjunct professor.

I have been part of a peer counseling community for some time, and I saw that my connection with people not only substantially improved my life (it helped to move me past considering suicide) but improved theirs as well. I wished I could use these skills not just as a volunteer but as a way of supporting myself as well. After that thought crossed my mind, I opened my email. The first one was for a coaching scholarship. I was not sure what coaching was, but I suspected that this could be the thing I hoped for. I applied and won it. I never regretted this decision. It paved a new way forward for my life.

It is not simple thing to earn a JD and practice law for seven years. It is not a simple thing to earn a PhD and enter a horrible job market afterward. And building a business is not a simple thing either. What is clear to me is that the painful experiences I had as an adjunct professor would provide the foundation on which I could build a business that mostly served BIPOC women in law and academia.

Ironically, the academic writing and publication process were crucial for me finding my joy in this world. I decided to apply for a tenure-track position one more time. I considered applying for a position in the school where I taught (and still teach). For political reasons that had nothing to do with me, I would not even be considered for the posted position. This conclusion underscored that there was little incentive for me, as an adjunct professor, to better the institutions in which I worked, although just by teaching I did. As Littisha Bates and Whitney Gaskins discuss about the impact of diversity, equity, and inclusion service for tenure-track Black women, because adjunct professor wages are so poor, our very teaching is service (and the only sort of service we are permitted).[7] Although this school refused to hire me, because of my work and that of many of my colleagues, including Thea Hunter,[8] who died because she could not afford health insurance, the program experienced a fivefold increase of majors and minors. No amount of publication and teaching accolades, once one finds themselves in the contingent career path, can shift the status many Black women hold in these institutions. We are constantly told that no matter how much work we do, we will not advance. Our labor will build the institutions but remain contingent.

Having failed, once again, to find a tenure-track position, I decided to publish anyway. Both Paula White, Eva Gibson, and Jessica Fripp as well as the anonymous authors of "Four Black German Women" argue that navigating academia requires building affinity groups that are crucial to moving one's research agenda forward.[9] A group of BIPOC women scholars who gathered to write formed a core component of the business I built and was essential both for my writing and for supporting my clients' projects. The first community I developed was the Academic Writers' Meetup. This allowed me to create both the time during which and the community with whom I could write. I did the research necessary to support these women with writing and adapted what I learned to my own practice because I also wanted to ensure that the scholars who came could write successfully. I had concrete and specific tasks I could do to move my project along daily. I knew what each step was. I had more support reworking this piece of writing than I had drafting the initial dissertation. But, most important, unlike grappling with the tenure clock, I was able to arrange my academic writing on a schedule that worked best for me, my family, my teaching, and my business. This often means that I can take advantage of only ten to fifteen minutes here and there, and I am pleased with that. Part of the resistance my path and view created was that I would continue to publish my work. Academic institutions were unwilling to hire me for the tenure track; however, I knew that my work was valuable and should be published. I refused to pretend that my doctoral research was no longer meaningful. Other scholars would still have to reckon with my work.

Women in law and academia who are Black, Indigenous, and people of color face parallel issues. I knew that because I worked not only in both industries but also through my business. It is remarkable that BIPOC women ever earn tenure because, as we see through this collection, there are few people who are willing to guide us through the process.[10] There are few people who are willing to make sure we do not accrue additional labor so that we can publish. There are few people willing to read our work and provide the content and structural edits it needs so we can get our work published. I am honored to be able to support brilliant women through this process and watch as they earn tenure and build the lives they crave.

We navigate this system knowing that we cannot care what others think about what we are doing as a career choice or what we are saying. Sayam Davis argues that she "learned not to rely on others for my self-worth but to unapologetically value myself, my work, and my purpose regardless of what others think."[11] The judgment I felt as I was repeatedly rejected for full-time employment has required a clarity about who I am and what I am doing that cannot be earned from outside of myself. Running a business has reinforced this lesson. I will not be everyone's cup of tea: that does not mean that what I have to offer is not valuable.

Building my own business has allowed me to parent in ways that are much more satisfying. Although my son headed to college in 2022, I have been able to be a presence to him in all parts of his life. I could spend much of our summers together. I could ensure that my workday was finished when his was. I could be off when he is. I did not feel like I was constantly choosing between him and my work. I could structure my time so that I am either fully with him or working.

Finally, I have created a life where I can fully indulge all parts of myself. I take time to be a musician and develop those skills—not only have I sung in opera choruses but also in a church choir, and I studied voice and performed in my own recital. I crochet and knit to calm my nerves. I can create the time in my days to meditate and nap without fear of reprisal or worry about what others think. I use this as a way to model for my clients expecting and doing more for themselves.

The challenges we have as Back women in the academy are structural. The overwork, lack of respect for our scholarly efforts, ill health, students demanding so much of us, earning tenure, etc. are all structural. Advanced capitalism and academia, like everything else, do not mesh well. If the industry tries to teach students and procure scholarship on the cheap, and it, alongside many other industries, refuses to face the reality that cheapening Black women's labor is the bedrock of institutional advancement, the view will always be challenging and tenuous. Further, we must recognize that the system needs to allow success stories so that it remains credible and we do not all insist that it be dismantled in its entirety. But we carry the workload in this industry with poor pay, poor workloads, and untold emotional and physical stress.

Given that corporate bodies (I will include academia in this) thrive on exploiting labor, owning my own business does not automatically free me from the burdens of exploiting my own labor. So that running my own business becomes a manageable endeavor, I must set sturdy boundaries with myself in all parts of my life.

I still teach part-time. I do not teach using a rubric of shoulds. It is work I love, yet I know that it will not be what I will do forever. I resist the pull to frequently rework my courses. I do not allow myself to be endlessly available for students. I start the year creating a clear container for us to learn together so teaching does not become the vessel against which I measure my life.

I could work all day on any component of my business. However, I am clear with myself that there is never enough pay that would justify me treating myself that way. There are no circumstances where I need to accede to the premise that I should exploit my own labor, even if the benefit accrues to myself. At its core, no one benefits when I exploit myself (or anyone else for that matter).

When I exploit myself, my family suffers. This does not mean that I selflessly do everything for them because I am setting up boundaries with my work. This does mean that I can work with my son to learn the skills he needs to live after he leaves my home. He can learn to clean bathrooms, load dishwashers, vacuum the apartment, and other things that make my life better but will enrich his life although he may not appreciate it now. The objective is not to find additional ways to exploit my labor.

When I exploit myself, my clients suffer. I cannot support them through identifying and strategizing how to create the full lives they want as lawyers and scholars, the very thing for which they pay me. Clients often suggest that I am a better investment than their therapists. That means that I must make sure I am well rested. I make sure my mental and spiritual health is in good shape. That is how I ensure I continue to enjoy my work and that my clients achieve the goals they set. They also see that, although I am not fully ensconced in academia, there is the possibility of not being exploited by these institutions. One by one, each client learns to say no. One by one, each client learns to prioritize themselves and the work they love, and the institutions fully benefit from that.

When I exploit myself, my students suffer. I get grouchy that I must do this work in the first place. My grading load increases because I am determined that they have enough work to justify tuition dollars, but it is more than I can possibly keep up with. Students stretch themselves in my courses. They pursue the work that makes them excited, and they work in mediums that best translate their passions and learnings. No one ever complains about the ability to drive the direction of their work as undergraduates.

When I exploit myself, my scholarship suffers. I hate writing because I am exhausted when I sit down to do it. I cannot think through what I want my work to convey. I end up procrastinating and not doing the work at all. I can respect it when I make sure I am in good physical and mental shape. I remember it is not one more thing to do but what feeds me.

When I exploit myself, most of all, I suffer. I do not get enough sleep. My weight increases, which means my blood sugar levels start to elevate, my blood pressure increases. Exhaustion robs my focus for the short term and for examining and evaluating longer-term goals. When I do not take care of myself, I rob myself of the ability to enjoy life.

My clients and I mirror the challenges of exploitation in our work. Creating work outside academia does not necessarily provide an escape hatch without consistent connection with myself. My academic career ended up being one planted squarely within and outside the institutions. The refusal to create tenure-track positions in academia has had a profound impact on Black women scholars. My life is one example of this; yet, without being part of contingent labor, I may never have built a business that supports me. In that we are dealing with the limits of advanced capitalism, I must beware that I do not exploit myself—that the business allows me to enjoy the view. It allows me to nurture myself, my family, my community, my clients, and hopefully the world. And that is where I find my joy.

NOTES

1. G. White, "Recession's Racial Slant."
2. Washburn, *University Inc.*, 371.
3. See Bates and Gaskins, "Taking One for the Team?," chap. 7 in this volume.
4. Porter et al., "To Be Black Women," 674.
5. Scott and GuramatunhuCooper, "Crossroads Post-Tenure," chap. 8 in this volume.
6. Porter et al., "To Be Black Women," 675.
7. Bates and Gaskins, "Taking One for the Team?"
8. Adam Harris, "Death of an Adjunct."
9. White, Gibson, and Fripp, "Navigating the Ivory Tower," chap. 10 in this volume; Anonymous, "Four Black German Women," chap. 16 in this volume.
10. See Chapdelaine, "We Are the Ones," chap. 1 in this volume.
11. Davis, "Tokenism in the Era of Performative Wokeness," chap. 9 in this volume.

CHAPTER 7

Taking One for the Team?

Reconciling Individual Ambition and the Greater Good

LITTISHA A. BATES AND WHITNEY GASKINS

Historically, Black women administrators in higher education have overwhelmingly been situated in two types of administrative positions: academic affairs or student affairs.[1] Arguably, diversity, equity, and inclusion (DEI) administrative roles are quickly becoming a third space for Black women. Because of the demand for more equitable and inclusive institutions, we have witnessed a surge in DEI administrative positions, which has left Black women wrestling to reconcile our own personal values, sources of joy, and academic ambitions with institutional expectations that we will engage in this work no matter the cost. In short, Black women are left taking one for the team. Utilizing a collaborative autoethnographic approach, we demonstrate the ways in which Black women find ourselves taking one for the team, how we make sense of our choice to do so, and how, despite the adverse impact of doing so, we find joy in our work. Drawing on our experiences as Black women who hold DEI administrative roles at a historically white institution, we recount the ways we significantly contribute to the institution yet are forced to reconcile our ambition for its greater good.

On the one hand, the legacy of leading the fight for social justice and equity is in our blood. Our lived experiences coupled with our desire to exist in equitable spaces draws us to these roles. In addition, the joy and fulfillment we experience because of our work is in some ways its own reward yet introduces complexities in the meaning of these roles for us. Many Black women are already engaging in equity work within and outside our institutions before these roles were created and bestowed on us. To be clear, we have agency, and although the feeling is one of being put upon, hence the use of the word "bestowed," the choice to accept these roles and engage in this work is one we thoughtfully undertook. We do our best to make sense of the negative impact of the work by capitalizing on the joy it brings us. On the other hand, there is an unspoken but noticeably clear expectation that Black women in the academy are to commit to these DEI administrative roles and tasks while continuing to maintain their faculty commitments of research, service, and oftentimes teaching. It is difficult to sustain the balance between administrative and faculty duties. Faculty are taught and even rewarded for taking an individualistic stance, whereas administrators are taught to consider the entire institution. Black women, regardless of our academic titles, are taught to be community minded, which creates internal conflict and a clash of values. For Black women who hold DEI roles, the internal conflict and clash of values complicates our already fraught existence in academia. As Heather Scott and Nyasha GuramatunhuCooper point out, Black women are consistently underrepresented in tenured roles in the academy.[2] These challenges are further exacerbated as administrative work generally is not considered in reappointment, promotion, and tenure review (RPT). This becomes even more problematic as universities and colleges are placing more emphasis on DEI work. Within these roles, Black women often feel as if we are forced to choose between advancing social justice and equity, and our own advancement within the academy, we are often pushed to take one for the team.

As Black women take up this important work, we must weigh the impact of these roles on our long-term academic trajectories. Moving into these positions marks a shift in our academic tracks. This switch is risky for those of us who have not first reached the pinnacle of faculty success—tenured full professor. Even though our institutions need us to do equity work, there is no academic reward inherent in it. Engaging in such work may bring us a sense of joy as well as moral and social satisfaction but not tenure and promotion. Yet the work we do in these administrative roles has a significant measurable positive impact on fundraising dollars, student recruitment, retention, and graduation, as well as the community.

BACKGROUND

Black women make up 4 percent of all full-time faculty in academia.[3] This underrepresentation has consequences for both the educational mission and individual faculty, and the impact on both is well documented.[4] The primary duties faculty are judged on during the RPT process are a balance of research, teaching, and service. However, Black women find themselves with an unbalanced workload in the areas of teaching and service. Like many Faculty of Color, Black women are more likely to engage in an overload of uncounted service due to their own experiences of marginalization, a sense of commitment to their community, and a desire to see cultural changes in their institutions.[5] In many ways we have no choice (or least we feel as though we don't) but to choose to engage in this work, for if we don't, who will move us toward equity?

Not all these efforts are voluntary; Black women are often sought out by institutions to take on more service to help the institution achieve the status as leaders in inclusive excellence and diversity.[6] These often-uncompensated disproportionate levels of service result in decreased research output and Black women not being able to win tenure or be promoted to full professor. The creation and formalization of DEI roles in some cases financially compensates Black women for their work, yet this work still does not count toward RPT. The trajectories of those who choose this path are forever changed.

Most of the research on Black women in higher education who hold DEI roles focuses on the executive level: chief diversity officers (CDOs). While no national data set exists that details the racial and gender breakdown of CDOs, we know that Black people hold about 59 percent of these roles in the academy.[7] This number is even higher once we account for what Joana Dos Santos refers to as unit-based chief diversity officers (UBCDOs) and all other "middle management" who have had DEI responsibilities tacked on to their roles.[8]

While this surge in DEI-related roles might suggest that the academy is committed to doing the work to create more equitable spaces, we often see little financial investment in DEI efforts. A study conducted by INSIGHT found that "though DEI costs have increased by nearly a third from the 2014–2015 academic year to 2018–2019, they account for an average of only 0.49 percent of university-wide budgets."[9] In addition to the lack of financial resources, we see a general lack of institutional support. This work does not count toward RPT, and those tasked with carrying out the DEI mission often hold little to no power to enact change[10] or are utilized as "fixers."[11]

In her in-depth analysis of Women of Color CDOs, Monica Nixon examines their lived experience of existing and thriving in their roles as well as how they came to inhabit those roles.[12] Much like our experiences, these women see their trajectory into their DEI roles as a "natural progression" informed both by their lived experienced as Women of Color and as an extension of their current work. The women in her study discuss the ways in which they navigate isolation, microaggressions, stereotypes, and challenges to their credentials and credibility. While none of these women aspired to the CDO role, they all accepted the challenge with the hopes of supporting marginalized communities, being a visible marker to Students of Color for what is possible, being an ally for the most marginalized in their institutions, and creating institutional change.

Our narratives align with those of Nixon's participants and many other Black women and Women of Color in academic CDO and UBCDO roles. We use this work as an opportunity to center our narratives as Black women by drawing on autoethnography—specifically, we utilized collaborative autoethnography.[13] This method allowed us the validation, freedom, and safety to recount our narratives while probing for overlap and making sense of our experiences. Although our individual narratives are unique, they are also painstakingly familiar. Writing this chapter has been both traumatizing and liberating. We hope that other Black women and Women of Color experience freedom in validation as they read on.

OUR NARRATIVES

Littisha

My academic experiences as a Black woman in higher education are likely no different from so many Black women who came before me and, sadly, will likely be the same for some who come after me. For the most part I was academically supported; in many ways I was evidence that the programs were "good and inclusive." My success as a Black woman and the financial and academic support that contributed to that success allowed these programs to see themselves as different and better, while not really doing much different or better. However, the invisibility of faculty that looked like me coupled with the microinsults, microinvalidations, and silences around the lack of diversity and equity were very loud and subsequently shaped how I navigate the academy.

As an undergraduate, I found safe space among my peers. We did our best as a community of Black students at a historically white institution to shield one another from racial trauma and isolation. We fostered safe space through Black Greek life and carefully curated social events—if you were a Black student on campus, you knew exactly where to find the other Black students at any given time. These experiences and the amazing Black staff who supported us are what I remember most; however, these experiences were all social. I vividly remember the first time I had a Black professor, in an Introduction to Sociology course; after the second class I changed my major from psychology to sociology. At the end of the semester, I was looking forward to taking another course with that professor, but he taught only intro, and then he was gone. I later learned he was an adjunct, and like so many in his marginal position, he did the work to draw students in and then was discarded.[14]

During my entire undergraduate career, I had one other Black professor. This experience or lack thereof created a void for me, one that I filled with love and support from Black women staff who helped me learn how to navigate racial trauma in the classroom and on campus. The invisibility of Black faculty is what inspired me to become a professor. I wanted to ensure that students like me saw someone like them.

I entered my graduate program as the only U.S.-born Black person and one of two Black graduate students. This experience was softened by the visible legacy of Black excellence in the department: we had the A. Wade Smith Conference Room and the Memorial Lecture on Race Relations. Dr. A. Wade Smith was a prominent Black sociologist who had once been chair of the department. There was a plaque with his name and face outside of the conference room—I used to walk the long way around the building so I could pass it every day. At that time, our department head was a Black woman full professor, Dr. Verna M. Keith. Her presence, along with that room and his legacy, motivated me. Most of what I know about being a Black woman in the academy I learned from Dr. Keith.

Despite those warm and fuzzy feelings around the legacy of Black excellence, I was still reminded of my second-class citizenship in the department. On more than one occasion I was reminded that I was a master's degree student, not technically a PhD student. Although most of my cohort came in with master's degrees or had GRE (Graduate Record Examination) scores high enough to be admitted directly to the PhD program, I was the sole master's-only admit. This meant that I would later have to reapply to begin the PhD program. Despite not being officially in the doctorate program, I was often used to help recruit and market the program to prospective Black and Brown students and potential new faculty hires. I finished both the master's and PhD program within five years with several tenure-track job offers.

Word travels fast when a new Black faculty member arrives on campus. Within my first year on the tenure track, I found myself drowning in students. I, my office space, and my family home quickly became safe spaces for Black and Brown students across the campus. I found myself being an academic mentor and life coach to students within and outside the sociology department. These increased demands on my time often created an internal conflict and a very real impact on my scholarship. I had a deep desire to support students, but I was being given a clear message that my publication and grant-getting records were marginal at best, so I should be doing less service work and more publishing and grant getting. The demands on my time steadily increased as I became a vocal advocate for equity and change across the institution, including confronting the isolation that plagued Black faculty with the proposal to launch a university-funded Black Faculty Association (BFA). The association was fully funded and launched in the 2014–15 academic year.

When I went up for tenure in 2016, my case was split 7–2 at the college-level committee. The committee noted that while I met my departmental criteria and thus should be awarded promotion with tenure, there was concern about my rate of publication. As painful as it was to read then and now, they weren't necessarily wrong. Like so many others, especially those in DEI spaces, I had made a conscience choice to spend my time on DEI and service work, despite the potential detrimental impact on my scholarship. For me the choice, though fraught, was one that enabled me to define success and choose joy, the joy in making a difference, supporting students to the finish line, and shifting university culture.

The time and labor of my equity work across the university would not count toward winning me tenure, yet it certainly increased my visibility and made me a likely candidate for the inaugural position of associate dean for inclusive excellence and community partnership in my college. When I first joined the professoriate, I had three primary goals. First, I wanted to ensure that Black students and other Students of Color could see themselves when they walked into the classroom. Second, I wanted to make a difference through my research. Finally, I wanted to move through the ranks of the academy, winning tenure and soon after promotion to full professor. At no point in time had I ever entertained the idea of being an administrator let alone DEI professional; however, like so many Black women in the academy, that is exactly where I have found myself—in the position to make a choice that in some ways didn't feel like a choice but a mandate. A choice to engage in work that gives me hope while also feeling like a burden, a choice that leaves me less productive in scholarship but an agent for change. In the end, a choice that leaves me feeling like I'm taking one for the team.

Whitney

While my experiences in the academy have been different than my coauthor, they have in many ways been much of the same. Like my coauthor, my experiences as a Black woman in higher education are no different than many other Black women in science, technology, engineering, and mathematics (STEM), yet the trauma is uniquely my own.

As an undergraduate, the College of Engineering and Applied Science (CEAS) was a hostile environment. In a profession that relies on collaboration, the interactions and experiences left me feeling isolated. Microaggressive behavior from both classmates and faculty often led me to question my place within the college. Instead of looking forward to gaining more knowledge about my field, my focus turned to graduating and leaving as soon as possible.

I left CEAS to pursue a master's degree within the College of Business (COB). The culture there was different. Although I still had to navigate the climate at the university, the COB students and faculty were more welcoming than were those in engineering. Students were willing to work collaboratively on projects and were overall more supportive. The faculty were open and supportive of my work. I did have uncomfortable experiences with one faculty member, but overall, the faculty in the COB did not make the environment feel less welcoming for me in comparison to my white male peers. In fact, the department chair helped me overcome some challenges and eventually became my master's thesis adviser. When I graduated from the program, I felt honored and excited as opposed to my undergraduate graduation, when I felt equally excited to have completed the program but equally relieved to be out of the space.

For my doctoral program, I returned to CEAS. It turned into a particularly challenging experience once again. I will always be appreciative of my faculty committee who supported me throughout my journey. Their support was critical. The general "hazing" of graduate students is not new, but the challenges were more unique than simply overworking a graduate student. In fact, passing the qualifying exam and defending my dissertation were among the least stressful times during my doctoral journey. From the first day, there were barriers and roadblocks placed in front of my path: changing graduation requirements, mid-program; questioning the validity of my research; and attacking members of my dissertation committee. But, unlike my undergraduate experience, the attacks felt more personal than systemic. Even with all the turmoil along my doctoral journey, I wanted to work in the academy because I felt that I could be an advocate for change.

After completing my doctoral work, I had originally planned to pursue a postdoctoral position. Instead, I chose to pursue a full-time faculty position immediately. My career began as a faculty member in the very place that was the source of so much trauma, CEAS. I became one of three Black faculty in the college and the first Black women to be employed as a faculty member. I was first hired as a visiting assistant professor in engineering education. For the first six months, I worked without an office while teaching first-year undergraduate courses. Once I was given an office, it was not long before it became a safe space for racially and ethnically diverse students within the college. The Black students were not used to seeing someone who looked like them in a faculty space. As the only Black woman in the college, I became the listening ear and the shoulder on which many of the students could cry. Being an ally to the students, though heartwarming, impacted the available time and energy that I had to carry out traditional faculty responsibilities. They would share stories of traumatic experiences, and I understood because I had experienced many of the same. Often, when the seats in my office were occupied, they would find a space on the floor. These students had come to see my office floor of as a safer space than the remainder of the college. Some students were not seeking homework support or even enrolled in my courses—they needed to embrace a homelike space. I became the de facto adviser for several campus organizations. It quickly became clear that, in addition to teaching and conducting research, I was also responsible for advising a large proportion of our college population.

Although many of the students had been in the minority in their secondary schools, college was a unique experience. In high school, a student who felt marginalized in their school could go home at the end of each evening and decompress within the comforts of home. College did not offer this same experience. My office became the space where they could be removed from the climate of the college, at least temporarily. This led to me to creating Sunday dinners. Every Sunday, my husband and I would reserve the African American Cultural Resource Center and provide a home-cooked meal for the students. For four hours, students would come, eat, and enjoy fellowship. Quickly, the Sunday dinners became informal study sessions for first-year students. Older students would join as well, becoming tutors and mentors for first-year students. I was unknowingly creating a nurturing, safe place for students in what many have described in research interviews as a hostile space. I was focused on creating safe space for students and educating them; I did not aspire to be an administrator, yet here I am. As the only Black woman to ever serve on the faculty, it is a welcome burden to change that narrative not only for the college but also for both the Black and the engineering community. Mentors within the college have told me that taking on this type of role would not be advantageous for my career, but they often do not understand the duality of our obligation. Being a trained engineer who was successful in industry has also provided me the privilege to leave the academy, if necessary—a luxury that others in these positions do not have.

Doing the DEI Work

As our narratives reveal, our moves into these roles were the result of our institutions creating these roles and our having high profiles in the institution as DEI champions. For Littisha, a new dean created this inaugural role. As a tenured associate professor, it was a bit easier to take the risk as she was protected by tenure, despite not yet being promoted to full professor. For Whitney, the dean wanted to bring back a role that had been vacant since the early 2000s. She was an untenured assistant professor; the risk to her could mean never receiving tenure.

Despite the risks and opposition, we took on these roles and have made a significant impact in our spaces. We have collectively raised over six million dollars; this does not account for the impact we have had on student recruitment and retention in our roles as faculty and administrators. We have developed and implemented culture-changing processes and procedures around equitable searches and hiring in our respective units. On top of this heavy administrative workload, we both struggle to maintain a faculty load.

Although we have been successful in advancing the DEI mission of our institution, we are consistently reminded that our work is not valued and exists on the periphery of academic prestige as it relates to RPT. Despite the fact that our institution, like others, proclaims investment in DEI, its actions reproduce the very inequity our jobs are designed to eradicate. This is especially true for Black women, who overwhelmingly hold these positions.

DISCUSSION

Black women and Faculty of Color who work in DEI spaces often take one for the team. We sacrifice our personal career growth in the hopes that our work will create less hostile, more inclusive spaces in which our students achieve better outcomes. We put our tenurable and promotable work (that is, research) on hold for the greater good of the communities our roles are designed to support. Despite all of this, it still brings joy to see our work making a difference. There is no better feeling than knowing our minoritized students, faculty, and staff will face fewer barriers and have allies in positions to support and protect them.

Based on the contribution to the university's image, financial bottom line, campus climate, and student success, DEI work should be valued enough to count toward RPT. Universities regularly claim inclusive excellence as part of their core mission and argue its value to the institution, yet their commitment to the work is not visible. The university will readily promote DEI work but not reward workers for their commitment and accomplishments. This failure to support the DEI administrators leaves us in a stagnant, undervalued position.

Based on our experiences, we have created recommendations that institutions can adopt to support faculty members who are engaged in DEI work and subsequently to increase the impact of their work. These recommendations include 1) not minimizing DEI work; 2) Creating pathways to achieve RPT through DEI work while in these roles; 3) Giving us resources as we take on this work; 4) #ListenToBlackWomen; 5) Empowering us to do the work that we are charged with accomplishing.

Recommendation 1. Diversity, equity, and inclusion work should be front and center; changing the culture of an institution is not an easy job. Do not minimize DEI work by treating it as a side project or tacking it on as additional job duties, DEI work is an all-consuming, full-time role. If the fruits of the labor are being promoted in strategic plans, in marketing materials and on websites, then the same commitment needs to be shown to the laborers who are doing the work.

Recommendation 2. For so long, institutions have focused solely on research, service, and teaching. We can change the culture of the RPT process. This requires changing what we value as tenurable and aligning what we say we value in processes and procedures. Academia must include a pathway to tenure that counts DEI work. We cannot say we value it and at best count it as mere service or at worse not count it at all. Leaders must understand how all-encompassing the work is and reward those who are doing the work that institutions claim to value.

Recommendation 3. A culture cannot be changed by having a lone soldier fight every battle. For the tide to shift, resources need to be allocated. Diversity, equity, and inclusion work cannot be completed within a silo, especially when many in the institution are comfortable with the status quo. Money and staff are essential to meet the long-term goals.

Recommendation 4. Help us how we want to be helped. As Black women, we are not able to draw on the same strategies as our white counterparts. As a result, our needs, both professionally and personally, are different, which also means the support and resources we require are also different. When we tell you what we need, LISTEN. We are often provided insight and feedback that do not align with our actual needs. We want leaders to listen when we speak and support us in the way that we request. #ListenToBlackWomen.

Recommendation 5. For too long, DEI leaders were simply figureheads. The challenges are, however, very real. We must be empowered to bring the change that our institutions claim they want. When we are at institutional tables of influence in a meaningful way and have a voice, we are more likely to be seen as an authority. When not empowered, our professional credibility and authority is questioned. Even when changes we make are evidence based, we do not have buy-in or real power to make meaningful changes. If the work is truly valued, those who are doing the work and considered experts must have their work and expertise supported, valued, and empowered.

Diversity, equity, and inclusion leaders carry a heavy burden of work within our universities. We are responsible for changing cultures; creating and revisioning practices, policies, and procedures; creating fundraising initiatives; developing programming and evaluation services, while not always having the resources or power to carry out such tasks. Without the weight of this heavy burden, these faculty leaders could survive and thrive in the traditional areas of their work. The workload is not ideal, but it is not the central issue; the lack of value of the work—DEI work—is the challenge.

Diversity, equity, and inclusion leaders are often left feeling unprotected as they carry out the work of creating a better environment for all stakeholders. As institutional leaders, we must take all stakeholders into account, which means we are often subjected to having our credibility, expertise, and humanity loudly and publicly devalued. It is clear from our narratives and the narratives of Scott and GuramatunhuCooper that there is no safe space for Black women in the academy. Even in such a momentous occasion as being promoted and receiving tenure, there is no chance for relief. These experiences leave Black women feeling drained, undervalued, overworked, and, worse, stuck in a position where we are putting in significantly more work than other faculty but receiving less professional and often financial reward, left taking one for the team despite our individual ambition, all for the greater good.

NOTES

1. Glover, "Existing pathways," 4–17.
2. Scott and GuramatunhuCooper, "Crossroads Post-Tenure, chap. 8 in this volume.
3. U.S. Department of Education, http://nces.ed.gov/programs/coe/indicator/csc#3.
4. Allen et al., "The Black Academic, 112–27.
5. Guillaume and Apodaca, "Early Career Faculty of Color," 1–18.
6. For an in-depth analysis of faculty workload, see Kuykendall et al., "Finding Time."
7. Jaschik, "Next Generation President."
8. Santos, "Who Are These Diversity Officers?"
9. INSIGHT Staff, "An INSIGHT Investigation."
10. Gravley-Stack, Kara, Chris M. Ray, and Claudette M. Peterson. "Subjective experiences of the chief diversity officer," 95.

11. Harvey, "Chief Diversity Officers," 92.

12. Nixon, "Women of Color University Chief Diversity Officers," 301.

13. Tevis, Hernandez, and Bryant, "Reclaiming Our Time," 282–97.

14. Thompson, "A View of the Margins from Academia," chap. 6 in this volume.

CHAPTER 8

Crossroads Post-Tenure

Should I Stay or Should I Go?

HEATHER I. SCOTT AND

NYASHA M. GURAMATUNHUCOOPER

Feminist scholar Sara Ahmed noted that "every research project has a story, which is the story of arrival."[1] In this chapter, our point of arrival is March 2019: the month and year we were both notified of our promotion and tenure. This date is significant because it raised the question teased by our title: Do I want to stay here, or should I find another job? This might seem like an odd question to entertain after a career milestone. However, the much-deserved celebration of a monumental accomplishment was tempered by the shadow of years of toil and the continued struggle to be seen (intellectually and physically), valued, and appreciated in the academy and institutional life. Our chapter follows the tradition of autoethnography and centers on our experiences as two tenured Black women at a large public university in the southern region of the United States.[2] We highlight the critical incidents that influenced the decision to leave or stay. Although the idea of Black women leaving or staying at institutions post-tenure is not new, our work serves as a catharsis for our own experiences. It is a chance for us to engage in honest and fearless meaning-making and give voice to experiences that have been kept close.

As Ahmed noted, the act of writing about one's experiences is grounded in revealing what one is feeling and thinking.[3] At the other side of our catharsis is a realization of joy—a type of joy that manifests as the ability to resist things that no longer serve us and the ability to hold firm to our priorities and values. In this chapter, we present two expressions of joy: one rooted in prioritization, and the other rooted in resistance. As the preeminent scholar of Black feminism, Patricia Hill Collins noted, "While living life as Black women may produce certain commonalities of outlook, the diversity of class, region, age, and sexual orientation shaping individual Black women's lives has resulted in different expressions of these common themes."[4] It stands to reason that the path to and expressions of joy present familiarity that ought not to be expected to be similar.

OUR CONNECTION

Though we answered the question of should I stay or should I go differently, our stories are intertwined, and it is fitting to elaborate on and celebrate our relationship. We have known each other since 2014. For two years, Heather was the only Black woman in our department. Nyasha joined two years later as the second Black woman. By the time we both earned promotion and tenure, there were four Black women in the department, and all of us have either moved to new institutions, industries, or positions. Our relationship began with Heather serving as the committee chair during Nyasha's interview process for a tenure-track position at a large public institution in the southern region of the United States.

Nyasha

I recall Heather breaking the interviewer/interviewee barrier: "We have five minutes to walk across campus. Ask me anything you want to know." We would be the only Black women in the department, and I was curious about her experiences and what mine might be like. That candid and unexpected offer made an impression on me. I ended up doing the same thing for Black women candidates during faculty searches. In fact, I remember giving her a big hug of gratitude when she dropped me off at the airport after my interview because her generosity was striking given what I had been told about what to expect during a campus interview. Once I was hired, our relationship became one of mentorship and friendship, knowing that we were navigating environments where our physical presence as Black women was not commonplace. We laugh about this now and often retell these stories. Our white colleagues, who had worked with us for years, often mistook us for each other despite our differences in complexion, hairstyles, physical build, and just generally not being the same person by any stretch of the imagination!

Heather

I felt tremendous delight when Nyasha accepted the offer of employment. It had been lonely as the only Black woman in our department. Our relationship blossomed as a peer-to-peer mentorship. We happily shared resources as we found and made our place at the university and in our discipline. We practiced sponsorship, extolling the respective talents of each other when university opportunities became available. We shared a concerted commitment to mentioning each other's names when we found ourselves with "a seat at the table." Although our energy and efforts were no match for the social and professional networks our white counterparts enjoyed, we knew through deeds spoken and unspoken that we had each other's backs, and still do.

THE QUESTION OF JOY

As we discovered in writing this chapter, defining joy is complex. Delightfully and unexpectedly (given our disciplinary orientation in contemporary Leadership Studies), Audre Lorde's "Uses of the Erotic: The Erotic as Power" gave us language to explore and formulate a definition of joy.[5] We have come to know joy in what we consider an active state: resisting ways of knowing and being that do not serve our connection to ourselves, and prioritizing people, places, and things that anchor us to the lives we seek to lead.

Both of our mothers are academics and well versed in the cultural and institutional politics of the academy. The messaging we received repeatedly was that joy would come after tenure. The covert message was, "Play the long game to get tenure, then you can do whatever you want." Joy was framed as the opportunity to follow one's desire, but only as a product of successfully assimilating into the norms of the academy. This positioned joy as an external product dependent on meeting the approval of proxies of the academy, such as promotion and tenure committees, department chairs, and academic affairs administrators. However, reading Lorde's work challenged us to think of joy in the academy as internally derived, requiring us to "examine the ways in which our world can be truly different" by "reassessing the quality of all the aspects of our lives and of our work, and of how we move toward and through them."[6] The catalyst of this examination is a clear understanding of values, needs, wants, and purpose. With this lens, joy develops as an internal and urgent reflection that demands external action. Joy is incomplete if it stays only internal. Urgency and action push it to become a public expression (what Lorde describes as living from within outward), thus completing the creation of joy that is dependent on one's agency rather than as a transactional product of labor to and within an entity.[7] When viewed as a product of agency, joy is self-connection, knowledge of what one is capable of, and a rejection of what wounds and violates the soul, even at the risk of losing status.

Cases of tenure and promotion typically do not dominate the news cycle. In 2021, the media was abuzz with news of Pulitzer Prize–recipient and MacArthur Fellow Nikole Hannah-Jones joining the faculty of Howard University as the first Knight Chair in Race and Journalism and spearheading the creation of the Center for Journalism and Democracy. In a public and magnificent display of unmitigated agency, Hannah-Jones turned down what can only be diplomatically described as a dubious offer of tenure and a teaching position at the University of North Carolina–Chapel Hill's Hussman School of Media and Journalism after being initially denied a tenured position by the Board of Trustees.[8] Hannah-Jones's own self-advocacy and support from students, staff, and faculty at UNC–Chapel Hill and beyond led to an eventual offer. The actual story of Hannah-Jones being denied tenure is not particularly noteworthy (albeit disappointing) because Black academics have long experienced institutional, social, and political roadblocks.[9] What Hannah-Jones's decision demonstrates is the power and glory of agency, specifically the agency that Black women can enact in the academy, despite attempts at sabotage by institutional agents.[10] Though Hannah-Jones's story is referenced in many ways in this book, we draw attention to it because it exemplifies a manifestation of joy that is premised on exercising one's agency as an act of resistance and prioritization.

THE DECISION TO STAY: JOY AS PRIORITY

Heather

I was welcomed to the university as an individual who could contribute to a burgeoning department and academic program. My transition to the role of assistant professor came after a successful career as a student affairs administrator. In retrospect, I did not realize the significant need for mentorship and guidance to be successful in the academy. I was offered little to no guidance in navigating the promotion and tenure process. Due to fears of being seen as an impostor, I did not ask my department leadership for support. I got busy doing what I do best in times of uncertainty: self-mentoring, researching, and finding information on every aspect of the promotion and tenure process on my own. In my second year, I began to seek out advice and guidance in earnest, but to my surprise, I was met with annoyance and dismissal.

An unintended encounter with the dean of my college further derailed my confidence. I recall being off campus during the summer months at a research colloquium, spending my "off contract" time in what I assumed was the way most faculty in pursuit of promotion and tenure did. I received an email from my department chair indicating my faculty performance agreement needed to be revised immediately. The chair had quantified a particular number of publications that I needed to produce, and the dean was demanding the language be adjusted to read that I would write and submit a certain number of publications in a span of time, and those pub-lications would be published and disseminated by that time. In the world of "publish or perish," this was most likely a fair revision and one that I did not question; however, I expressed a desire to fully understand the pro-cess. Upon my return from the research colloquium, I requested to meet with the dean to discuss publication expectations. The dean reluctantly agreed, and I was met with a dour countenance and annoyance that I did not fully understand the publication expectations. I recall being told, "No one is going to give you promotion and tenure. You must earn it and you will not earn it if you do not meet the expectations set forth." The expecta-tions were never ones that I attempted to shirk, nor were they expectations I was incapable of meeting. After all, I had successfully completed doc-toral coursework, conducted a full research study, written a dissertation, and had two babies in the short span of 21 months, all while working a demanding full-time job as an administrator.

As I reflect on my experience with the dean, it was evident that they deemed me not worthy of sharing space in the academy because I did not understand the process. Being truthful and forthcoming about my lack of understanding of how to navigate the promotion and tenure process result-ed in the very thing I feared: judgment. Explaining the process of promotion and tenure and supporting me through that process would not lessen my aptitude, ability, and commitment required to successfully attain promotion and tenure. I felt shame in admitting needing help and further clarity to understand the models of achievement in the academy. Despite the way I was shamed, I completed a successful third-year review and continued to seek out information on creating a pathway to promotion and tenure.

As life often does, my linear line to success developed a curve when my husband of nineteen years was diagnosed with a rare form of cancer. In the throes of vibrant professional careers and raising two brilliant young girls, we were facing the "in sickness and in health" vow we had pledged to each other. We established a plan for soldiering through this unexpected journey, rallied our village to care for our children, and apprised our employers of the fight ahead. I was met with great care and concern when I shared the news with my department chair. Blessed with the same response from his supervisor, my husband developed an admirable and ambitious plan to continue working during his extensive and demanding treatment. Per my department chair's suggestion, I contacted the university's Department of Academic Affairs to discuss options to amend my promotion and tenure timeline. My portfolio was due a few months from the date we received my husband's diagnosis. I recall working up the nerve to call the vice president of academic affairs, not in a ploy to gain sympathy but to educate myself on the options I had regarding my promotion and tenure timeline. Without pause, they said to me quite casually, "Your husband's cancer diagnosis should not impact your ability to move forward with your promotion and tenure process." I instantly felt defeated. We had sent our children to live with my parents temporarily. I was sleeping on a chair in a hospital room for days at a time while learning how to administer IV medication, clean a port catheter in my husband's chest, and administer a twice-daily injection, all to be told that these tasks and my newfound role as a caregiver should not interfere with my ability to condense four years into a digital portfolio, solicit external reviewers, and maintain my teaching and research. I shared academic affairs' response with my department chair, who wisely advised me to contact human resources. After securing documentation from my husband's medical team to attest to my role as a caregiver and the scope of my responsibilities, I was granted leave under the Family Medical Leave Act (FMLA), and my tenure clock was paused.

I share my story to demonstrate the very real lack of empathy that is present in the academy. Had I not had the support of my department chair, I might have easily succumbed to the challenges I was facing and not completed the promotion and tenure process. After a grueling year of supporting my husband through several months of chemotherapy and a stem cell transplant, I completed and submitted my promotion and tenure portfolio. Although submission should have brought a sense of relief and pride, the battle and preceding events tarnished the joy and sense of accomplishment. During the process of assembling my dossier, I recall a moment of reflection where I thought, "Wow, I did all of this!" There was never a moment of celebration or opportunity to reflect on my positive contributions to the academy. A momentous point in my career that should have been joyous was steeped in confusion, sadness, and survivor's relief of having endured. After all this, I decided to stay.

In thinking of my connection to Nikole Hannah-Jones's story, my agency came in the form of prioritizing my family. This seemed (and still seems) radical in a culture that calls for maximum intellectual, physical, and emotional labor as a demonstration of commitment and at the expense of self. Making a choice based on my family's needs was just as poignant as making a choice in resistance to institutional and structural barriers. I had numerous reasons for maintaining my geographic connections to the institution. I heavily rely on the support of my parents in caregiving for my two young daughters. A nationwide job search was not realistic for me as it would uproot my family. Despite the lack of opportunity for professional growth and profit at the institution, I made the choice to stay because I prioritized my family's need for stability.

At the height of the pandemic, I accepted a role as interim department chair. This felt like the right next move after tenure. I had committed myself to the institution and had become comfortable with the idea of making the institution my home post-tenure. Ironically, I was offered the appointment of interim chair on April 1 (also known as April Fool's Day in the United States). I recall asking the dean who offered the appointment if this was a joke. I had worked hard to determine the formula for a successful promotion and tenure bid, and receiving this offer was validation that I was on the right path. As suddenly as the offer was extended and accepted, the opportunity became an unrealized dream. The department and college that were my academic home were unceremoniously dissolved, and I found myself not only displaced but also given a new academic home that came along with a title in a discipline and field that was not a part of my academic identity.

In the complexity of these moments of upheaval and profound disappointment, I reaffirmed that my joy was rooted in prioritizing and protecting my family. I come back to this often as I think of the young women I am raising and prepare them to make their mark in the world. I realized there is room to engage in both active motherhood and my professional self who delights in exploring and advancing women's leadership. I became resolute in forging a new path forward for my fulfillment and survival.

I was awarded a research leave for the Fall 2021 semester. This time away from my faculty role offered a temporary respite and the opportunity to undertake research that brought me joy. I had committed to expanding my research not only in the arena of women and leadership but to couple that research with initiatives that would assist in preparing Black women for success in the pursuit of promotion and tenure. Solidly committing myself to this space, I began to explore opportunities for growth at the institution. To my delight and surprise, I was offered an opportunity to join my alma mater in an administrative leadership position that combined my passion for leadership and inclusive values.

I left the institution at which I had earned tenure in the summer of 2022—on my own terms and for a role that speaks to my passion and purpose. I am grateful for the opportunity to continue my academic career at an institution that aligns with my values in a role that gives me a chance to advance inclusive leadership. Having endured a lifelong educational experience where there was a lack of representation of Black women, I want to advance representation in higher education and am resolute in that I want my own daughters to see themselves represented in academia. I find joy engaging in work that may make the path easier for those who follow behind me. Having learned that despite the fickle nature of professional relationships and the landscape of higher education, if I can find opportunities that continue to align my passions and purpose, I can use my strength to find and advocate for my joy while prioritizing my values.

THE DECISION TO LEAVE: JOY AS RESISTANCE

Nyasha

The academic job market can be a grueling and uncertain experience. I count myself among the fortunate ones who landed a tenure-track job, because a single job posting can attract hundreds of qualified applicants. Admittedly, I had little understanding of the tenure-track life. Even in my neophyte state, I was looking forward to contributing to our academic program, especially because I was the only one in the department with a terminal degree in leadership studies. I was ready and willing to lend my disciplinary training to develop our program. Over the next few years, I dedicated myself to pursuing excellence in teaching, research, and service. Each of my annual reviews noted my work in all three areas of evaluation as exceeding expectations. I was buoyed by a strong commitment to excellence. I developed new courses, served on internal and external committees, maintained scholarly productivity, and built a presence on campus and in my discipline.

This hard work came with a significant amount of emotional labor brought on by the awareness that a) I was only one of two Black women in the department (at the time), and students often questioned and resisted my presence in the classroom; b) I was an international faculty member living in the United States as an immigrant (from Zimbabwe) with a "difficult" name to pronounce; and c) I taught course topics that challenged the mental models of white students who viewed me as aggressive, anti-American, and demanding. These aspects of my lived experience made me work even harder, assuming the pursuit of excellence and a record of success would prove me worthy and quell perception of flaws. I started to grow weary but persisted. This theme of pushing forward and working hard shows up in my journey consistently and ultimately became a key factor in my decision to leave after earning tenure and promotion.

In 2016, I was invited to be part of a mentoring group for Black women faculty at our institution. The group was created and facilitated by a formidable Black and multiethnic woman scholar and educator who understood the culture of our institution and its relationship with Black women. This group was (and is) an integral part of my experience in the academy. I was safe, celebrated, challenged, and nurtured in our monthly meetings. I had translators and a cheat code about how to navigate the ebbs and flows of institutional life. Being part of this mentoring community helped me understand the institutional currency valued for promotion and tenure. Though the process may have been documented in handbooks, my mentoring group helped me make sense of what was being overtly and covertly conveyed by the institution through administrators. With the assistance of my mentoring group, I applied for and earned promotion and tenure one year early—something administrators had repeatedly warned me not to do because "only superstars could do that." As it were, I was a superstar.

My official notification came in March 2019. I remember reading the letter and emitting what seemed like a cross between a sigh and an exhale. It was over. The sweat equity of four years was punctuated by a form letter from the university president. I tucked the letter into my purse and went on to teach two classes back-to-back. When I got into my car after teaching my last class for the day, I cried. They were not tears of joy. My tears reminded me of my relentless pursuit of excellence so that I would not be seen as lacking by the various review committees. I thought by building a reputation for excellence and hard work, I was positioning myself for career progression, specifically into administrative leadership positions that would allow me to merge my passion for global learning and leadership development. If I exercise fearless honesty with myself, I thought the institution would reward me with new and challenging opportunities because I worked hard and produced excellent work. I explicitly voiced interest in taking on new roles and remember getting the message that I was too valuable within the department, meaning that I was more valuable as labor in the classroom and in service. My labor was important, but my ambition was inconvenient.

When I should have been celebrating my tenure and promotion, I was questioning my future. I knew it was time to leave because no opportunities existed for upward mobility. If I needed further confirmation, I found it in a sudden reorganization. Our department and academic college were eliminated in 2020. As it turns out, hard work and excellence are no match for institutional politics. I would no longer be associate professor of leadership studies. Instead, I was to be associate professor of interdisciplinary studies, a nebulous title I could not identify with at all and refused to put on my email signature. In the middle of a global pandemic, I secured another tenure-track position through networking and moved my family to another state.

I do not regret leaving. I am clear that it was a necessary decision to increase my salary, create new networks, and achieve career progression. Despite my accomplishments and accolades, the institution did not take an interest in my development and progression. The institution wanted only my labor and what I could produce for its own sake. Part of my frustration and fuel for leaving was the abysmal pay. As a tenured professor, I was going to make $55,000, significantly less than a new assistant professor in my discipline. Even with salary studies and multiple collective and individual attempts to discuss this issue with the department, college, and university leadership, my salary was not going to change (despite these leaders expressing shock at just how little my colleagues and I were paid). Without context, this might seem like a preoccupation with money; however, I view pay as a diversity, equity, and inclusion (DEI) issue, particularly within an institution that professed a commitment to DEI. Statistics show that Black women are paid at lower rates across industries and subject to lifetime losses owing to gender and racial gaps in compensation.[11] My agency was rooted in recognizing that the institution would not change, therefore I needed to change. I resisted and resented the notion that the institution had all the power, which meant choosing to leave the security of tenure, risking the uncertainty of the job market, and trusting that my teaching, scholarship, and service record would position me as a strong candidate. Watching Nikole Hannah-Jones's expression of agency in a very public way spoke to my own private expression of agency through resisting the saddle of an exploitative relationship with the institution.

As of May 2022, I have left the academy altogether. The moxie I developed to leave my previous position helped me quickly recognize that the culture of my new department and institution would not serve me well. The lack of alignment, comfort with mediocrity, and anti-Blackness couched in a religious ethos made me realize that I needed to urgently leave the academy. I wrote an eight-page, single-spaced letter to my department chair and provost informing them of my intent to resign after only eighteen months. In my own voice, I clearly outlined the reasons I was leaving. Both the department chair and provost asked me what it would take to keep me. My response was that they would have to "move heaven and earth." Moving heaven and earth meant less teaching, more money, more autonomy, opportunities for special projects, an administrative position, and an increase in professional development funds. I knew they would not and could not move heaven and earth for me. I can laugh at this now, but their idea of enticing me to stay was offering to appoint me as associate department chair with responsibilities for graduate programs at three instructional sites in different parts of the state, with no additional compensation or reduction in my teaching load. It was incredibly easy for me to hold steadfast to my decision.

Now, I have started my own leadership development consulting practice. I use my disciplinary knowledge and skills to help individuals and organizations identify their leadership capacity and actively create and nurture organizations that prioritize diversity, equity, and inclusion. I also now work in the corporate space as a program consultant within a growing leadership development company, helping organizations diagnose learning needs and design impactful leadership training programs. I enjoy what I do, work less, and make more money. This career and industry shift has given me space and time to dream, think, and rest. Working in a corporate environment, I am unlearning, relearning, and learning what work means to me and how I show up. I work hard from 8:00 a.m. to 5:00 p.m. and take breaks throughout my workday, including a full hour of lunch. At 5:00 p.m., I shut off my laptop, go for a walk around my neighborhood, and do not think about work again until 8:00 a.m. the next day. These days, joy looks like waking up in the morning with the sun, exercising for half an hour, taking a shower, and heading upstairs to my home office to start my workday. Joy also looks like choosing which clients I work with in my consulting practice and accompanying them on their individual and collective leadership journeys. Joy looks like creating new end-of-the-week self-care routines with my daughter as we plan for the weekend without worrying about a writing deadline, grading papers, or committee service. I am still connected to higher education and the academy on my own terms. I returned to my alma mater as adjunct faculty and teach a class I am passionate about. I am coediting a journal issue on decolonization and antiracism pedagogy in leadership education, and I am writing book chapters that are deeply personal. I write what I like. I do what moves me. I know what I do not want. I am clear about my boundaries. Someone recently asked me whether I would ever go back to the academy full-time. I do not know the answer to that. For right now, the answer is no, and it feels good.

SEEKING JOY AT CAREER CROSSROADS

The decision to stay or go after tenure is highly personal and contextual. We both had different push and pull factors that drove our decisions. We turn to the concept of self-leadership as a framework to guide those who may also be wondering whether to stay or leave after tenure. Parallel to our definition of joy is the concept and practice of self-leadership: a purposeful approach to self-determination.[12] A more expanded explanation of self-leadership emphasizes individuals enacting agency by intentionally using reflection and awareness to establish self-direction and self-motivation to effectively lead themselves before leading others.[13] Self-leadership rests on a strong sense of self.[14] Nikole Hannah-Jones is an exemplar of self-leadership. Though we do not presume to know her internal dialogue, her decision to decline the offer of tenure and a teaching position at the University of North Carolina–Chapel Hill demonstrates enactment of self-leadership. The public events and narrative that played out signaled to us as Black women in the academy that we could exercise agency and are not beholden to institutions. We, too, are examples of self-leadership.

We focus on self-leadership's reflection and awareness components to develop a list of questions to employ when faced with career crossroads.

- What are my values and priorities?
- What do I like and dislike about my current role?
- Do I see a future in the same or new role here? If not here, where?
- Do I have a community of support within the institution?
- How might my decision to stay or go impact my well-being and/or my family?
- What do I stand to lose or to gain?

The questions require fearless honesty with oneself. Reaching a career crossroads challenged us to resist the status quo and prioritize ourselves in a challenging environment.

Our narratives demonstrate that though Black women faculty may traverse familiar difficulties on the path to tenure, our decisions to remain or leave an institution are individual and guided by personal values and context. What is crucial is one's ability to exercise agency in making the decision. Michelle Dionne Thompson's chapter in this volume revealed joy in working with women committed to proving the impossible to be possible. Much like Thompson's clients, we too came to recognize that it was possible to center ourselves and our values and challenge the norms of the academy. Joy comes from exercising agency. In its active state, joy is an act of resistance and protection of one's values. Whether one stays or goes, there is bravery in both decisions and the possibility of joy.

NOTES

1. Ahmed, *On Being Included*, 2.
2. Creswell and Poth, *Qualitative Inquiry and Research Design*.
3. Ahmed, *On Being Included*, 2.
4. Collins, "Learning from the Outsider Within," 16.
5. Lorde, *Sister Outsider*, 53–60.
6. Lorde, *Sister Outsider*, 55.
7. Lorde, 58.
8. Asmelash, "Nikole Hannah-Jones Declines UNC."
9. Jackson, "I Am a Black Woman in Academia."
10. Lee, "Surviving a Difficult Tenure Process," 48–58.
11. Wilson and Rogers, "Black-White Wage Gaps Expand."
12. Manz, "Self-Leadership," 585.
13. Browning, "Self-Leadership," 14.
14. Neck, Manz, and Houghton, *Self-Leadership*.

CHAPTER 9

Tokenization in the Era of Performative Wokeness

Lessons from the Tenure Track

SAYAM DAVIS

When I was on the job market, I was obsessed with my discipline's Academic Job Wiki, a space where job seekers could post information about different positions, such as whether they had been contacted for an interview or campus visit or whether they had received an offer. People also occasionally posted their thoughts about particular departments, and someone had written how the department that had offered me a job was full of wonderful people. This poster added that whoever landed this position would be a very happy person.

While delighted to start my academic career in a department with a positive reputation, I also knew I couldn't take those anonymous words of praise at face value. As a Black woman in academia, I was inhabiting a space never meant for me.[1] Throughout my entire educational experience, I was often the only person from the global majority, let alone the only Black person.[2] My new home would be no different. The department was all white and, despite its friendly reputation, had only ever hired one other tenure-track minoritized scholar. This person decried their tokenization among other things when resigning. As marginalized people know all too well, we are the ones who are expected to do the heavy lifting in addressing and counteracting racial injustice even when we have the least amount of power to effect change. It didn't help that I would also be moving to a city that lacked the diversity to which I was accustomed and therefore easy access to a community of people who could empathize with my experience. Most important, however, it didn't matter how nice the people in my department were. Even though working with well-meaning people is arguably better than the alternative, what really mattered was how committed my new department was to dismantling inequities that were baked into the fabric of this country and its institutions.[3]

In some ways, my department really has been as wonderful as that anonymous poster made it out to be—a proverbial unicorn in a field known for its stuffiness and tradition. Many of my colleagues are proactive in reimagining literary and cultural studies, and we have worked well together in diversifying and decolonizing our curriculum. I have never felt the need to hide my research agenda, one rooted in centering discussions of race, particularly Blackness. And when I have sought to expand my audiences and tackle my discipline's elitism by fully embracing public scholarship, colleagues have held up these interventions as a model. I am well aware that very few departments in the country, let alone the world, would let me bring all of my different passions together in the way that I have done. I have never felt defensive about my work and am allowed to shine on my own terms. At the same time, as someone who has always fit precariously in higher education, I have learned not to rely on others for my self-worth but to unapologetically value myself, my work, and my purpose regardless of what others think. This is the only way to truly find joy in life.

Even with the seeming support of my department, I still deal with my fair share of workplace microaggressions. There's the colleague who patronizingly told me that I looked like a little doll because apparently my A-line dress warranted such sartorial critique. Or the faculty member who jokingly called me an *esclava*. Sure, it was in the context of being a slave to our jobs, but as the only Black person that they see on a daily basis—I am practically the only Black person who ever walks the halls of my floor—some self-awareness would be appreciated. And if I had a dime for every time someone mistook me for a student or custodial staff or for some other Black woman on campus, I wouldn't have to worry about the fact that my institution never increases my salary enough to keep up with cost of living because I'd have enough money to retire already. But these incidents, as harmful as the sting of repetitive microaggressions is, are nothing compared to what my friends in other departments and institutions go through. And besides, my respect tank (to borrow from Gary Chapman's "love tank") is full enough to neutralize the daily insults that come with the territory of being Black in academia.[4]

As such, the tenure and promotion process was not as harrowing as it could have been. My chair enthusiastically strategized with me about how to present my case to external reviewers because my work was so inter-disciplinary and therefore not necessarily legible to everyone. Colleagues shared their own experiences and tenure file materials while offering feed-back on my tenure narrative. Everyone was generous with their time and expertise, and they made me feel like a valued member of the department.

More important, there was no indication of behind-the-back politick-ing. While I had done everything to ensure a rock-solid case, as many Black women know, it doesn't really matter if you have excelled in what-ever metric you confront. Take the recent case of Nikole Hannah-Jones and the University of North Carolina (UNC) at Chapel Hill. Playing the rules of the game so well that you outperform your colleagues does not protect you. If your department deems you a bad fit, they will find a way to push you out. I watched, horrified, as some friends confronted this reality. I understood I was one of the lucky ones. Could I really take the words of that anonymous wiki post to heart?

In sixth grade, I competed in a district-wide writing competition. Because I had a tae kwon do tournament later that day, I didn't stay for the awards ceremony. When I found out the following Monday that I had won first place, I proudly put my trophy next to the gold medals I had earned for winning my sparring division. Even at that age, I knew the barriers I was toppling as the Black student who beat out everyone in a predominant-ly white scholastic competition and the little girl who outcompeted all those boys in a male-dominated sport. I was doing it all, and it felt good. I couldn't wait to tell my parents and excitedly thrust my trophy into my mom's face when she picked me up from school that afternoon.

But something unexpected happened. My mom's initial joy at my suc-cess slowly turned into an emotion I could not place. She shook her head and sighed, "Because you missed the awards ceremony, no one saw you get your trophy. No one knows the district winner is Black."

At the time, my eleven-year-old self was incredulous, and I exploded in the way that only a tween can. How dare she chastise me for missing an awards ceremony? I had done everything asked of me. I kept up with my studies while pursuing my extracurricular interests, and I put in the time and effort to excel at whatever I took on. But as the years went on, my mother's disappointment accrued new meaning each time I was confront-ed with assumptions that I didn't belong. I weathered much of high school as the only Black girl in my grade. I never once had an instructor who looked like me. For my mother and so many others, Black representation and evidence of Black excellence mattered, not as a token of exceptionalism but as an irrefutable claim that these spaces are just as much ours. For so many, the hope is that the visibility of Black excellence will crack the doors open just a bit wider so that "the only Black girl in my grade" is no longer a thing.

However, in my experience, that has hardly been the case. It didn't matter that my fellow students knew the high quality of work I produced. Even though my high grades and test scores proved otherwise, I was presumed incompetent. My classmates had written an inferiority narrative for me and conveniently ignored any evidence that would force them to reassess their expectations. When I got into various prestigious colleges, students shamelessly told me to my face that I should be grateful for affirmative action. How do I convince people of my humanity and value—let alone that of other Black folk—when they've been taught their whole lives that people like me possess neither?[5]

In fact, the whole system maintains this charade. In high school, for instance, I was awarded a National Achievement Scholarship, receiving $2,000 from the National Merit Scholarship Corporation (NMSC) as part of their program to advance the educational aspirations of Black students. I was also a National Merit Finalist but never had the opportunity to compete for that award. I was informed by NSMC that I had to choose one competition or the other, and since achievement scholarships were announced weeks before merit scholarships, I couldn't risk the sure thing when there was scholarship money on the line. I never forgot how I was siphoned off into the less impressive award and essentially erased.[6] There is an assumption that Black students are underrepresented because of lack of competence without acknowledgment that the system was built to diminish our achievements and maintain the status quo. No number of trophies or other markers of success have erased white people's skepticism of my abilities, let alone allowed me to find myself in spaces with folks who look like me. That's not an accident. It's by design.

I spread all my notes about the various job applicants onto the conference table and took a deep breath. It had been seven years since we had been granted a tenure line, and I was teeming with excitement for the possibilities. My department, acutely aware of its entanglement with institutional racism, had publicly stated its goals of recruiting and retaining people who reflected the demographics of our local community and our field of study. As a newly tenured associate professor, imbued with the confidence that comes with job security and upward mobility, I marveled at my seat at the table and our committee's mandate to dismantle the power structures that had kept our department so white for so long. It was wonderful to dream of shedding my token status and welcoming a new colleague from a racially minoritized group.

But every step of the way I saw the work of highly qualified, dynamic, cutting-edge scholars be questioned, judged, and deemed inadequate. These were scholars with a track record of success who should have been celebrated; instead, their contributions to the discipline and the classroom were framed as lacking or not what we needed. I saw strong candidates being rejected for flimsy, subjective reasons, such as their scholarship was too contemporary, their archive was too limited, or the curricular diversity they offered wasn't what we were looking for.

The mental gymnastics some of my colleagues used to discredit the work of minoritized applicants were shocking on their own, but to come from a department that had embodied such convincing performative allyship made the slap in the face reverberate much more deeply. Only one colleague emphatically fought for our stated vision, speaking up about the moral imperative and practical incentives of hiring someone whose lived experience and scholarly agenda fully embodied the DEI criteria that we had claimed were important to us and that would better prepare our students for a diverse world.[7] Colleagues dismissed this argument because we are technically not allowed to hire based on race. What went unstated, however, was the assumption that the only reason nonwhite faculty would ever be hired is because of their race. Furthermore, people tend to reward those who remind them of themselves.[8] White faculty hiring white people is not a neutral act but one based on race, even though they claim their criteria are objective.

In our discussions of candidates, my rebuttals were rebuffed, and my pleas, ignored. I pointed out the major blind spots in our curriculum and how this hire could go a long way in rectifying our shortcomings. Colleagues flippantly reminded me that because we are a small department, we have lots of holes that need filling. They reduced diversity to a difference of research interests. Finding a colleague with research interests they preferred was more important than creating a better environment for minoritized and historically excluded faculty and students.

When all my arguments in favor of what candidates' proven track records of excellent research and teaching could bring to our department failed, I tried to appeal to what I thought was our collective goal of diversifying our department by sharing my own personal experiences, engaging in the emotional labor that accompanies pleading with colleagues to no longer be tokenized.[9] I reminded them of my extra burden as the only racialized minority in a sea of whiteness. I recounted the emotionally draining experiences of supporting our minoritized students, of how students seek me out as adviser for research projects dealing with racial difference or for help navigating a predominantly white institution, of how I don't just address our own students' anxieties but field requests from students across campus.[10] I hoped that sharing my daily racialized reality would have some sort of effect. It didn't. In the end, my seat at the table and the vocal support of my one colleague (as well as the tepid support of a couple others) were not enough to bring change in a department that was content to reproduce its whiteness. Eventually, the reality dawned on me: our department had no interest in tackling its tacit support of whiteness.

Looking back on it, I had somehow allowed myself to believe—despite my initial trepidations—that my colleagues were different. I had allowed myself to buy into the narrative that because they were "wonderful people" they would do what was necessary to make our corner of the world a little more equitable. I don't know if I ever actually believed it, but I needed this conviction because it was the only way to motivate myself in a world addicted to white supremacy. And, of course, there was no denying the role of the systems in place at my university—like those governing the National Achievement Scholarship. Inequity and racism are built into hiring practices from recruitment to selection (e.g., ignoring qualified candidates that aren't the right "fit," devaluing community-engaged scholarship, recruiting most heavily in supposed "peer" institutions).

Soon after this experience, COVID hit, and the racial inequities associated with the pandemic were yet another reminder of how perilous this world is for Black and Brown bodies. Then Breonna Taylor, Ahmaud Arbery, George Floyd, and countless others were killed by agents of the state or vigilantes emboldened by our country's indifference and silence.

In response, Black Lives Matter (BLM) signs popped up all over my neighborhood. But they were not fooling me. If my neighborhood's racist posts on Nextdoor were any indication, those same people probably wouldn't hesitate to call the police if they saw a "suspicious" Black person get too close to their property. This performative wokeness and the very real pain, violence, and death that it ultimately masks rather than extinguishes are nauseating. The debilitating stress that these high-profile incidents cause is compounded by my having to navigate a work environment where people claim to care about things like racial justice and equity but then won't do the bare minimum to dismantle whiteness or consider the ways that they benefit from it. I liken our departmental DEI statement displayed so prominently on our website to those BLM signs. The department has succeeded in perfecting the DEI statement genre while avoiding real DEI work, such as improving the conditions of Black, Brown, Indigenous, and melanated people (BBMIP) students and faculty.[11] As Paula White, Eva Gibson, and Jessica Fripp convincingly argue in chapter 10 of this volume, this type of performative allyship "makes white people 'feel good' about themselves without introspection, action, or accountability. Consequently, Black people must continue performing, assimilating to the behavior and discourse of whiteness."[12]

The talk makes the lack of action that much more violent. One of the most dangerous things about liberal institutions and left-leaning people is their aversive racism.[13] In dispelling the myth of the Klan and other right-wing extremists as the biggest threat to racial progress, Dr. Martin Luther King named white moderates with their devotion to order rather than to justice as "the great stumbling block."[14] But in my experience, liberals have caused the most pain. These supposed allies say the right words to appease those who want change and then gaslight us when we speak up about change not coming. Most of my colleagues seem completely unaware of the violence they have inflicted. I wonder if they really are this obtuse. When I told one colleague that I was thinking about leaving the department partially because the lack of diversity was wearing on me, he lamented that it was hard to address these types of issues because as a small department we so seldom are granted faculty lines. That he was a main reason that none of the highly qualified minoritized applicants were hired did not seem to cross his mind. The supreme irony is that this particular person was instrumental in getting me hired and has been a supportive colleague throughout my time with the department. Once again: My own Black excellence wasn't opening doors. In some ways, it was being instrumentalized to keep them stubbornly shut. Not even calling out this tokenization seemed to work.

The violence of the hiring process washed over me during that conversation. I quietly seethed, knowing that correcting their version of events would have done nothing more than provoke his defensiveness. As I disassociated from the conversation, the words of Nina Simone's "Mississippi Goddam" flooded my mind: "I don't trust you any more / You keep on saying 'Go slow!'"[15]

The inability of my department to hire a minortized faculty member and the subsequent gaslighting left me so numb that I was on the verge of quitting.[16] I have no interest in waiting another seven years for the next opportunity to hire and then watch again as my colleagues use code words to argue why marginalized candidates aren't good enough. Suffering from the "one-minority-per-pot syndrome," my department would only feel compelled to replace its token if I left.[17] That would be one way of opening the doors for others, at least. Unfortunately, my achievements and contributions over the past decade weren't enough to convince them of what BBIMP scholars can bring.

My mother's disappointment that no one saw me pick up my first-place trophy causes me to ruminate on the shortcomings of representation then and now. Centuries' worth of devaluation and denigration don't dissolve because of one awards ceremony. Nor do the exhortations of a token Black colleague and a white colleague accomplice effect meaningful change. I might have made it, but there is no guarantee that I can bring others with me.

I am sure that if my colleagues read this essay, they will dismiss my arguments because that is what always happens in these instances. When a former PhD student wrote a scathing critique of my department soon after she graduated, my colleagues were hung up on her tone (she was angry and belligerent) instead of the value of her words. They weren't willing to perform the introspection necessary to address her criticisms, and so they learned nothing.

By speaking my truth and sharing my experiences, I am aware of the bridges that could be burned and the implications it could have on future employment.[18] But I know the greater danger is for me to silence myself.

As Zora Neale Hurston purportedly argued, "If you are silent about your pain, they'll kill you and say you enjoyed it."[19] Meanwhile, Gwendolyn Etter-Lewis maintains that our testimony provides "a means of enfranchising and empowering people whose lives have previously been shaped by 'colonized history' written from the standpoint of outsider."[20] Maybe my experience will help other minoritized people navigate an inherently unfair system or, even better, push white people to do the necessary work to dismantle it. John Lewis, who faced much more than job insecurity and hostile work environments, knew the power of good trouble when he told us, "Do not get lost in a sea of despair. Be hopeful, be optimistic. Our struggle is not the struggle of a day, a week, a month, or a year, it is the struggle of a lifetime. Never, ever be afraid to make some noise and get in good trouble, necessary trouble."[21]

Perhaps my department will take my words to heart and commit itself to change, or perhaps I will find a different space where there are others like me, where I can escape tokenization, and where colleagues move beyond performative wokeness.[22] What is clear is that the onus is not on me to change the system. As Hannah-Jones so eloquently put it when leaving UNC: "For too long, powerful people have expected the people they have mistreated and marginalized to sacrifice themselves to make things whole. The burden of working for racial justice is laid on the very people bearing the brunt of the injustice, and not the powerful people who maintain it. I say to you: I refuse."[23] Since academia is an institution that was *never* meant for me, my positioning as a scholar outsider (to pay homage to Audre Lorde's *Sister Outsider*) has taught me never to rely on academia to dictate my worth. Armed with Lewis's optimism, I believe in finding joy wherever I can and doing everything in my power to help the next generation find their joy—within or without academia.[24]

NOTES

1. "The nation's most prestigious universities were not established to educate women, people of color, or the working class. On the contrary, they were designed to serve the interests of wealthy white men . . . While many of the formal barriers have been lifted, academic institutions remain, at their core, profoundly inhospitable to the experiences and points of view of those formally excluded." Harris and González, introduction, 7.

2. In coining the term *global majority*, Rosemary Campbell-Stephens astutely points out that only 20 percent of the world is white, but this global white minority minoritizes and marginalizes the other 80 percent, those of the global majority. See Campbell-Stephens, *Educational Leadership and the Global Majority*.

3. According to the most recent national data, Black women make up 2.1 percent of tenured professors. At my institution, we are only 1 percent. In my current city, the percentage of the population that is Black is in the single digits, whereas two-thirds of residents are white, a very different demographic to my majority-minority hometown. June and O'Leary, "How Many Black Women Have Tenure?"

4. Chapman, *5 Love Languages*. Yolanda Niemann reports that minoritized women should expect these types of comments and the associated stress: "People comment on things about you that they do not notice about your white colleagues. These include your dress, opinions and contributions during meetings or events on or off campus, food and music preferences, etc. You will face negative reactions for not meeting stereotypical expectations, which can also result in severe stress." Niemann, "Lessons," 489.

5. Gutiérrez y Muhs et al., *Presumed Incompetent* (2012), chronicles various minoritized women in academia who have confronted similar experiences.

6. I wondered if I misremembered what had happened, but my experience was not an outlier as evidenced by "The Racial Insult Built into the National Merit Scholarship Program," 30–32.

7. My colleague and I argued how historically excluded faculty's lived experiences and the intercultural competence gleaned from such experiences enrich scholarship and teaching. See Madyum et al., "On the Importance of African-American Faculty," 65–84.

8. Gaertner and Dovidio, "Understanding and Addressing Contemporary Racism," 615–39.

9. Niemann details the effects of tokenization: "Tokenized persons feel isolated and lonely, not only on the campus, but sometimes in their predominantly white communities-at-large. Tokens experience attributional ambiguity; they do not know whom to trust." She also expresses her incredulity that diversifying is still such a hot-button issue: "There is simply no excuse today for an all-white department or for a unit that has only one token faculty member of color." Niemann, "Lessons," 473, 475.

10. This cultural or race tax is well documented. See Rockquemore and Laszloffy, *Black Academic's Guide to Winning Tenure*. Like myself, Yolanda Niemann reports a responsibility to support students from historically excluded groups: "As a woman of color, I felt duty-bound to respond to students who felt marginalized in the institution, especially ethnic/racial minorities." Niemann, "The Making of a Token," 345. Karen Pyke conveys the toll this unpaid labor takes on

minoritized women who "perform a disproportionate share of care labor and 'institutional housekeeping'" and whose labor is "*not* optional, nonessential, unskilled labor; rather, it is vital to the day-to-day and long-term operation of the university." Pyke, "Service and Gender Inequity among Faculty," 86–87. As Kristian Contreras articulates in chap. 4 of this volume, Black women must also fight against the warped images that higher education perpetuates where we are cast either as Mammies or Strong Black Women, stereotypes that create expectations of our emotional and invisible labor.

11. Louisa "Weeze" Doran coined the term *Black, Brown, Indigenous, and Mela-nated People* (BBIMP). As she explained in an Instagram post, "My existence isnt rooted in opposition to whyteness. . . . I am not a 'person of color' as though the gold standard for humanity is the absence of!" See https://www.instagram.com/p/CG5SRpBHQz2/?hl=en.

12. The repercussions of this type of stress on historically excluded faculty's emotional, mental, and physical well-being can be found in Zambrana, *Toxic Ivory Towers*.

13. Joel Kovel coined the term *aversive racism*, a phenomenon that is particularly prevalent among white liberals. Kovel, *White Racism*. As Samuel Gaertner and John Dovidio explain about aversive racism, "Many whites who consciously, explicitly, and sincerely support egalitarian principles and believe themselves to be nonprejudiced also harbor negative feelings and beliefs about Blacks and other historically disadvantaged groups." Gaertner and Dovidio, "Understanding and Addressing Contemporary Racism," 618.

14. "Shallow understanding from people of good will is more frustrating than absolute misunderstanding from people of ill will. Lukewarm acceptance is much more bewildering than outright rejection." King, "Letter from a Birmingham Jail."

15. Simone, "Mississippi Goddam."

16. Deena González conveys how others have suffered through similar existential crises: "The cumulative effects, the destructive power of unaltered structures, of traditional bases of privilege and identity, eroded the confidence many had at the beginning of their careers." González, introduction, 334.

17. As María de la Luz Reyes and John Halcón contend, "Many colleges and universities operate under an unwritten quota system that manifests itself as reluctance to hire more than one minority faculty member per department." De la Luz Reyes and Halcón, "Racism in Academia," 305.

18. The editors of the 2012 volume of *Presumed Incompetent* witnessed this fear when seeking chapters for their book: "A significant number of women decided not to contribute to the anthology for fear of retaliation. They believed that they would be penalized for airing their home institution's dirty laundry in public, and they were not prepared to become pariahs. One woman felt that

writing about her experiences would not only burn bridges at her current institution but also undermine her future career prospects." Gutiérrez y Muhs et al., *Presumed Incompetent*, 11. As Niemann argues, this fear was warranted: "I have also been informed that I was not considered a candidate for positions in some universities because search-committee members did not appreciate the message in 'The Making of a Token,' and/or they feared I would write about them some day." Niemann, "The Making of a Token," 353–54. I have personally witnessed retaliation against colleagues who have spoken up about inequities. After much reflection, I have chosen to use a pseudonym and not to include the name of my institution as an acknowledgment of my lack of power and the precarity of my position even as a tenured professor. As an anonymous reviewer pointed out, "Black women often feel pressured to empty their emotional reserves in front of folks who couldn't care less . . . the courage to be vulnerable comes with the risk of rebuke." I have been vulnerable. I have been rebuked. And while I honor myself by telling my story, I also show myself love by protecting myself to a certain degree.

19. This quote, which is found all over the internet, is often attributed to Zora Neale Hurston. However, thorough searches of her writing have yet to uncover the source.

20. Etter-Lewis, "Black Women in Academe," 83.

21. Lewis (@repjohnlewis), Twitter.

22. Over the years, my institution has failed to retain many minoritized women scholars, usually doing the bare minimum when these sought-after colleagues have been offered employment elsewhere.

23. Hannah-Jones, "Nikole Hannah-Jones Issues Statement."

24. Lorde, *Sister Outsider*.

CHAPTER 10

Navigating the Ivory Tower
A Community Approach

PAULA W. WHITE, EVA M. GIBSON,
AND JESSICA A. FRIPP

Expectations of Black faculty are more far reaching than teaching, scholarship, and service. As Ebony McGee noted in the *Chronicle of Higher Education*, underrepresented faculty members also battle the pull to engage in extensive service activities as well as educate communities on diversity, equity, and inclusion (DEI).[1] Jeremy House highlighted that Black faculty members allow their careers to hang in the balance while supporting their colleges' diversity initiatives.[2] As Black faculty are creating opportunities to support their campus community, they are met with microaggressive behavior from faculty, administration, and students; handle negative evaluations; and are critiqued more harshly regarding scholarship on topics related to diversity initiatives. Additionally, Black faculty members provide a level of mentorship to Black and Brown students, another form of invisible labor not considered in the evaluative process. As Patricia Matthew notes in the *Atlantic*, the imbalance of service requirements between white and Black faculty as well as associated burdens of doing culturally responsive work are unrewarded.[3] These items are minimally evaluated on annual dossiers, with most faculty retention/tenure/promotion (RTP) committees demonstrating focused attention on research and scholarly activities. Without adequate opportunities to balance the needs of their academic position, junior faculty (especially Black faculty) are at greater risk of burnout, fatigue, job dissatisfaction, and potentially vacating their positions early.

Furthermore, many institutions are not committed to the work of diversity. From an administrative perspective, it is uncomfortable, time-consuming, controversial, and expensive. It is much easier to appear diverse or antiracist. In a post–George Floyd era we see an influx of DEI marketing from university websites to course syllabi. This is performative allyship and focuses on image and reputation instead of change. White performative allyship makes white people "feel good" about themselves without introspection, action, or accountability. Consequently, Black people must continue performing, assimilating to the behavior and discourse of whiteness. Black women, in particular, face barriers designed to prevent them from achieving mainstream and long-term success. Lori Walkington argues that as double minorities, Black women scholars are viewed as less capable, leading to fewer full-time, tenured positions for Black women faculty and assumptions of Black women graduate students as affirmative action recipients incapable of graduate-level work.[4] To combat these myths and stereotypes, Black women forge communities of resistance. Faced with the challenges to "retain themselves," Black women scholars create their own retention programs to grow and sustain community. Gloria Thomas and Carol Hollenshead conducted a case study at a U.S. research university that revealed the resistance strategies of academic women of color (including Black women), addressing five areas: organizational barriers, institutional climate, lack of respect from one's colleagues, unwritten rules governing university life, and mentoring.[5] These themes are reflected in the individual views narrated below.

This chapter will portray the perspectives of three pre-tenure African American women at a predominately white institution, where support for African American women is not often forthcoming. In addition to the tenure mandates required from all tenure-track faculty members, these women also experienced emotional burdens resulting from encounters with microaggressions and the demands of invisible labor. As African American women often experience emotional and psychological violence from faculty, administration, and students; receive unfavorable peer and/or student evaluations; and face harsher critiques of scholarship related to topics on social justice and diversity initiatives, the authors sought avenues to solicit support. As a means to seek respite, the authors became active in an affinity group on their campus (the African American Employee Council) and developed further bonds, which led to subsequent collaborations and shared professional projects. They worked closely together to foster a sense of belonging to improve collegiality and retention. This chapter will discuss challenges the women faced individually juxtaposed to the outcomes resulting from their collective approach to professional development. Moreover, this chapter will discuss how these women used mentorship and collaboration to navigate professional and academic spaces.

INDIVIDUAL VIEWS

Dr. White

I recently completed my first-year on the tenure track amid a global pandemic. My experience as a junior academic has been much like my experience over the past year—remote. I have and continue to navigate the ivory tower in a struggle with isolation and invisibility. Since my doctoral studies, I am often the only "one" in the room. This sort of double-consciousness often causes me to feel like an accessory rather than a colleague—meaning my race and gender contribute to the aesthetics of the institution more than its work. Especially true in my current position, as I am the only Black woman in my department. If not for Black tenured colleagues, I would know little of on-campus opportunities for funding my research or the "hidden" challenges of navigating the tenure track. Similarly, Black campus organizations kept frustrations at bay, as they provided an otherwise fragile network where I could outsource the support and mentorship I desperately needed for retention. This year and those before it have taught me that searching for joy in the academy is just as important as creating it.

After completing the PhD from a predominantly white institution (PWI) in the South, I accepted a non-tenure-track position at another PWI in the "deeper South." I emphasize the region of these institutions because of its influence on campus politics and culture for Black faculty. In this case, both institutions had landmarks and buildings on or surrounding campus that reflected Jim Crow politics or Civil War history. So, Lost Cause ideology and white supremacy were embedded in symbols, mascots, and university branding. No amount of diversity training or antiracism workshops could distract me from the overwhelming influence of "tradition" or "heritage" on campus. Moreover, I found some of these ideologies reflected in the behavior of my colleagues, campus administrators, and students. To survive in this environment, I had to commit to assimilation, which meant learning the language and culture of white academia. Doing so required a full-time masquerade; it was mentally and emotionally exhausting.

I earned two degrees from a historically Black university (HBCU). At the HBCU, I gained an idealistic perspective of academia and the Black professorship, one that was centered around community and mentorship. My decision to pursue the professoriate was heavily influenced by the work and mentorship modeled by Black professors. I witnessed them meeting with my classmates about personal concerns affecting their studies and career choices. These conversations were pivotal to student success; many received internships and scholarships, took student leadership positions, and enrolled in graduate school. Some of my most impactful moments as an HBCU student were outside the classroom, specifically office hours. By my junior year, I realized that my professors were available for more than grade disputes and lecture notes. I can recall many office visits that turned into conversations about my future and the anxieties of young Black womanhood. I grew personally and intellectually when I engaged in face-to-face meetings with my professors. We were able to connect over the shared experiences and marginalities of Blackness and womanhood. This helped me find joy—to reimagine academia as a communal space, a place where I could belong. Those moments of care and grace gave me the courage to pursue a master's degree and later enroll in a doctoral program.

However, when I began my doctoral studies, opportunities for community and mentorship were few and far between. For the first two years, I was the only Black graduate student in my department. Additionally, the department experienced high turnover among Black contingent and tenure-track faculty. Despite diversity and retention issues, I was able to form a few relationships with professors—many of whom serve as my current mentors. As I neared the dissertation stage, I eagerly sought out additional guidance and resources. The Black graduate student association connected me to Black faculty across campus, which changed my experience and relationship to the university. The most impactful organization during my doctoral studies was the Sisters of Fulbright (SOF), a community of Black women PhDs and doctoral students that provided support for research and professional development. The Sisters of Fulbright was specifically invested in helping Black women doctoral students navigate their programs and complete the dissertation. Mentorship in this group helped me complete the PhD, as well as acquire fellowships, conference invitations, and additional funding. Moreover, the encouragement and resulting joy I received from SOF countered the impostor syndrome and anxiety I developed in predominantly white academic spaces. Though my experience at PWIs were largely non-communal, Black faculty at these institutions encouraged me not to leave my program or the university because of isolation. I strongly believe I would not have completed the PhD or survived my first academic job without the support and visibility of Black faculty.

I experienced the most invisibility and isolation in my first academic job after completing the PhD. For three years, I worked as a permanent, but non-tenure-track instructor on two branch campuses. There were no academic departments on the branch campuses, so there were few to no opportunities for camaraderie, collaboration, and professional development. I did not have an office, and faculty meetings as well as social events were held one hour away on the main campus. Likewise, I attended monthly departmental meetings with colleagues I barely knew. These experiences as well as being overlooked for faculty research opportunities fueled my job market search until I received a tenure-track offer from my current institution.

Dr. Gibson

My view has been shaped by a mixed bag of experiences, both positive and negative. Prior to transferring to a PWI, I worked at an HBCU for two years. My decision to change institutions was primarily driven by proximity considerations, but it impacted other aspects of my personal and professional development. My new setting required adjustments in my approach and engagement strategy. At my previous institution, I was one of many faculty of color, and the majority of my students looked like me. This provided a sense of comfort and familiarity. In my new university, Black faculty make up 7 percent of the total faculty on campus, while Black students make up 20 percent of enrolled students. This change in demographics prompted a more intentional and thoughtful process. I realize that I stand out more to both faculty and students, so my impact on others may carry greater consequences, both positive and negative. On the positive end, students have shared with me that I have been the first Black instructor they had in all their years of schooling. I am very vocal about the importance of culturally sustaining practices as I prepare future professionals and am very proud as I witness my white students develop into culturally conscious practitioners. On the negative end, working in a PWI also means that many of the people around me do not understand the complexities of being Black. It is tiring to continue to explain aspects of my culture and being. Additionally, it is even more frustrating to be expected to educate others without compensation. I became strategic and intentional in an effort to preserve my mental health and wellness while seeking joy. I connected with other Black faculty both within my university and across other universities and connected pods of professional support networks. One pod, affectionately called my "SistaScholars," consists of two additional Black female professors at different universities who share my research interests. We met at a conference and have since cocreated multiple publications and presentations together. It is also important to note that we focus on social justice issues and culturally affirming practices. My time working with them is heart work and fulfilling. Although I initially connected with them for professional support, I quickly realized that I bonded with them on a personal level and experienced joy in our interactions. My second pod consists of two other Black female professors at my university. Although our research interests vary, we connect on a routine basis and discuss issues relating to navigating the university. These relationships motivate me and impact my view of academia. These particular communities play a significant role in my current position, yet I must acknowledge the Black women who have also assisted along the way. Throughout my journey, Black women have contributed to my development and success in impromptu, yet important, ways. My first publication transpired owing to my connections with a Black professor. During my first year teaching in academia, she reached out to me and gave me the opportunity to write a chapter for a textbook she was editing. I am forever grateful for her willingness to support my professional development. My second year in academia presented some similar opportunities as another Black female professor invited me to write a chapter for a book and another invited me to take part in a grant proposal. Even when I transitioned from the HBCU to my current PWI, I was still showered with the loving kindness of Black women in the academy. While preparing for my dossier review, a Black colleague shared her dossier with me to provide an example of expected format and content. Another Black colleague used her connections to provide me with opportunities to serve as a grant reviewer, present at conferences, and obtain service as well as leadership positions. Although I cannot fully express my gratitude for the Black professors who have poured into me over the years, I would like to acknowledge the joy they supplied me and honor their legacy by pouring into others. Despite the struggles of navigating a PWI, I have been blessed to have multiple publications, presentations, and awards, and I owe many of those accomplishments to my connections with these women.

Dr. Fripp

Most of my early academic experiences were marred with invisibility and impostor syndrome. Before my current appointment at a teaching university in the South, I was hired as a clinical faculty member with no option for tenure at a research-focused institution. As a clinical instructor, I was given arduous teaching and service expectations; additionally, I was often mistreated by colleagues within my program area, as my position did not hold the academic merit of others. Particularly, one colleague of mine (on the tenure track) held a similar research agenda and created an environment of unspoken competition and academic hazing. She became increasingly more combative and condescending toward me as students gravitated to my research interests, knowledge, and real-world experiences. As we taught separate course sections related to the same content, my expectation was she would be a resource, a sounding board, and part of my support system. However, anti-Black racism was the tie that bound us to the coursework and kept me burdened with feelings of inadequacy. Her invalidations of my experiences were subtle, as she found ways to circumvent blame for my feelings through gaslighting and false interpretations of what I reported. If a student used the content of the course to bully me, if an encounter in a faculty meeting made me feel uncomfortable, or if I felt targeted in the feedback I received from a manuscript submission, she found ways to hold me responsible for other people's behavior. Thinking back on my personal experiences, chapter 8 in this volume, written by Heather Scott and Nyasha GuramatunhuCooper, resonated with me. As they described feelings of judgment, I was often left feeling confused, bruised, humiliated at times, and distrusting of others, particularly those in the academy.

According to David Mihalyfy, critique in academic settings is common; however, sometimes one must discern if the feedback borders on bullying.[6] Of the four indicators outlined in this article, I most related to the concept of general, nonconstructive feedback. Reflections on my time in that department were marked by the lack of metrics to adequately score my performance, devoid of any concrete evidence that would support the need for change in my current way of teaching. I received minimal guidance or support to ready myself for a tenure-seeking line, and more items added to my workload ensured I would never find time to prepare myself to be competitive on the job market. I felt physically stuck and emotionally harmed in that environment. I became painfully aware during my time at this university that that colleague on the tenure track was not "my person." Furthermore, I had to come to terms with whether this particular university suited my needs and my future career aspirations. With that understanding, I went on the market and found a tenure-track position. Though my experiences with this university contributed to frustrations and disappointment, I found an unexpected community with Black faculty members who were in my age bracket. We lovingly referred to ourselves as "the unicorns," as many students indicated they never expected to see young Black instructors who commanded the classroom. These women became unofficial sisters, mentors, and friends who empowered me to take advantage of my career experience. They believed in something I had yet to see; furthermore, their encouragement informed my self-worth, provided necessary belonging, and created a sense of joy toward a hope deferred of reaching my full potential.

Now that I am fully invested at my current institution, the community among Black faculty has created a sense of safety and protection. I was able to pair with a tenured Black faculty member who shared grant-writing opportunities with me and presented opportunities for us to present together. She provided a fresh perspective, advice, support, and guidance, whereas previous mentors had been lacking. I am forever grateful for her ability to steer me on my tenure journey. She and other colleagues continually provide me with relevant feedback concerning my manuscripts and offer quality recommendations to improve my overall academic performance. With their guidance, I enjoy the benefits of being published, have received early promotion, and submitted my tenure application in Fall 2022. I was also recently named the associate dean of the College of Behavioral and Health Sciences. Looking back on the previous experience enabled me to know what I did not deserve, which forced me to remove myself from a toxic environment. I went from being ostracized to recognizing my personal and professional worth. Knowing who I am and what I bring to the table are qualities I lead with, now understanding that I add value to and gain joy in each space I enter.

SHARED VIEWS

Performativity

As faculty members at a predominantly white institution, each of us has firsthand experiences of the ways whiteness becomes the standard for behavior and performance within the academy. Navigating these unspoken "customs" gives birth to emotional burnout, as Black people feel compelled to masquerade as a "safe Black" to appease white comfort. It is important to note these types of negotiations (between who you are and who they prefer you to be) prevent us from walking in full authenticity. Additionally, muting the posture and identity of Black women reduces exposure to Blackness. Having appropriate representation increases the benefits to the campus culture, as students, faculty, and staff are exposed to different presentations of Black identity without the social politics and labeling (e.g., being aggressive, loud).

Invisibility versus Visibility

Each author has been told by students that we are "the first Black professor" that they have had. This reaffirms why retention of Black faculty is critical to student enrollment, as faculty and staff should reflect student demographics. From our experience, students perform better in the classroom and matriculate more successfully throughout college when they are taught by and engage with faculty that "look like them."

Representation and Mentorship

The importance of representation, identifying Black connection, and mentorship became pivotal parts of each woman's perspective. According to Walkington,[7] Black women in the academy are often viewed as "tokens," have limited access to resources and support, and often feel like outsiders within the context of historically white spaces.[8] Though Black women in the academy are intellectual equals to their white counterparts, little space is made to invite them to the proverbial "seat at the table." As Sayam Davis references in chapter 9 in this volume, finding a shared space, where she can escape tokenization, might be an option, but changing the system is not her responsibility. To this point, authors White, Gibson, and Fripp recognized this disparity and became intentional about identifying individuals on their paths who guided them, mentored them, and provided encouragement toward their success. These relationships are invaluable and cannot be ignored. Such connections solidified their identity as Black women in a space where people have consistently attempted to transmute their power. Additionally, these connections allow Black women to reimagine and redefine female Black identity within the academic ivory tower as opposed to engaging in respectability politics and accepting tokenism as their role. Although the history of respectability politics contributed to greater access, allowing Black women more opportunities to take space in the room, the necessity to tolerate respectability as a current practice is reduced. Black women can find their value in their authenticity while navigating the balance of freedom, joy in the midst of turmoil, and respectability.

Each author's specific views are unique, common themes emerged along their collective perspectives. As a result, the authors sought support to motivate and encourage them throughout this experience.

COLLECTIVE SUPPORTS

The university African American Employee Council (AAEC) was created in 2020 as a result of public displays of racial injustice throughout the nation. The AAEC was formed organically, started by a series of text messages between Black employees. Based on this correspondence, Black employees began planning a university town hall open to students, employees, and alumni to process recent events. The virtual town hall was held the following week and attended by over five hundred participants. Facilitators led a discussion covering emotions, needs, mental health supports, and next steps to create a collective safe space. As a result, the AAEC was officially formed to promote unity, provide support, and build community among Black employees and students at the university. The council created bylaws, a constitution, officers, and committees to lead the charge. It also committed to advocacy and collaborative efforts to enhance communication and champion equity, access, inclusion, and social justice. Since the creation of this group, monthly meetings have been held to offer support and continue work in these areas. One product of the AAEC that particularly impacted the authors of this chapter was the creation of the Faculty Affairs Committee.

The Faculty Affairs Committee (FAC) was developed to assist Black faculty members as they navigate through the demands of retention, tenure, merit, and promotion. This committee seeks to build faculty connections and a sense of community across campus, provide mentorship, and supply a safe space to process departmental or programmatic concerns. The FAC created recommendations and voted on goals for the group. Based on majority vote, participants selected the following goals: (1) assist faculty with the retention/tenure process, (2) collect and archive Black faculty publications, (3) share scholarship opportunities, and (4) host webinars.

The FAC met on a monthly basis and successfully accomplished all four goals within the academic year. Additionally, committee members recognized the value in sharing a safe space with other scholars to promote greater productivity. As such, they proposed a writing retreat to build a broader sense of community among Black faculty members. This initiative, fondly named the Beloved Community Writing Retreat, was inspired by the work of Dr. Martin Luther King Jr., who often spoke of his vision of a beloved community that actively works together toward shared goals. The beloved community concept emphasized a spirit of support and synergy as well as collective joy. The program sought to create such a community for tenure-track Black faculty at the university. A formal proposal was created and included the following objectives for participants: (1) demonstrate the ability to engage as a productive writing collaborator, offering and accepting feedback to and from peers, (2) develop strategies to enhance competency and confidence in the production of scholarly and creative works, and (3) formulate an action plan to prioritize writing and create a manageable framework for incorporating academic writing into the workload.

A budget was developed to support program goals at an off-site location. The proposal and the budget were submitted to two different college deans and fully funded. After funding was secured, Black faculty members were encouraged to apply for the Beloved Community Writing Retreat. Applications were evaluated, and five were selected to participate in the retreat at no cost. Daily agendas included time for goal setting, guest speakers, independent writing, and concluding accountability checks. Guest speakers featured Black tenured professors, the provost, and other university representatives. Participants completed a pre-assessment and post-assessment to evaluate the impact of the program. Days were dedicated to scholarly endeavors, but evenings were devoted to fellowship and community building. Participants formed a closer bond and collective products included the following: (1) five manuscripts in progress, (2) one grant submission, (3) two completed manuscripts, (4) two completed presentations for future conferences, and (5) one manuscript proposal. Although some outcomes were measurable, other results were intangible. The collective joy felt and expressed during this experience was powerful! Additionally, participants reported an increased level of support and a desire for similar programs and continued engagement.

FUTURE ENDEAVORS

While being Black in the ivory tower can pose unique frustrations and barriers, the authors found solidarity and support as they embraced a shared view and community approach. The shared view has been so powerful that the authors have committed to continuous engagement in both the professional and personal spheres. Participants in the Beloved Community Writing Retreat collectively agreed to meet on a monthly basis to share progress on scholarly goals. Additionally, retreat organizers have started discussions with participants and financial supporters about making the retreat an annual event. The provost and respective college deans have expressed support for future programming. The FA committee is in the process of formally establishing a mentorship program dedicated to support Black faculty in the promotion and tenure process. In an effort to expand this sense of community, FA committee members have created plans to connect with new faculty members entering the university.

CONCLUSION

Black women academics and arguably Black academics at large cannot sustain successful and healthy careers without community and finding joy within those connections. Many white colleagues lack the cultural sensitivity and experience necessary to collaborate with Black faculty and students. Mandated workshops and training on diversity cannot replace actual diversity in the academy. Universities must be willing to invest in retention and professional development of Black faculty, beyond what they contribute to white faculty. The shared view and community approach discussed in this chapter illustrates that the benefits of mentorship, intentional community, and collaboration go further than empty gestures of allyship and support; this collaborative process fosters a dynamic unity and comfort within the walls of academia. It is our hope that every Black woman can find and create inviting and collaborative spaces in the ivory tower.

NOTES

1. McGee, "Ready to Be an Ally?"
2. House, "Faculty of Color Hurt Their Careers."
3. Matthew, "What Is Faculty Diversity Worth?"
4. Walkington, "How Far Have We Really Come?"
5. Thomas and Hollenshead, "Resisting from the Margins."
6. Mihalyfy, "When Is Criticism Bullying?"
7. Walkington, "How Far Have We Really Come?"
8. Walkington, "How Far Have We Really Come?"

CHAPTER 11

Seeking Corrective Policy and Practice

TIFFANY MONIQUE QUASH

> For some to pass through the door, to enter a room, requires being given permission by those who are holding that door.
>
> —Sara Ahmed, *Living a Feminist Life*

I dreamed of being a well-rounded and academically motivated college student as a child. At the age of nine, I heard my first Black Womxn college president speak, and at ten, I went on my first college tour and was determined to become an academic before the conclusion of that tour.[1] These experiences motivated me in the classroom to become a stronger student, but I was unaware that higher education, as it is currently conceived, would not consider allowing a Black Womxn to fully enter the ivory tower. As I grew older, my idea of the ivory tower increasingly resembled a fantasy world.

To me, the ivory tower looks a lot like an off-white pristine fortress surrounded by a moat with a locked gate. To proceed through the gate, individuals are hand selected by a mysterious force. When I close my eyes, I can see myself banging my hand against the door, trying to get in as I watch mostly white men, with a sprinkle of Black men among them, walking in a line, wearing regalia in the dead of night.[2] Frustratingly, when I open my eyes, I am still banging on that door to be let in, to be seen, to be heard, and to feel validated and vindicated. These feelings of alienation from the academy are compounded by a traumatic experience I endured as a doctoral student at a primarily white institution, when I was compelled to navigate a hostile work and education environment created by a Black male faculty member.

In this chapter, I examine the policies and practices for filing a complaint against this type of behavior—which I consider psychologically abusive—at this particular institution. I will demonstrate how this institution and its administration continued to protect this faculty member, despite his harmful behavior toward a student like me. After I recount my experiences, I will offer some suggestions for how institutions and administrators can prevent future harm to graduate students and conclude with a reflection on how to find joy even in the face of bureaucratic complacency and inadequate policy responses. At the core of this chapter is the idea that institutional policies and practices are biased against Black Womxn.

Because of the intersection of race and gender, Black Womxn are "multiply-burdened," as Kimberlé Crenshaw puts it, and experience discrimination compounded by this intersectionality.[3] Because higher education has long been dominated by white, cisgender men, this multiple burden has translated into institutions that do not prioritize the academic preparation of Black Womxn. As Sherri Wallace, Sharon Moore, and Carla Curtis have argued, this failure is especially pronounced at primarily white institutions, as opposed to historically Black colleges and universities.[4] For Black Womxn doctoral students, this broader discrimination is manifested in the lack of proper mentoring and advising provided by the institution to them,[5] as well as the lack of visible Black Womxn in leadership positions.[6] As a result, to thrive in their programs, Black Womxn students need to look to alternative sources of support, such as networking across academic disciplines, attending campus events, and seeking out professional development opportunities that might be outside of one's area of study. Yet no matter what alternative strategies Black Womxn develop to survive and thrive in higher education, nothing can prepare you to endure a senior faculty member creating a hostile work and education environment.

GUILT AND SHAME

Ever since I was a child, I have felt the heavy weight of being an intelligent Black Girl in white-dominated spaces. Whether it was because of my physical appearance or because I spoke up when I had a concern or perhaps something else, it was abundantly clear that I was not welcomed in spaces constructed by and comprised of mostly white, cisgender men. Furthermore, it was abundantly clear that bringing attention to a negative encounter with a supervisor, or someone with authority, was unacceptable, particularly in educational settings. For example, in 1996, when I was sixteen years old, I secured a summer internship at NASA Langley in Virginia. My goal was to become a computer engineer, and I felt the internship opportunity would guide this path. But my dreams were shaken when I was verbally harassed by two straight, white, cisgender men—my supervisor and his colleague—for three months. I was criticized for my thought process and how I held firm to my beliefs as a youth, which they considered uncharacteristic of someone my age. I was unsure to whom I should speak about this behavior. I did not want to be perceived as a troublemaker by others in the program, including the coordinator or the other students, and I was concerned by how my family might react , so I arrived at work every day and accepted the verbal abuse. When the summer was over, I received a copy of the supervisor's assessment of my internship, in which he stated: "My apprentice needs to have a counselor or the [coordinator] engage in a tough, frank conversation/discussion with her to modify her expectations and behavior before she gets too far in life to reverse her attitude. I am deeply concerned. Concerned enough that I have plans to discuss my perceptions with her prior to her departure." Needless to say, my "expectations and behavior" during this internship were not disruptive and would likely have been lauded as "self-assuredness" had I been a young white male instead of a Black teenage girl.

I had not thought about my NASA supervisor, my experience, or that assessment until I started to reflect on my experiences as a graduate student. In both cases, the men involved were ill-prepared to mentor a Black female. In fact, I suspect that these men felt threatened by my presence and knowledge as a Black female and possibly sought to sabotage my future. Moreover, like my experience at NASA, as a graduate student, I realized that I had little control over situations that impeded my educational experience, even as I watched white male colleagues successfully navigate similar impediments. In each case, at some point I started to conclude that as a Black Girl and Black Womxn, I would never be welcomed in these educational spaces the same way that white males were.

When I was an undergraduate, faculty members would frequently use the words "paranoid," "angry," and "unreasonable" to describe how I advocated or voiced my opinion in the classroom. I knew immediately that this was coded language for someone being perceived as a loud Black Womxn. When each semester began, I silenced myself in thought and behavior to figure out how to navigate this space better than I had the previous semester, attempting to change how I interacted with people so that I could be perceived as likable by colleagues, the faculty, and administration. I had internalized the guilt and shame of being a complainer. This self-silencing led to further guilt and shame, and it meant that I had to set aside who I was and who I wanted to be after I achieved my degrees.

When I was a master's student, this guilt and shame began to lessen. Even though I received my master's degree from a primarily white, teaching-focused institution, I believed that institutional policies and practices were in place to assist students in developing into professionals suited for the "real world" connected to their majors. And, indeed, this was my experience for the most part. However, as I continued my graduate studies into a doctoral program at a primarily white, research-focused institution, I discovered that institutional practices and policies had been developed to mold future academics into replicates of the white, cisgender, straight founders of higher education institutions.

Now that I have completed my doctorate and am "molded into an academic," I recognize that the ivory tower was neither spatially nor bureaucratically ready for me because I did not, and do not, embody the historical ideal of a white, straight, cisgender man. And likely because I do not embody this ideal, I again encountered verbal abuse from a male educator who was supposed to have my best interests, as a student, in mind. And likely because I am a Black Womxn, when I tried to file a complaint about this educator, the primarily white institution I attended offered me only indifference and obstruction. As a Black Womxn, filing any complaint against a male authoritative figure meant that I was a threat to heteronormative leadership ideals and to those in positions of power who assumed such ideals.

But I filed the complaint, anyway. By remaining quiet, I might not have been a "problem" to others, but remaining quiet was creating problems for me that I needed to fix to save myself. I developed this attitude of self-preservation in the hopes that the guilt and shame would dissipate and joy would thrive.

THE ABUSE

When I asked an administrator about the presence of Black students at the primarily white, research-focused institution in the Midwest where I completed my doctorate, I was told that I was the first Black student in the program in at least five years, the only Black student at the time in my academic program, and one of the very few Black students in my school. Thus, I was fully aware that my physical presence as a Black Womxn at this particular higher education institution disrupted expectations of what a doctoral student should look like. Yet, rather than my supposedly "disruptive Blackness" on mundane expectations, the trauma of completing my degree was due far more to my realization that this institution allowed a Black, cisgender male with tenure to engage in hostile behavior toward a student with impunity, an impunity facilitated by the establishment's convoluted reporting policies and practices.

The incident occurred at a coffee shop, so it was in public. The previous summer, I had been an unpaid teaching assistant for this faculty member, and I wanted to reconnect with him. My main purpose was to apologize. Because of commitments that I needed to fulfill outside of higher education, I was unfortunately unable to finish the last few weeks of the summer term, and because the position was unpaid, the situation was more informal than a paid job. Not only did the faculty member reject my apology, but he also brought up other grievances that he had with me. The conversation between myself (TQ) and the faculty member (FM) went like this:

TQ: I wanted to apologize for what occurred [during the summer].

FM: Thank you, but your apology is not acceptable. You should have apologized then. You tried to take over my class. You ruined my relationship with [a student] and disrupted my course. I don't trust you.

TQ: I tried to speak with you in . . . (Both of us look through our phones.)

TQ: August . . . I mean September.

FM: That was too late. You never made an appointment to discuss the course. You never wanted to talk about my knowledge. You only wanted to discuss what was going on with you. I don't trust you. I don't trust anything you will say. If you had a problem with the course, you should not speak with another doctoral student. I don't trust what you say to other students. Everyone likes a good gossip. You bad-mouth the department to other people outside of the department and you talk to them. If you need to speak to someone then you need to speak with [other Black administrators]. But you should never speak with another doctoral student.

At this point I was crying because I was unsure of what he was talking about. For some reason, the faculty member mentioned problems he had with another Black male scholar in the field. I have never understood why he shared this information with me. Through the tears, I told him that I never spoke poorly of him. The fact that this individual attempted to restrict my discussion with any of my colleagues was astonishing.

The conversation suddenly turned to my qualifying exams. He was on my course prescription committee, and he told me that he had never had a student who had taken as long as I had on my "revamp" (as my adviser called it). This part of the exam process meant that my submission was satisfactory but that they (my adviser and this faculty member) wanted more development of the project. I responded that a key reason for the delay was that during the qualifying exams, I had had a partial hysterectomy, with the surgery date changing at the last minute due to unforeseeable pain. He told me that I should have taken a leave of absence, which was not possible to do on such short notice. I told him that emotionally, much had come up, but I had sent all previous documents to my adviser, who was ultimately in charge of my qualifying exams. He replied that he had not received anything from my adviser. I was dubious of his answer, because I had sent all the information to my adviser, and my adviser had then tried to communicate with this faculty member. I insisted that I had sent the exams, but he ignored me and said that my actions were "unacceptable."

My intent to connect with this faculty member had been to catch up and apologize; instead, he used the meeting to berate me for over an hour. After he was through, I immediately called my wife to pick me up. I began texting my adviser, who was on the phone with the faculty member. I told my wife and my adviser that I was confused and hurt by the entire conversation. I cried on the car ride home. I cried through the night and only found comfort when I composed myself enough to draft and send an email to my adviser and the faculty member outlining my next steps. In the days that followed, these events occurred:

- I turned in the exam's last question on time.
- The faculty member accused me of turning the exam in late. My adviser told him to look at the time stamp and that I had gotten the question in on time.
- Via my adviser, the faculty member accused me of plagiarism, wanted to remove himself from my exams, and stated that I had failed from his perspective.
- The faculty member met with the interim department chair to remove himself from my committee. He was told that he had to stay on the committee due to his written and verbal commitment to me of being on my committee.
- Days later, the faculty member wanted to remain on my committee.

The final word came from my adviser and not this faculty member. My adviser advocated on my behalf to have him removed from my qualifying exams with the permission of the associate dean, and I passed. But no matter my joy at my success, I could not help but remain deeply troubled by the actions of this educator. In my entire academic and professional career, I have never plagiarized, never cheated, nor ever been accused of these actions by anyone. I followed the proper chain of command by communicating with my adviser, and yet this faculty member still wanted to fail me. My frustration, anger, and sadness at the situation was made worse when I considered that he was a tenured faculty member and I was a student and that he had the power to derail my entire education. And to top it off, his actions were in a public space, which greatly increased my humiliation. I couldn't help but ask myself: Is this who the institution wants as a representative? Because I could not believe the answer would be yes, I sought redress through the proper channels, but I was only further frustrated by the institution's policies and practices.

POLICIES AND RESPONSE

I first spoke with the Title IX office. The Title IX officer, a white Womxn, stated that the faculty member's behavior was not enough to fall under the policy of discrimination, harassment, and/or sexual misconduct. I insisted that he had demonstrated hostile and intimidating behavior toward me during that meeting. But, again, according to her, this was not enough to file a complaint with the Title IX office. The staff member went on to say that he did not exhibit discriminatory actions against me because we are both Black. I found it interesting that the Title IX officer decided that our supposed racial similarities negated the possibility of other types of discrimination, and particularly gender bias. And, indeed, I later found out that this faculty member had a habit of not being supportive of "strong-willed" and independent-thinking Womxn who were not willing to massage his ego. Was this enough to indicate that he had little respect for Womxn who exemplified the trait of standing up for themselves? Unfortunately, no.

I then went to the Student Advocates Office. This office has "retired . . . faculty and staff members who volunteer their time and expertise to assist students in resolving academic, financial, and conduct problems."[7] I spoke with the director of the office (who remained by my side throughout my hearing against the faculty member) and told them that the faculty member *never* filed paperwork for plagiarism and that there was no evidence of his accusation.

I eventually contacted the appropriate dean for my school of study. By that time, I had spoken with a representative from the Title IX office twice, someone with the school's psychological services (aside from my therapist), and a representative from legal services; submitted a bias report; met with the department chair the following day to file a formal complaint; sent an email to the dean of the graduate school and the dean of the Office of the Vice President for Diversity, Equity, and Multicultural Affairs; and emailed the Office of Research Compliance to address how this faculty member's work mirrored my work and was working with the Student Advocates Office's director to prepare all the documentation for an official hearing. The hearing was comprised of faculty members within the school. Every mentor I spoke with about this situation was adamant that I should focus on completing my dissertation and graduating from my institution. From beginning to end, this experience lasted a total of one and a half years of my life as a graduate student. I was unable to sleep, broke out into nightly sweats, experienced daily anxiety attacks, and had difficulty eating.

Throughout that time, my mentors and others within my institution referred to the behavior of their Black, male, tenured colleague as a "rite of passage" or "how things are done." I contested these remarks by saying "this is not right" and reminding others that I, too, am a human. As a response to these glib, offensive remarks, I decided to publish about the incident during the fall of my final year.[8] But even the joy of publishing was tarnished. For one, I had to relive the incident as I got it down on paper. But I also had a feeling of dread that he might someday have a hand in deciding if my academic work is publishable. What if he is on the board of the journal where I submit my article? What if he tells others in the field that I am "a problem" and they are sitting on the editorial board? Even if he will never have this power, the very fact that I considered it demonstrates the continuing detrimental effect of the incident on my mind.

Even though I was angry, disappointed, and sad over his behavior and the institution's lack of response to it, I still graduated. I completed my dissertation during the COVID-19 pandemic. I walked across the stage a year later to be hooded by my dissertation chair. But my feelings of joy were tempered by feelings of emotional emptiness and vulnerability. I was graduating from an institution to which I gave so much time and energy but that did nothing to reprimand this faculty member or even acknowledge his transgressions.

POLICY CHANGES AND SOLUTIONS

In thinking about how my institution could have better responded to this situation, one key area is in the process of filing a complaint. A complaint can be complicated for the individual filing it. As Sara Ahmed explains, to file a complaint, one must follow the proper procedures, locate the correct offices, and gather a wealth of evidence, all of which can be exhausting. And once a complaint is filed, higher education institutions often mishandle it. My personal experiences with many of the offices at my institution, and particularly the Title IX office, suggest that, at the very least, complaints are often not taken seriously within higher education. Katherine Hanson, Vivian Guilfoy, and Sarita Pillai note that such mishandling is often influenced by discriminatory practices and that there is a long "history of [Womxn students who] were ignored, intimidated, or otherwise given the message that they were not welcome" to file a complaint.[9] Moreover, in many cases students must prove how the verbal harassment continued to create a hostile educational and work environment, which causes them to relive the experience multiple times.

To help all students file a complaint, regardless of race, gender, sexuality, or other identity positions, institutions need to properly explain and make easily accessible the proper materials. Such accessibility could be facilitated by making these materials available on the internet, allowing students a greater degree of privacy when filing. Such accessibility could also expedite the process, as it could remove the influence of faculty and administrators, who can sometimes be unsure of the proper protocols, or unwilling to follow them, which can then draw out the proceedings. Above all, to make changes to policies and practices around filing complaints, institutions need to understand that they cannot continue to do "business as usual" in the hopes that situations will "go away." The more resistant institutions are to changing or challenging their current processes, the more incoherent those processes will appear to their faculty, staff, and students.

Similarly, institutions should be more transparent about the number of cases filed and the corrective actions taken. This information should be made easily available to the entire campus, which again could be facilitated through the internet, and ideally via a centralized web page. If problems persist, faculty and staff should be required to attend informational sessions and familiarize themselves with the policies and procedures related to hostile academic and education environments.

I AM A PHENOMENAL BLACK WOMXN

Throughout my ordeal, I had the unnerving fear that the door to the ivory tower would never be open to me, and I still feel this way because I refuse to be obedient in the spaces confined by the ideologies of the white patriarchy. As I encountered, such oppressive ideologies are so pervasive that they can even influence a Black male who willingly disregarded the experience of a Black Womxn, despite such experiences being an area of his supposed expertise. My doctoral journey is a reminder that receiving an education can come with the price of psychological harm when the educational environment is characterized by hostility. The harm was compounded when I tried to file a complaint against the behavior and received only inconsistent messaging from the administration and lack of support from my department, the graduate school, and the institution. While I remain grateful for the opportunity and privilege of receiving an education from an esteemed institution, I cannot forget that in *many* spaces within higher education, Black Womxn continue to be perceived as instigators: loud, angry, and opinionated. The ivory tower needs to do better to protect historically marginalized groups, such as Black Womxn, and recognize the harm that outdated policies can have on students in these groups.

Many may conclude that I succeeded by completing my degree from a primarily white institution and that this process did not break me because I have a PhD. This process did not break me intellectually, but it left scars in places that require constant care. I do not forgive that Black male faculty member; the deans; the graduate school; my school; *some* of the faculty and staff; or the institution. I will never get back the time that I lived in fear in my home and in my mind because of the abuse I endured. Yet, I continue to find joy in the very fact that I am now a *Doctor* and that no one can ever take that away from me.

NOTES

1. In using the letter *x* in "Womxn," I (re)focus the conversation on Womxn without men.
2. To (re)focus this essay on the experience of a Black Womxn, the *w* in white is in lower case.
3. Crenshaw, "Demarginalizing the Intersection," 139–67.
4. Wallace, Moore, and Curtis, "Black Women as Scholars," 45.
5. D. Davis, "Mentorship and the Socialization of Underrepresented Minorities," 278–93.
6. Monroe et al., "Gender Equality in Academia," 215–33; Stanley, "Coloring the Academic Landscape," 701–36.
7. Indiana University–Bloomington, Division of Student Affairs, "We Listen."
8. Quash, "Academic Hazing Is Abuse."
9. Ahmed, *Complaint!*; Hanson, Guilfoy, and Pillai, *More Than Title IX*, 82.

Part III

The Enigma of Joy

CHAPTER 12

Sail Fast

ANNETTE KAPPERT

I define "joy" through an early primary school memory of being selected to represent my school at Festival, the then-main national salute to all things Jamaican, aiming to visualize our history and our culture, and marking the day when Jamaica became independent from the British. My contribution was to recite the Right Honourable Louise Bennett-Coverley poem "Colonisation in Reverse": "Wat a joyful news, Miss Mattie, / I feel like me heart gwine burs."[1]

Forty years later, the consequences of colonialization and slavery remain entrenched in my mind and in my daily experiences. I, too, challenge the concept of postcolonialism because not only does it suggest closure but also, as Stuart Hall queries, "When was the colonial ever post?"[2] As such, the theories that inform this chapter, the questions that it may generate, and the writing styles employed have all been decolonized,[3] or, as Alexander writes, "the non-linear narrative evokes storytelling in the manner of West African oral cultures, in which memories and objects are invested with meanings from which the story is woven."[4] Hence, guided by the Ancestors, in my analysis of the dichotomy of the self and the other, I seek to explore two main concepts of joy: joy begins with the self, and it is only by creating joy for others that we, too, may become joyful.

This chapter autoethnographically interrogates the author's personal experience in higher education via ship metaphors. It acknowledges the illusiveness of joy for Black women by highlighting how our own self-deprecating voices, as well as the daily actions of others, can rob us of our joy, and it explores how the construct of impostor syndrome wreaks havoc on the internal dialogues of Black female educators (BFEs) in higher education. Ultimately, I hope the chapter will appeal to educational leaders, teachers, and scholars for them to see the gifts in others that they do not see in themselves, to move forward to more diverse epistemologies and practices, to reflect on their role in sustaining feelings of joy for others, and to create environments and cultures in which we can thrive in higher education. Perhaps in doing this, we all will be able to experience that which makes us joyful. As such, I invite you, the reader, to reflect on personal moments of joy and to use them as leverage on your journey, and I specifically remind the few fellow Black educational leaders to be courageous, hopeful, and ready to challenge yourselves in unlearning what has been taken for granted for too long.

"IF DIS A FOOT NUH FINE IT, DIS ONE WILL"

After completing her maiden voyage in July 1948, the Annette 2 docked in University Harbor to unload her precious cargo.[5] The distinctive razzle-dazzle two-tone black-and-white paint on her hull made her one of a kind.[6] Furthermore, unlike the ships of the British Royal Navy, who carried figureheads proclaiming allegiance to the British monarchy and its heirs, the unusual black female figurehead, normally only ever used for pirate ships, of the Annette 2, represented her strength and independence. However, despite being an awesome feat of creativity, she also came with a stark reminder of the number of foreign vessels being allowed to enter British ports. As such, the berthing was a major news story, and all along the dock people came to catch a glimpse of the unusual vessel.

The Annette 2 was very proud of her cargo; the manifest read:

The Annette 2 Commercial Cargo Manifest
Net worth $32000 of which $62000 is graduate debt (not including interest and taxes)
1 x case Pedagogical Content Knowledge[7]
10 x bales Higher Educational Leadership Experience[8]
4 x boxes Cultural Capital[9]
2 x boxes Rare Black Cultural Capital[10]
4 x casks Funds of Knowledge[11]
2 x rolls Self-Doubt[12]
1 x bag Hope[13]
5 x containers Ambition[14]

However, one day she noticed something rather peculiar. She had been sitting in the harbor for several months with her cargo still intact, whereas other ships had come and gone and she herself had bidden farewell to the Cutty Sark and the Sovereign of the Seas. For such a grand vessel, the burden was becoming unbearable, and she began to get a familiar sinking feeling. You see, she had been in this position several times over the expanse of her career, and each time she hoped it would be better in a different port. As she reflected on her previous berth, she knew that there were things she couldn't voice, things that to some that would seem trivial or could be weaponized and used against her, and she was reminded of a story she had been told by a senior officer:

She stood in the lineup feeling proud; she had managed to tame her unruly curly hair into a sleek ponytail. She looked down at her shiny blue shoes and thought about how well they matched her suit. Next to her was the captain and several other senior officers, all similarly groomed. They worked for a private cruise ship company, for which image was essential. With the drawbridge lowered, a stream of crew members anxious to get in out of the cold had entered. The captain sprung forth to admonish one for not wearing their name badge. She followed suit and tackled one whose hemline failed to meet the required length; knowing she would be late for work but afraid of the repercussions as the captain was watching, she sent the crew member back into the cold to change her clothes. Later she told me about the Imps that had reminded her of her high school days when her uniform had been too short; as there was no more hem to let down, her mother had added pieces of cloth to the shoulders to lengthen the tunic, her hair had conveniently hidden the stitch marks. "Imps" was the apt name she had given to her impostor syndrome self, and yes, she said there was a direct correlation with the small mythical creatures often described as mischievous talented pranksters.

She recalled how she and the other senior officers had taken it in turn to flex their leadership prowess until all crew members were in their respective positions. Then she had gone back to doing more mundane activities, but as she shivered below deck, she thought about the other crew members in their small, cramped cabins and the lack of equipment to do their jobs properly. She hinted of her fear of voicing the ways power, privilege, and oppression functioned within her daily experiences, because to the outside world all must look perfect.[15]

I remember her telling me that for her, all was far from perfect, and later that day, having missed lunch and feeling crabby, she had been summoned above deck and admonished for pointing out an error in the ship's log. She said, "As I sat through the collation of my wrongs, my Imps kicked in—'Know your place, you tragic mulatto'—and the sharpness had stung, causing her eyes to well up." Misunderstanding her frustration, the captain had snapped at her and told her to grow up!

She recalled as she walked down the old colonial staircase, with her head hung low to hide her emotions from the passengers, her Imps mocking her again: "Not so clever now are you, Dr. Kappert?" Awash with self-pity, the Ancestral voices gathered around to comfort her, and she heard them say, "Weeping may endure for a night, but joy cometh in the morning."[16]

Joy, strangely enough, had always been an elusive concept for the Annette 2—it never seemed to hang around very long. No matter how much she tried, it was as if she would need to develop "backs of steel," as discussed by Prisca Anuforo, Elizabeth Locke, Myra Robinson, and Christine Thorpe, to be able to hold on to it.[17] She thought about her initial sense of joy when first arriving at University Harbor. Perhaps if she hung on a little longer, this time things would get better, and sure enough, one day the harbormaster stopped by, looked up at the Annette 2, and shook his head. He climbed on board and seemed to be searching for something: Was it the five containers of ambition, surely the rare black cultural capital, and what about the bales of higher educational leadership experience? Annette was once again full of joy and with renewed confidence and couldn't help humming her favorite tune: "The Big Ship Sails on the Alley Alley Oh."

The harbormaster picked up the case of pedagogical content knowledge, and the Annette 2 groaned, mistaking it for the now-rotting floorboards underfoot. The harbormaster paused and thought for a moment. He was a traditional man and didn't like all these foreign vessels in his harbor, and he knew nobody, well not in his circles anyway, who could possibly want any of this strange cargo, but it was the law, and by berthing the Annette 2 he had met his quota and could tick the box. Muttering to himself, he picked up the bag of hope and disembarked ship.

The Annette 2 then realized that despite all her attributes, if she wanted to stay in University Harbor, she would need to get rid of the five container loads of ambition. She was so tired, and the two rolls of self-doubt seemed to be fermenting in her hull. She had weathered many storms, had almost been shipwrecked, and had never been afraid of hard work, but just sitting here and being the brunt of other ships' jokes was too much. Speaking of jokes, she recalled being sent on a quest to find the ivory tower only to discover that "there are towers and there is ivory, both quite real; but their combination in the idea of an Ivory Tower was both imaginary and consequential."[18] She was tired of such microaggressions, the microinsults,[19] and "the psychophysiological symptoms resulting from living in such extreme environments."[20] In fact, she had requested not to visit British ports anymore given the insidious patterns of racism and discrimination, but it was her improbable friend, the USS destroyer Turner Joy, who had reminded her "we're not ok" in many of the other ports.[21]

The Annette 2 recalled the most recent debate she'd had with the German MV Monte Rosa about legacy and inheritance, the latter wise beyond her years having begun as a cruise ship, then a warship, and finally used as a floating prison until she was captured by the British and renamed the HMT Empire Windrush. They had discussed the impact of taking on your capturer's name, being forced to carry human cargo, and the importance of thinking through our feelings, to analyze and theorize racism through them, rather than being immobilized by the fear that we are not strong enough, which in its self would be a show of strength.[22] How she had looked forward Rosa's return to discuss her own legacy, how and what she would be remembered for, and whether she had managed to bring joy to herself and even to others. But this was not to be, as Rosa experienced engine trouble and had sunk off the coast of Gibraltar, leaving the Annette 2 to ponder such questions on her own.

Then one day she realized, having visited so many ports and seen and heard so much, that perhaps this was the legacy she could leave behind, not the narratives she had inherited but positive and uplifting stories of joy and gratitude.[23] The more she thought about it, the more she began to consider how narratives are passed down and the impact they have on the present. She thought about the seafarers who explored themes of identity, journeys, and racial discrimination.[24] She could recall numerous stories about ships being forced to substitute joy with misery and fatigue, and the warning words of Edwidge Danticat in *The Farming of Bones*: "Misery won't touch you gentle. It always leaves its thumbprints on you; sometimes it leaves them for others to see, sometimes for nobody but you to know of."[25] But she couldn't recall one single uplifting and positive story, and as if on cue, the Ancestors whispered, *"If you want to build a ship, don't drum up the people, to gather wood, divide the work, and give orders. Instead, teach them to yearn, for the vast and endless sea,"* from whence we came.[26] Maybe, just maybe, if she was able to share her personal moments of joy, it may encourage others to do the same, and she knew then that University Harbor was by no means her final port of call.

As the gulls screeched overhead, she recalled the advice of Toni Morrison in her book *Song of Solomon*: "Wanna fly, you got to give up the [bird] shit that weighs you down."[27] So the next morning the Annette 2 simply decided to sling her hook; she gave five short blasts, hoisted her sails, and hit the open waters. And in her wake, I am told, you could hear the gentle voices of the Ancestors whispering in the wind, "If dis a foot nuh fine it, dis one will."

CONCLUSION

In this chapter I have sought to explore two main concepts of joy: joy begins with the self, and it is by creating joy for others that we, too, become joyful. We are reminded that the concept of impostor syndrome excuses leaders from providing spaces for women to grow in higher education and placing the blame on themselves, yet the construct of impostor syndrome is often mistakenly used as a catchphrase for women who lack confidence. As a BFE, I do not lack confidence, but I do sometimes feel ill-equipped to self-actualize in an institution in which I am constantly reminded that I do not belong, or one in which I should consider myself fortunate to be in; where I am repeatedly asked, So what are your qualifications? I used to resent such microinsults and the microaggressions and institutional harassment and maligning of Black women as mentioned in this book by LeAnna Luney and Cassandra Gonzalez, but now I am very well equipped and call on my Ancestors, and they retort, "How much time do you have?"[28]

As such, the myths, metaphors, proverbs, and stories used throughout represent the inner or interactive dialogues and positions that I continuously use to navigate the meaning of "my ordinary world." According to Joseph Campbell, this is where storymakers and storytellers exist before the story begins; it is a familiar place and offers audiences crucial and personal details to help them to understand the context on which the story is built.[29] The use of academic literature has helped locate the meaning and value of personal and professional stories within the realm of educational research and aided interpretation, especially for those who are privileged enough not to have shared these experiences. For those who "know," I hope that by being transparent about my journey and my stories, I not only begin to heal myself but also help you find your joy: "For while the tale of how we suffer, and how we are delighted, and how we may triumph is never new, it always must be heard. There isn't any other tale to tell, it's the only light we've got in all this darkness."[30]

In closing, I hope that you, the reader, experience the same joy while reading as I did in writing. I conclude in reminding you that pain strengthens our experiences of joy, albeit never on a permanent basis, but like the Ancestors, waiting in the wind and surfacing at the very moment you need it.

"Jacmandora mi nuh choose none!"[31]

NOTES

1. Bennett, "Colonisation in Reverse" (1966), 16–17.
2. Hall and Du Gay, *Questions of Cultural Identity*, 243.
3. L. Smith, *Decolonizing Methodologies*.
4. K. Alexander, "Julie Dash," 226.
5. The title of this section is Jamaican patois meaning, "If you can't achieve something one way, try another way."
6. The Dazzle design was first used on vessels in World War 1. Vessels had assorted designs to avoid making classes of them recognizable to the enemy. The Dazzle Ferry, affectionately dubbed " Razzle Dazzle," was commissioned by Liverpool Biennial and is the only operating Dazzle ship in the United Kingdom.
7. Cochran, De Ruiter, and King, "Pedagogical Content Knowing," 263–72.
8. Chavez, "Women and Minorities Encouraged to Apply."
9. Bourdieu, "The Forms of Capital."
10. Carter, "'Black' Cultural Capital," 136–55.
11. Moll, "Reflections and Possibilities," 275–88.
12. Wehnert, *Passing*.
13. Elbaz, "Hope, Attentiveness, and Caring for Difference," 421–32.
14. Wrench and Hassan, *Ambition and Marginalisation*.
15. Boylorn and Orbe, "Critical Autoethnography," 234–38.
16. Psalm 30, King James version.

17. Anuforo et al., "Backs of Steel™," chap. 13 in this volume.

18. Shapin, "The Ivory Tower," 10.

19. Luney and Gonzalez, "Quotidian Life of Anti-Black Womanness," chap. 14 in this volume.

20. W. Smith, "Black Faculty Coping."

21. Allen Stewart, *We're Not OK.*

22. Tate and Gabriel, *Inside the Ivory Tower*, 59.

23. Kappert, "Professional and Personal Experiences as Leverage," 98.

24. Seafarers' Stories, National Archives, https://www.nationalarchives.gov.uk/education/resources/seafarers-stories/.

25. Danticat, *Farming of Bones*, 353.

26. Antoine de Saint-Exupery, "Citadelle" (1943), 687. et al, (1943).

27. Morrison, *Song of Solomon*, 179.

28. Luney and Gonzalez, "Quotidian Life of Anti-Black Womanness," chap. 14 in this volume.

29. Campbell, *Hero's Journey.*

30. James Baldwin, James Baldwin: Early Novels and Stories, 862.

31. In Jamaican folklore, Jackmandora is the keeper of stories, and the phrase is uttered at the end of every oration. It literally translates to mean: I am but the messenger, I am not responsible for its content.

CHAPTER 13

Backs of Steel™

The Experience of Black Women Leaders in
Contemporary Academia

PRISCA ANUFORO, ELIZABETH LOCKE,
MYRA ROBINSON, AND CHRISTINE THORPE

NO TURNING BACK

Racism and sexism are interwoven into the fabric of
American society. To fully understand their impact
on Black women requires a thoughtful appreciation of the two terms. *Racism* is best defined as discrimination based on differences in color, whereas
sexism is defined as discrimination based on gender. The ideology of racism is the belief that members of each race possess characteristics or abilities specific to their race, ones that classify them as inferior or superior.
Sexism is prejudice, stereotyping, or discrimination based on sex, which
is typically shown toward women.[1] Black women encounter the struggles
associated with both racism and sexism. Therefore, we Black women, and
especially those in leadership positions, find ourselves at the intersection
of racism and sexism facing unreasonable expectations, challenges, and
assumptions.

Professional Black women's experiences with work-related stress are
rooted in the social, political, and economic context of the work environment that is characterized by race and gender-based discrimination.[2]
Many Black women in leadership wrestle with questions about how we fit
into our workplaces or how to address the unequal perceptions held about
us as compared with women and men from other racial groups, or both.
We experience the stress of being "the only" Black woman and in some
cases "the only" Black person. The psychological wear and tear of stress
takes its toll on the mind, body, and spirit and requires that we protect
ourselves with backs of steel™.

Stress is identified as situations in which demands are perceived as exceeding one's capacity to comfortably respond.[3] For Black woman, strength of body, mind, and spirit became their means of survival.[4] Survival and success for Black women in leadership roles requires developing an inner strength that is derived from such sources as their families, faith, and connections to "sister girls,"[5] sources that tend to provide encouragement, support, understanding, and friendship. Our family grounds us and gives us a sense of purpose and direction. Our faith provides us with a safe place where we can be vulnerable. "Sister girls" are a mixture of female relatives, other Black women in the workplace, and Black women who serve as mentors and are "there" for us.

Much has been written in the literature about leadership and being Black and female as double jeopardy.[6] Women in senior leadership saw a modest increase from 17 percent to 21 percent from 2015 to 2019.[7] While this statistic highlights the corporate sector, it does infer that Black women are experiencing professional disenfranchisement inclusive of academia. Black woman still fall behind on ascending to leadership roles and being promoted, also encountering microaggressions more frequently than do their white counterparts,[8] prompting the question, *When will the joy come?*

This chapter discusses the experiences of four Black women in various leadership roles in an urban university setting and how we leverage those experiences to influence policies on diversity, equity, and inclusion. For us, the joy is already here in the various leadership positions we occupy and the impact we make.

GOING UP YONDER?

The ascension of Black women to executive leadership positions in the American higher education system occurs within the context of barriers to inclusion, equity, and diversity. Discrimination is pervasive in academia.[9] Historically designed to weaken the aspirations of women of color to domestic and global leadership positions traditionally held by majority males, Black women have transformed the narrative to one of resilience, consistency, and sustainability in the presence of changing societal conditions.[10] This transformational experience has led to *backs of steel*, a term we have developed to represent the phenomena that support Black woman executives as we deconstruct antiquated paradigms and create new standards of excellence in today's academia.[11] The conditions that created the concept "backs of steel" have given rise to the responsibility to respect the journey and support the leadership qualities and ideals embraced by Black woman of past, current, and future generations.

Workplace discrimination owing to societal identification has helped strengthen the backs of steel among Black women to upper-level management positions.[12] True leadership requires backs of steel to transform existing rigid structures of decision-making to higher levels of inclusiveness that benefit the changing academic model. In the presence of barriers to success, Black women continuously collaborate to become collective organizational change agents in spite of workplace discrimination. From business, education, and nonprofit organizations to the healing arts and humanities, Black woman leaders are beneficial for community advancement and corporate bottom lines.[13] However, backs of steel have created a ripple effect in the professional and personal lives of Black women leaders. Developed through years of societal, cultural, and familial indoctrinations, the expectation to manage everything from social unrest to the daily management of home and office requires Black women to reconstruct boundaries to handle these expectations while actively engaging in self-care.[14] There exists the belief that Black women must be strong both physically and mentally in all situations involving family, work, and any other crisis that may surface. This myth, which permeates within the Black culture, negates the impact on the health of these women who are expected to be "all things to all people at all times." The result of this "superwoman" syndrome is high rates of heart disease, stroke, obesity, and other health concerns because Black women tend to put themselves last. The influencing factors that contribute to backs of steel are cultural identity, cultural values, environment, and perseverance (figure 1).

WHAT IS BACKS OF STEEL?

We postulate that backs of steel is the totality of our lived experiences culminating in resilience. Developing backs of steel is a process that begins in the early formative years of our life and is influenced by culture. In

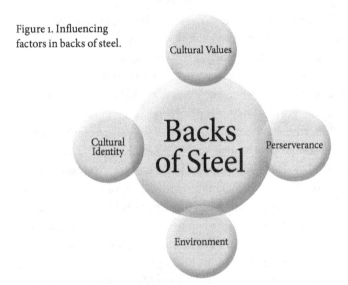

Figure 1. Influencing factors in backs of steel.

exploring our journeys as individuals and Black women leaders in academia, the following themes emerged: cultural identity, cultural values, perseverance, and environment, culminating in resilience or backs of steel. The interconnectedness of these four areas deserves attention. Upon exploring the sources of support for Black women in academia, we share common resources that provide us with safe spaces to engage in mentorship to develop strategies throughout our academic careers. The resources for support that are most prevalent include family, faith, professional counseling, and identifying with like-minded colleagues who share similar career experiences. Each of these resources serves to meet multiple dimensions of our wellness. Drawing on these resources has helped Black women experience release and renewal to tackle each day while challenging us to identify gratitude and purpose in our lives and workspaces.

NAVIGATING CULTURE: ONE BACK AT A TIME

Several definitions of "culture" exist and have evolved over the years. "Culture" is defined as "transmitted and created content and patterns of values, ideas, and other symbolic-meaningful systems as factors in the shaping of human behavior."[15] People are products of their environment. The common thread we have as leaders is the value we place on education and success. Our success is not only ours but that of our families and communities as well, which becomes a critical responsibility to the past, present, and future generations that we carry. In boardrooms, these values affect how problems are defined and resolved and what behavior is expected and accepted. In addition to being the matriarchs of the home, Black women have the added expectation to be bulwarks of society. A Black woman who is influenced by the superwoman syndrome believes she must balance the high demands of work, family, and social obligations at the same time and with the same intensity. In addition to these responsibilities, she must also be active in uplifting her entire race. Her responsibility to the Black community is to *lift as she climbs*. Failing to do so may result in experiencing strong feelings of guilt, group betrayal or selling out, and general ambiguity.[16] Commitment to self-preservation, personal health, and well-being lags far behind her commitment to her career, family, and community.

When considering safe spaces at work, we can acknowledge them as those spaces where we can speak openly and freely about our reflections and interactions with trusted individuals who can identify with our concerns and provide guidance. Our experiences, often shared in the narrative form of storytelling in such places, give us a platform to vent through our lens and debrief.[17] These safe spaces welcome the luxury of vulnerability, where Black woman can grapple with their thoughts about questionable behaviors and interactions that challenge the intersections of race and gender.[18] The utilization of safe spaces enables Black women to process feelings, find confirmation and validation for perceptions of uncomfortable interactions with colleagues, and seek solutions to either revisit the problem or prepare for it should it occur again.

When our chosen trusted individuals are mentors, the expectation of this relational dynamic is one where sound advice is provided from someone who has been in our shoes and can coach us through the uncertainties of our career path.[19] Mentors, unlike family members who are more likely to experience the emotional brunt of our professional bruises, have been incredibly influential in helping us understand how academia works and identifying ways we can position ourselves for success. The trajectory of each of our journeys is shaped by a handful of key mentors. Our mentors have reminded us to be bold when speaking up, to build community with other Black women in academia who recognize the strength in our union, to generously share lessons learned, to reduce isolation and loneliness, and to actively seek moments to edify and advocate for one another.

CULTURAL IDENTITY: WHO ARE WE REALLY?

Cultural identity is attributed to public norms that shape people's way of life, including beliefs on how to appear and interact with others.[20] Although cultural identity helps us aspire to, climb, and reach the pinnacle of power, there are risks associated with the cultural identity of Black women leaders. Our posture of strength, persistence, and natural high tone of voice is often interpreted as angry, loud, boisterous, and bossy. These stereotypes are negatively associated with leadership and block Black women from leadership roles. As a result, Black women who are perceived as angry tend to receive lower performance evaluations and lower recommended raises.[21] Cultural identity creates a double jeopardy paradigm for Black women, whose successes are often slighted or disregarded, with their success attributed to external hegemony.[22] The constant need exists to prove our legitimacy and ourselves. Again, having a back of steel in situations where one's contributions are slighted or discounted enables us to ignore those voices; instead, we reaffirm ourselves, as valued members of the team.

CULTURAL VALUES: WHAT ARE WE MADE OF?

Cultural values are desired objectives that drive the actions of individuals and how they see others.[23] The concepts of respect, communication, spirituality, upbringing, family, and community expectations are driven by cultural values. The Black woman value for spiritual/religious life is a major tenet that transcends all aspects of life.[24] To address stressful encounters, especially those stressors arising from the work environment, such as racism and sexism, Black women rely on their spirituality. Praying or calling on a higher power is often used as a coping mechanism and is considered an emotion-focused coping response. It is common to pray before, during, or after a "tough" meeting. Black women often ask for prayers from the "village" (parents, sisters, brothers, aunts, uncles, pastors or spiritual leaders, and the sisterhood) to overcome a difficult situation. The belief in a higher power is a source of strength.

Our faith in God centers us when we have professional experiences that leave us questioning why. Our faith, exercised in the form of prayer or faith-based counseling, has been the balm that heals and reminds us that a higher power has placed us to be a light in the halls of academia. We turn to prayer for guidance, reassurance, and peace in our souls as it reminds us that God is in control. Our prayers serve to mitigate the emotional response to the stress-causing situation. Therefore, when a Black woman says she is praying about a stressful situation or the situation is "in God's hands," she is not abdicating her responsibility to deal with the stressful situation and is actively engaged in behaviors that will bring about positive results. Placing trust in God and unwavering faith have traditionally formed the foundation of Black women's ability to cope with the vicissitudes of life that they commonly encounter. Spirituality as a mechanism allows us to deal with racism, microaggression, and sexism and focus on the Supreme Being who has the ultimate power to determine our fate. This Afrocentric perspective is holistic in that it recognizes the interconnectedness of all things and the oneness of mind, body, and spirit.

The following four excerpts were written by chapter authors, who work in leadership roles.

NO SINGULAR JOURNEY

My journey to academia has been nonlinear and strategically planned from my early years as a volunteer in a physical therapy department to my current role as an executive director of a graduate physical therapist education program. To arrive at this point in my journey, I capitalized on every opportunity to build the intellectual, physical, and spiritual fortitude required for success within a complex and disparate health care system. Growing up in the Deep South with strong family and community ties and in the absence of coordinated health services, I lived what I would later strive to change in my community. The whole of my life has been inextricably linked to the physical well-being of others, so the linear pathway did not lead me to higher education. Being taught that success and joy were synonymous with education and that I have the right to both was sufficient for me to begin my journey to higher education and the new experiences, struggles, and joys it would bring.

On a daily basis, I work to maximize my culture and intersectionality as an African American, a woman, a mother, a wife, a physical therapist, an educator, and a national leader in physical therapist education to benefit the unique individuals with whom I work and from whom I learn. I am in awe of the resilience of my colleagues and students and the similarities of our struggles, experiences, and joys. Our collective lives inspire the next generation of physical therapists to embrace the struggle that directly confronts us all.

My story is not singularly mine. It exists, as I do, within the fabric of a greater purpose filled with the joy of transforming higher education through the lens of health professions. Our purpose as higher education leaders is to transform others' challenges and struggles into an overwhelming sense of purpose and achievement. I call this joy, and it is real, alive, and thriving.

ENVIRONMENT: IT TAKES A VILLAGE

Individuals are parts of the larger fabric in the community. The African proverb "It takes a village to raise a child" means that family and community invest in the individual. These investments may be in the form of good counsel/advice; monetary support; physical assistance, such as driving one back to school or even paying a visit at the school; and buying books or computers, etc. The collectivist mindset and high-context communication of African American culture implies that there are expectations which may not be explicitly stated. Familial expectations within the African American community demand that each generation exceed the accomplishments of the former generation. Over time, these expectations become internalized, prompting one to want to do better for themselves and make the family proud. As one ascends to a leadership role, the expectation and desire to pay it forward becomes a driving force that allows one to persevere through the tough times.

In addition, upbringing plays a crucial role in who we become, how we respond to life events and success, the desire to aspire to something great, and understanding the concept of self. Black women are raised to be leaders, confidants, and problem solvers in the family. Most of these values are learned and passed down through oral history and actions by family members. When confronted with certain issues at work emanating from the leadership role, one reverts to those values of strength, respect, and problem solving for survival and victory. Giving up or failure is not an option.

PERSEVERANCE: WHERE OUR STRENGTH LIES

In difficult situations, we persevere until the end. Perseverance leads to developing the back of steel. It is the ability to withstand challenges and obstacles with our crown still on our head. It implies that we do not give up easily. However, it does not imply the lack of bruises and batter; instead, it is having success despite the bruises. It is asking the question, If not I, then who? It is falling and getting back up.

Many Black women leaders have no option except to develop that back of steel both during their climb to the top and in efforts to maintain that leadership position. Race-related factors play a major role in reporting life satisfaction within the African American population, as well as affecting self-esteem and sense of mastery.[25] Black women in academia strategically seek and create the necessary support systems that help validate why we need to show up, speak up, and remember the value we bring to academic spaces. Our need to expand and allow ourselves to be present among our colleagues is one that enables us to display our intellect, strength, and comfort while being Black and female. Through the reassurance and mentorship received from our avenues of support on and off campus, Black women learn how to navigate challenging interactions and creatively foster teachable moments to improve the work environment. Thus, these cultivated support systems take many forms given the multidimensionality of our lives.

THE GREATER PURPOSE

When I was interviewing for the role of dean, it was a mutual vetting process because I wanted to understand the culture of the people I would be working with closely on a daily basis. Upon taking the role, I would be the only woman at that level of academic administrative leadership. Thus, it was essential for me to assess the space I would be moving through and the interactions I would encounter. Prior to accepting the position, I took it on myself to walk through the building on two separate occasions where my office would be located to feel the energy and watch people while they engaged in the business of higher education. What I observed was a spirit of community. The faculty and staff, all of whom are in the health and human services field, led by example when teaching and training the students. One finds a special passion for service to humanity in this segment of academia, and for this group in particular it was clear that they functioned as an interprofessional team that was committed to addressing disparities in the community. It was obvious that they loved what they did and did so with their heart on their sleeves. To see this level of dedication to the future of health professions, I was moved to join them in furthering their mission to train compassionate and highly skilled professionals.

Since joining and leading this dynamic college as now the only black woman dean, I am continually renewed in my desire to deepen the vision, mission, and core values that as a community we have fostered together. I find great joy in the work I do because I see where we all understand the greater purpose of why we are here and what we are called to do. Over the years, I became more aware of a spiritual presence among the faculty and staff that has influenced our perspectives on how to support one another and work through professional and personal challenges. I have come to understand that the spiritual lens allows us to see humanity in one another, and that is where the joy comes from.

CONCLUSION

Policies in most higher education institutions are made at the top or through governing bodies. To influence any policy and improve working conditions and advancement of Black women in leadership, we need a seat at the table where these policy decisions are made. Vying for and being nominated to serve on committees where these policies are made is essential. The Sistah Network speaks to this need for affinity groups to emerge in higher education, as they have been present in the corporate sector, to provide support for mentorship and career growth.[26] Establishing a Sistah Network within the organization allows for similar voices and support to shield us from the challenges and to share in the joys. Efforts should be made to organize informal groups of Black women with the same aspirations within and outside the organization. Such informal groups serve as a sounding board and support system for their members. Building alliances and support outside the homogeneous group serves to educate others and acclimatize them to the cultural nuances of the African American heritage. Volunteering to lead or participating in committees and groups advocating for change is necessary. Many institutions are setting up diversity institutes or committees to show that they are part of the change. However, without the voice or presence of the Black woman in leadership in such organizations, it becomes a token of what it was meant to be.

Finally, the joy is already here in the work that we do—with training our students as future professionals, collaborations with colleagues, paying it forward through advocacy in the conference rooms and boardrooms. In getting to the ivory tower, these three things are true:

1. We have not done it alone.
2. We have done it against resistance.
3. We have developed resilience and sustainability leading to support our "backs of steel."

It took many years to dismantle the barriers that prevented the ascension of Black women to executive leadership positions in the American higher education system. As more Black women leaders with backs of steel continue to emerge in academia, the closer we approach our goal of inclusion, equity, and diversity in higher education. The joy comes from surviving the struggle and reaching the ivory tower. Our professional frame of reference shapes our purpose and joy in the work we do. Joy is being impactful or making a difference in spite of the challenges we face daily. Being the only one in a high-level meeting as often is the case forces others to acknowledge our presence. The joy is in sitting at the decision-making table.

NOTES

1. Barker, *Social Work Dictionary*.
2. Bacchus, "Coping with Work-Related Stress."
3. C. Smith and Carlson, "Stress, Coping, and Resilience."
4. Biakolo, "Black Women Are More."
5. Berkowitz and Padavic, "Getting a Man or Getting Ahead"; E. Bell, "Bicultural Life Experience."
6. Rosette and Livingston, "Failure Is Not an Option."
7. LeanIn.Org and McKinsey & Company, "Women in the Workplace 2019."
8. LeanIn.Org and McKinsey & Company, "State of Black Women in Corporate America."

9. Luney and Gonzalez, "Quotidian Life of Anti-Black Womanness," chap. 14 in this volume.

10. Wingfield, "Women Are Advancing in the Workplace."

11. Shung-King et al., "Leadership Experiences and Practices."

12. Kramer, "Recognizing Workplace Challenges."

13. Pace, *Women of Color Get to Senior Management*; Schnall, "When Black Women Lead."

14. DeSouza et al., "Coping with Racism."

15. Kroeber and Parsons, "Concepts of Culture," 3.

16. Gilkes, "Going Up for the Oppressed."

17. Grey and Williams-Farrier, "#Sippingtea."

18. Porter et al., "To Be Black Women."

19. M. Lee, Mazmanian, and Perlow, "Fostering Positive Relational Dynamics."

20. Yep, "My Three Cultures."

21. Motro et al., "Race and Reactions to Negative Feedback."

22. Barsh and Yee, "Special Report."

23. Donohue, "Religiosity and Multicultural Experiences."

24. Elk et al., "Developing and Testing the Feasibility."

25. Broman, "Race-Related Factors and Life Satisfaction."

26. E. Allen and Joseph, "The Sistah Network."

CHAPTER 14

The Quotidian Life of Anti-Black Womanness in Ethnic Studies Policy and Procedure

LEANNA T. LUNEY AND CASSANDRA GONZALEZ

In this chapter we narrate our stories as two Black women in higher education (HE). We—two former doctoral students—share our unique and collective narrative teaching and learning within an Ethnic Studies (ES) Department through storytelling and Black feminist and structural intersectional analysis. We provide broader implications about deficiencies in university-level policy that allow misogynoir to persist as a form of violence and its emergence in a department promoting decolonial, liberatory, and bottom-up praxes. Grounded in our experiences of commonplace misogynoir in an Ethnic Studies Department enabled by institutional policy, protocol, and commonplace practice, we conclude that Black women and femme joy necessitates radical reckoning and redress. We propose planting decolonial seeds, reparations, and intergenerational and nonacademic redress as pathways to reckon with misogynoiristic harm against Black women and femmes in the ivory tower.

OUR COLLECTIVE NARRATIVE

We situate our collective narrative within a Department of Ethnic Studies at a Research I university. University policy regarding harm done on campus merely addresses discrimination, harassment and workplace hostility, and related violations, which are most relevant to this chapter. Such policy defines "discrimination" as occurring when an individual suffers an adverse consequence on the basis of being in a protected class. "Harassment" is unwelcome verbal or physical conduct related to one's protected class that unreasonably interferes with an individual's work or academic performance or creates an intimidating or hostile work or educational environment. A hostile work or educational environment is harassment determined from subjective and objective perspectives that must be sufficiently severe, persistent, or pervasive that it unreasonably interferes with, limits, or deprives an individual from participating in or benefiting from the campus's education or employment programs and activities. The Office of Institutional Equity (OIE) is a university-level entity that enforces the university's antidiscrimination and harassment policy.

According to the bylaws on class-protected discrimination or harassment of our former Ethnic Studies Department, all cases are managed under the university's antidiscrimination and harassment policy, and all potential cases of discrimination and harassment must be reported to the OIE. Our collective narrative describes misogynoir in which the university's current antidiscrimination and harassment protocol could be directly enacted, as well as indistinct experiences of misogynoir that current policy disregards. We refer to ourselves as "Narrator One" and "Narrator Two" throughout the following to indicate which author is telling their part of the story.

THE QUOTIDIAN LIFE OF MISOGYNOIR IN ETHNIC STUDIES

Narrator One

I, Cassandra Mary Frances Gonzalez, am of African and Latinx heritage and am an Afro-Latina woman. However, I have no emotional or cultural connection to *Latinidad*. Instead, I grew into womanhood through the culture passed down to me from my Black mother—from one Black woman to the next generation of Black womanhood. Further, phenotypically, I present as a Black woman with what are traditionally considered "Black" facial features, and it is rare that people perceive me as a biracial or non-Black woman. Culturally and visually, I am a *Black woman* and thus self-identify as a Black woman, not a Latina or Afro-Latina woman. Despite repeated assertions of my gender and racial identity, my Blackness was frequently erased, and I was often categorized as a Latinx student, not as a Black doctoral candidate, throughout my time in the Ethnic Studies Department.

As a result, I endured several microaggressions and instances of lateral violence from the Black, Indigenous, and People of Color (BIPOC) faculty, especially cisgender men. My Blackness was frequently scrutinized and policed by faculty, and my Latinx heritage was often highlighted to diminish my experiences and knowledge production as a Black woman. For instance, several of the Latinx professors knew that I am not English-Spanish bilingual; nonetheless, two professors frequently spoke to me in Spanish with complete awareness I could not understand what was being said. One professor stated, immediately after meeting me and learning that I do not identify as a Latina woman, that they would speak to me only in Spanish to teach me the language. Taken at face value, this exchange might seem like a friendly language lesson. Yet, I felt that the professor's persistence to teach me Spanish served to diminish my Blackness to make me legible as a Latina or Chicana woman, despite my discomfort with this treatment and vocal declarations of my racial identity.

Forcing cultural attributes was a manifestation of anti-Black harassment, but other interactions also demonstrated misogynoir through gendered racial descriptions. A cisgender male faculty member frequently described me as "mixed" despite my adamant and explicit distaste for the racial descriptor—that is, "mixed" can be colloquial within the African American community for attempting to distance oneself from their African heritage or believing that multiracial individuals are superior to non-multiracial Black individuals. These interactions and labels were applied to me when I spoke on Black feminist issues or voiced a contrary opinion to the faculty member when discussing Black women and girls. Being called "mixed," particularly in front of other students, was demeaning and meant to attack my Black feminist epistemology by indirectly asserting that the knowledge I produced was not authentic due to my Latinx background.[1] Other instances of misogynoir that I experienced included comments on my hair, ranging from suggesting that my flat-ironed hair was an attempt to "code-switch" away from Blackness to reaffirming my Blackness when I wore braids in my hair. In other words, my hairstyles were used to demarcate how I performed my Blackness, and I was treated as though they were subject to others' approval.[2]

Alongside the disrespect of autonomy and self-naming, I was excluded from emails and word-of-mouth communications regarding Africana studies professional opportunities. For example, in several instances, student groups requested a Black doctoral student or professor who specialized in the criminal legal system and criminal justice. Other Black doctoral students were recommended, despite their having different areas of focus than did I. Such exclusion resulted in student groups' unfulfilled requests for insights or collaboration with a criminal legal system and criminal justice scholar, and I missed opportunities for engagement with undergraduate students.

I also felt that my research on sexual trauma and Black women and girls was trivialized owing to my academic training in sociology and lack of engagement with humanities-based disciplines. This sentiment was especially strong when a male BIPOC graduate student asked if I was concerned that my research would continue a scholastic pattern of pathologizing Black men as violent sexual predators. He expressed this in the presence of a handful of faculty members, some of whom then listened to our conversation. I answered that my research is motivated from the desire to give back to my Black women kin and create interventions that reduce harm to Black women and girls, intra-racial implications and politics notwithstanding.

In fact, I was vocal about the intentions of my research and goal of benefiting Black women and girls. My admission was occasionally met with inquiry on how my research could reify the belief that Black men and boys are natural predators to be policed, a growing attitude in the wake of social uprisings for racial justice amid police killings of Black men. This was also an assertion of misogynoirist beliefs, that research and activism centering Black women and girls must be compared against the possible— and, admittedly, real—repercussions of state violence against Black men precisely because it is often Black men who harm and traumatize Black women and girls. That crime is largely intra-racial was not particularly considered; rather, I was made to feel that my research was another form of encouragement and complicity in racist, state-perpetrated violence, which was reinforced when the department made "social justice" statements condemning acts of violence against historically marginalized groups, as male victims were given the most space. Further still, the department downplayed, if not outright erased, the gendered nature of racist acts of violence against Black women and girls.

UNIVERSITY ANTIDISCRIMINATION AND
HARASSMENT POLICY

Narrator One

Another interaction with a tenured faculty member resulted in my referral to the OIE. After confiding in a mentor outside my department about unclear funding allocation and requirements for comprehensive exams, they believed I was being deliberately deceived to hinder my progress and thriving in the program, so they made a report of possible discrimination on my behalf.

I met with an OIE representative and harassment advocate but was informed that the actions and verbiage used toward me did not fit the university's definition of prejudice, discrimination, or harassment. Although the Ethnic Studies Department was informed that a report was made on my behalf, no one in the department followed up or reached out to me. I was left alone without departmental or institutional protection or guidance, relying instead on the support of Black women in my life, graduate student colleagues, faculty outside my department, and my mentor to persevere despite the concerted attempts to obstruct my doctoral journey and continuance to eventual professorship.

Misogynoir was present in departmental policy, specifically after my adviser and I raised concerns about the graduate handbook and other guiding documents. In another instance, my adviser removed a faculty member from my dissertation committee as she believed it was in my best interest. During this time, I had experienced a parental death and was under the extraordinary stress of completing a dissertation and settling my personal affairs. As such, I did not object to the removal, nor did I consider it to be an offensive or unprofessional decision on behalf of my adviser. Shortly after the removal was final, the faculty drafted an updated handbook. The updated version held what I considered hostile language dictating the process of faculty removal from a committee. Absent from this new handbook edition were similar guidelines dictating appropriate behavior and boundaries for faculty. The reason for this addition was a blatant targeting of my adviser through implying there was an established protocol for removing a faculty member from a committee despite this being excluded from previous editions of the handbook. To my knowledge, the department never investigated *why* my adviser removed the committee member.

Narrator Two

Ironically—and perhaps a demonstration of the protection of a white woman's ego in juxtaposition to preserving the dignity of Black women graduate students and other graduate students at large—the uppermost administration of our department unhurriedly implemented policy with guidelines around professional and personal boundaries between faculty and graduate students. The updated policy mainly made graduate students responsible for upholding professional and personal boundaries when interacting with faculty, but little responsibility was placed on faculty members themselves. I, LeAnna T. Luney, was particularly impacted by a faculty member overstepping professional and personal boundaries in the workplace, which was rooted in racially gendered and classist issues and resulted in a promise for implementing new policy. Unfortunately, the agreed-on policy change was not applied after a faculty member exploited her white privilege and power to enact anti-Black and racially gendered harm against me.

I am a dark-skinned Black woman and femme who identifies as a first-generation college student from rural Kentucky. I am the daughter of working-class and imprisoned parents who raised me in a historically and predominantly white region. I come from a large, close-knit family and grew up in and out of extreme poverty. Considering the liberatory potential of naming and openly discussing one's struggles with poverty at the intersection of Black girl- and womanhood,[3] as well as the mission of ES disciplines to center the experiences of the subaltern critically and intentionally, I often and openly discussed how prevalent impoverishment was for me in the past and its remaining prevalence for my family.

In 2019, I received a message from family disclosing that my first cousin had been jailed for involvement with the mass distribution of firearms. My family explained that my cousin was homeless and sleeping at his friend's home when he was arrested for being in a house where guns were sold throughout the local area. Although my family sprang into action gathering their pocket change and cashing in monetary favors, I relied on the social capital I had built over the years in academia. I and my family acted with the understanding that my cousin was innocent and wrongfully accused of the crimes of a white family from my hometown.

I contacted an affluent white female faculty member because she had potential contacts who were well informed on projects and initiatives regarding prison abolition. My intent was that the faculty member could provide me with information on community bail funds, counsel, reporters, or other resources to prepare my family for fighting a criminal case on behalf of a Black man in a small rural county in Kentucky. Instead, the faculty member offered a loan to finance my cousin's bail amount in full. I felt pressured to accept her seemingly generous offer on behalf of my family and as a first-generation Black woman socialized to colloquially "keep family first," and with promise that my family would reimburse the faculty member in the future. In the moment, I felt as though the faculty member truly wanted to help my family. Yet, as time progressed and I learned more about the faculty member loaning money to other students and her strong-arm tactics holding me responsible for repaying the loan, I felt that the faculty member had preyed on my willingness to help my family, despite the risk of crossing professional boundaries and power dynamics between the two of us.

Over the next year and a half, the faculty member and I communicated rarely, but we eventually agreed to a reasonable payment plan for my cousin to reimburse the faculty member. In February 2021, I contacted the faculty member to provide her with my cousin's contact information with intentions to remove myself from the emotionally and cognitively draining situation, as I was completing my dissertation, on the job market, and preparing to move during the COVID-19 pandemic and shortly after the racial uprisings of 2020. I received a text message from the faculty member insinuating that she held me personally responsible for financially repaying the full amount of my cousin's bail, plus an interest fee that was never mentioned beforehand. For the first time, I confided in a colleague (that is, Narrator One) and the academic adviser we shared about the loan that my family had been offered, my acceptance of the loan, the anxieties I held about accepting money from a white liberal, and my intentions of filing a report with the OIE.

My own research about Black women and femme undergraduates' experiences and insights at the university, and the coping strategies and techniques they employed to survive anti-Black gendered racism at the institution, informed my awareness about the OIE's stringent and finite conceptualizations of harm. In addition, I had heard of and documented instances in which the OIE reframed Black women and femme victims and survivors as perpetrators against their aggressors. During a two-hour-long meeting, a white female OIE representative asked me to restate my story and describe any emotions I held about the matter.

Although the representative seemed to understand the intersectional and nuanced issues of power and oppression in my case—confirmed by her inkling of the faculty member's white savior complex,[4] the underlying issue of generational poverty at the intersection of Blackness, and expectations about Black women undertaking the plight of the Black men around them regardless of consequence[5]—she informed me that the formal adjudication process, or investigation into my case, was unwarranted for various reasons. The first reason she provided was that the current OIE and university policy on protected-class discrimination harassment and workplace hostility requires that harm based on race, gender, and class be more explicit than presented in my case. Other reasons included a lack of sufficient evidence, the faculty member's status, my ability to complete my academic studies and continue virtual teaching and learning in the workplace, and my upcoming graduation from the university.

Our meeting concluded without genuine redress for the racially gendered and classist power play I had been subjected to. My options were to have the representative speak with the faculty member to explain to her why her actions were harmful within a broader framework on power and oppression, speak with the chair of the Ethnic Studies Department, or speak with both the faculty member and the chair individually. I opted to have the representative speak with the chair of my department and to request that he and the uppermost administration in the department design and carry out policy that included language on monetary boundaries between faculty and graduate students from a power and oppression perspective, with hopes of preventing faculty loans of money to graduate students in the future. With the memory of how misogynoir had impacted me through the Strong Black Woman and Welfare Queen archetypes, and witnessing how OIE protocol misjudged Black women and femmes in their quests for protection and reprimand for their aggressors on campus, I preferred that the OIE representative exclusively speak with the chair of the department.[6] Logically, I knew that the faculty member would not benefit from the university's rudimentary script on diversity, equity, and inclusion that the OIE representative would offer her, because she is a self-acclaimed scholar of ES, and I felt that she was aware of the misogynoir-motivated violence that Black women and femmes endured in the academy. And in my soul, I believed the harm done to me and the facts of my case could not compete with one white woman—the OIE representative—hearing the case of another white woman—the faculty member.

The OIE representative recommended that I file a formal complaint indicating a breach of the university's Professional Rights and Responsibilities (PRR) for faculty members and academic leaders. My academic adviser requested a formal investigation under the PRR policy with the chair of our department and the College of Arts & Sciences social sciences divisional dean and asked that the chair speak directly to the faculty member about the matter, direct the faculty member to cease all communications and interaction with me, and establish departmental guidelines and regulations regarding monetary transactions between faculty and students. The department chair's response included telling the faculty member to cease communications with me but disregarded my adviser's ask that he address the faculty member's interaction with me because the OIE found no violation of antidiscrimination or harassment policy at the university level. The chair also stated that he passed the responsibility of creating the new policy to the associate chair of graduate studies. My adviser eventually reported my case to Faculty Relations, which had created the PRR policy, to initiate a formal investigation under the PRR. Subsequently, the department chair exacerbated the harm against me by inviting me to events that the faculty member was hosting or attending and never responded when I informed him that I would not attend events that the faculty member attended. Although all parties involved with my case were aware of the harm that I endured at the intersections of Black womanness and class, no one provided redress owing to policy inadequacies failing to capture abuses of power in contemporary time—where misogynoir-motivated classism comes in the form of white liberalism, even in an Ethnic Studies Department, and protections to comprehend and prevent such occurrences remain moot.

INSTITUTIONALITY AND MISOGYNOIR

There are 384 colleges and universities in the United States that offer degrees in ES.[7] These programs espouse a pedagogy that centers the knowledges, sociopolitical histories/herstories, and lifeworlds of marginalized peoples. Yet our lived experiences within the ES disciplines reveal how these "critical" pedagogical efforts marginalize Black women and propagate misogynoir. We maintain that misogynoir in ES persists because of inadequate institutional policy, protocol, and support to comprehend and redress contemporary and mundane functionalities of anti-Black womanness.

Institutionality and *misogynoir* inform how we conceptualize our collective narrative. They reveal that our experiences within an Ethnic Studies Department underscore the academy's deep-rooted herstory/history of mistreating Black women and femmes and that our experiences exist as part of a long lineage of misogynoir in HE. We concur that white supremacist logics of violence, assault, and offense at the nexus of Blackness and womanness have both subverted radical and accurate comprehensions of violence within HE institutions and also color current conceptualizations of misogynoir in some of the most critical and radical departments in colleges and universities—and ES specifically.

The Institutionality of Ethnic Studies

For many, the university is a space to dismantle white supremacy and transform it into a space of educational and economic opportunity, empowerment, and reclamation of nonwhite lifeworlds. Though activists challenged the nation-state and HE to implement the core values of grassroots activism, stakeholders institutionalized calls for a shift in power by reconstructing demands and regulating how and why the academy met demands. Resultingly, colleges and universities portrayed themselves as tolerant of *difference*, which aided the nation-state's agenda to appease grassroots protest and organizing, recruit higher numbers of nonwhite peoples to campuses, and answer calls for racially and herstorically relevant pedagogy by institutionalizing Black/Africana, Ethnic, and Women and Gender Studies programs.[8]

Roderick Ferguson's concept of *institutionality* characterizes how colleges and universities used the development of ES, incorporating *difference* into the academe, to pacify grassroots demands for redistributions of power in the academy.[9] Both the nation-state and HE institutions agreed to integrate difference in colleges and universities without changing power distribution, mollifying grassroots demands against white supremacy and promoting a culture of multiculturalism and quantifiable diversity instead. Focusing on the development of ES demonstrates that although these programs espouse a pedagogy that centers the knowledges, sociopolitical histories/herstories, and lifeworlds of nonwhite peoples, an Ethnic Studies Department subjugated us to misogynoir because of the colonial, anti-Black, and patriarchal nature of academia and the institutionalization of grassroots demands for transformative shifts in power.

Institutionality explains the violence that we faced. For example, the quotidian nature of institutionality appeared in Narrator Two's account on the department and university comprehensions of violence, where policy was rooted in ironclad conceptualizations of discrimination, harassment, and workplace hostility. Institutionality for the Ethnic Studies Department also occurred as faculty updated the handbook to protect one faculty member instead of the Black women involved in Narrator One's research—Narrator One herself, her adviser, and the participants in the study—while simultaneously beguiling Narrator Two with plans to create new policy to protect students from faculty coercion. The institutionalization of ES meant that the department abided by the university's bylaws instead of creating their own in which comprehensions of violence were contingent on Black women's and femme's intersectional and intricate experiences of misogynoir in the everyday.

Misogynoir

Black women's theorizing and pedagogy have been essential in creating the foundation for ES and especially curriculums utilizing Africana, critical race theory (CRT), and feminist and intersectional theories. Despite these disciplines intellectually benefitting from Black women's labor and theorizing, Black women and femmes experience marginalization and lateral violence from their BIPOC colleagues that is both anti-Black and sexist, culminating in misogynoir. Created by activist and scholar Moya Bailey, *misogynoir* is the "particular brand of hatred directed at Black women in U.S. visual & popular culture."[10] Misogynoir describes how racism and sexism intersect to harm Black women and femmes, relying on racial stereotypes of Black inferiority while reinforcing sexist notions of male and heterosexual superiority.[11]

As a concept, misogynoir provides an analytic framework that centers the dehumanizing assumptions created about Black women and femmes. It is rooted in gendered and racist beliefs about Black women's and femmes' sexualities, bodies, behavior, and creative and intellectual abilities. Misogynoir demands the undermining of Black women and femmes to uphold white supremacist and patriarchal thought that is inherently antagonistic to the well-being and flourishing potential of Black women and femmes because it demands their submission to and acceptance of the violence and marginalization that is done to them. Because of the subjugated and intersectional positionalities of Black women and femmes, misogynoiristic views and oppressions can be utilized from other disenfranchised populations of BIPOC folx—especially from nonwhite men.[12]

Misogynoir is the bedrock on which microaggressions and institutional harassment and maligning of Black women and femmes within the academy take root, even in departments that profess to challenge and dismantle white supremacy and patriarchy. Misogynoir illuminates the intricacies through which male entitlement of misogyny and white supremacist beliefs in anti-Blackness manifest among academics and administration who declare themselves to advance intersectional and radically critical scholarship and activism while actively participating in demeaning and violent acts on Black women graduate students and faculty, then penalize when Black women graduate students and faculty advocate for themselves and one another.

Our collective narrative emphasizes mundane functionalities of misogynoir. Dehumanizing stereotypes about Black women and femmes, Black inferiority, and male and heterosexual superiority compose the foundation of misogynoir. For instance, various persons in the Ethnic Studies Department and the OIE—who already held a reputation of characterizing Black women and femme complainants as perpetrators—used the Welfare Queen archetype against Narrator Two, which informed the gravity of violence displayed alongside unwavering descriptions of harassment and discrimination. Furthermore, misogynoir illustrates the required mistreatment of Black women and femmes to uphold systems of oppression. As demonstrated in Narrator One's account, people in the department excluded her from Africana Studies opportunities and pushed her to adopt Latinx cultural attributes and racial identity when she declared her Black feminist research endeavors. Regardless of ES's revolutionary roots, the institutionality of it perpetuates misogynoir against Black women and femmes because it has become *of* the academy and not merely *in* the academy. Ethnic studies requires the dehumanization and undermining of Black women and femmes through misogynoiristic policy and practice, like all entities of the academy—even in the silos we invent to protect ourselves from quotidian institutional violence and to dream of joy as Annette Kappert conveys in her essay in this volume, "Sail Fast."

We analyze our collective narrative through the lens of institutionality because of the Ethnic Studies Department's structural displays of misogynoir, which occurred as many faculty members maligned our shared adviser—who was the only tenure-track Black woman in the department—and eventually pushed her out of the department. The Ethnic Studies Department instated a culture of anti-Black womanness that not only affected us individually but also shaped departmental policymaking and protocol—demonstrated when the department altered dissertation policy to protect faculty members' positions on dissertation committees (allowing them to fulfill service workload requirements for promotion), upheld the university's definitions of discrimination and harassment, and failed to install policy prohibiting monetary exchanges between faculty and staff. The department's creation of policy rooted in the degradation of Black women antithetically affected our livelihoods and left us questioning if we would ever find joy in the ivory tower.

OUR JOY NECESSITATES RADICAL RECTIFICATION AND RECKONING

Our interwoven narratives expose the everyday realities of misogynoir in the ES discipline. We endured racially gendered offenses and found little systemic support from our department because of the university's apathetic approaches to understanding, preventing, mitigating, and redressing quotidian and nuanced forms of misogynoir against Black women. Through it all, regardless of meager departmental and university policies and procedures, we remained agentive, sought out support systems to persevere, expressed our joy, and advocated and cared for ourselves and each another, similar to what Prisca Anuforo, Elizabeth Locke, Myra Robinson, and Christine Thorpe call resistance in their chapter in this volume, "Backs of Steel™."

Nonetheless, the neoliberal inner workings of HE encourage and condone administrative decisions that forgo the implementation of antimisogynoir protocol that might protect the well-being and welfare of Black femme students, faculty, and staff. Even worse, predominantly white colleges and universities boast diversity, equity, and inclusion and wellness campaigns that oftentimes yield underfunded and culturally irrespon-sive services and programming. Universities' surface-level performance of concern for mental health and wellness, combined with hard-line defi-nitions of prejudice, discrimination, and harassment, leave individuals to combat misogynoir—and other systems of oppression—on their own and without systemic support. Under these circumstances, Black women and femmes bear the brunt of misogynoir, utilizing our coping strategies and creating practices of love and care for ourselves, as well as networks through which we love and care for our comrades.

Yet we question the sustainability of Black women and femmes taking on misogynoir at the individual level and in our communities. Although we have established enclaves of support for ourselves and our academic families to fight the pressures of anti-Black womanness, we are *human*—meaning, although we create and practice resilience in the face of every-day occurrences of misogynoir, we become traumatized and depleted, often without remorse from our departments or universities. If curated in light of the quotidian life of anti-Black womanness in ES policy and proce-dure, our joy necessitates radical rectification and reckoning.

Planting Decolonial Seeds

Ethnic studies academicians must account for individual and systematic complicity in misogynoiristic practices cloaked by academic professional-ism, tenure, and promotion. The university forces us to achieve its stan-dards for success, by which we may abandon decolonial techniques of community. As we yearn to decolonize the academy and build space for Black women and femmes to fully embody joy, we must hold ourselves accountable, building kinship and love in the process. Is your work meant to build coalitions and collaborations, or is it just for tenure? Are your contributions to departmental research and curriculum for the liberation of Black women and femmes globally, or is it for promotion? Are you will-ing to mentor, support, and encourage future Black women and femme scholars to find their paths? And, perhaps most important, are you recti-fying harm against Black women and femmes, or do you explain your actions with an air of innocence and condescension? Though Black women and femmes within the ivory tower search for joy, ethnic studies—and related disciplines—must plant the seeds of decoloniality, nurturing pathways for us to transform the academy into a world of love and kinship for Black women and femmes.

Reparations

Establishing a reparations action plan is essential to redress misogynoiristic violence against Black women and femmes. By all means, reparations should be implemented without solely relying on Black women and femmes to lead initiatives and policy campaigns to remedy departmental and university wrongdoing. The culture in HE is to bombard Black women and femmes with additional service work and refuse to acknowledge the labor of support they often provide to other faculty, students, and staff. Joy in the ivory tower is a possible dream, but it lingers beyond the bounds of possibility so long as Black women and femmes are overly troubled with laborious exploitation. Au contraire, joy is the absence of exploitation, not being submerged in it.

We encourage HE institutions to lessen the labor of Black women and femmes by fully supporting their endeavors. Doing so could include monetary trusts for Black women and femme scholarship and programming. Unlike grants for program development, a trust or endowment might garner buy-in from the campus community and ensure that institutions secure monies reserved for exclusively Black women's and femmes' research, curriculum development and professorship, professional development, and programming. Black women and femme faculty, students, staff, and community partnerships should determine stipulations for trusts. Building these types of trusts require HE administrations to divest from university entities that uphold white supremacy so as to reallocate funds to programming exclusive to Black women and femmes.

Intergenerational and Nonacademic Redress

Colleges and universities must rely on an intergenerational approach to rectify harm against Black women and femmes who were formerly in the academy. Because HE institutions have made little to no redress to Black women and femmes regarding misogynoir—and because our intellectual lives are so intimately interwoven with our academic foremothers and siblings—those of us presently in the academy bear the weight of centuries-long anti-Black womanness. In addition, our statuses as scholar-activists, outsiders within the academy, and other roles through which we bridge communities and higher education indicate that we carry the heaviness of misogynoir against Black women and femmes existing outside the walls of colleges and universities. To radically reckon with misogynoir by taking the weight off of Black women's and femmes' shoulders, colleges and universities must pull their weight in taking accountability for perpetuating misogynoir intergenerationally and outside the academy.

NOTES

1. Collins, *Black Feminist Thought* (2009), 22.
2. Pitts, "'Uneasy Lies the Head,'" 716–35.
3. hooks, *Talking Back*, 29.
4. Bandyopadhyay, "Volunteer Tourism," 331.
5. Beauboeuf-Lafontant, *Behind the Mask*, 83.
6. Moya Bailey, *Misogynoir Transformed*, 2–12, 85–89; Collins, *Black Feminist Thought*.
7. Cavill, "Growth of Ethnic Studies Programs."
8. Ferguson, *Reorder of Things*; Rojas, *Black Power to Black Studies*.
9. Ferguson, *Reorder of Things*, 7–8.
10. Bailey, "They Aren't Talking about Me."
11. Bailey, *Misogynoir Transformed*.
12. Bailey, *Misogynoir Transformed*.

CHAPTER 15

Marronage in the Ivory Tower

CÉCILE ACCILIEN

I am born of enslaved Caribbean ancestors who likely undertook *marronage*, the process of freeing oneself from slavery by running away, usually to the mountains. On plantations throughout the Caribbean, marronage historically provided a survival strategy whereby enslaved people developed and maintained different skills to achieve their freedom. These people came to be called Maroons, and stories about them are well known in the Caribbean.[1] For example, Haiti, where I was born and lived until I was about twelve years old, is filled with tales of both female and male Maroons, such as Zabeth and Makandal, who escaped plantations in search of freedom.

Maroons defied the colonial capitalist system that dehumanized people to achieve its goals—exporting sugar, indigo, and other goods to Europe—and I have found inspiration in marronage to resist the power structures associated with academia. As Sara Ahmed has written, the ivory tower was not created for women of color.[2] Microaggressions, insults, and impostor syndrome are the result of a belief instantiated in the academy that there should be a few people of color there, but not too many. Because of the ongoing reinforcement of the belief that we *do not* belong, people of color are constantly both hypervisible and invisible. These facts are made literal when we consider that some of the most prominent institutions of higher learning in the United States were built on profits from the slave trade or the ownership of enslaved people or both, which these institutions often refuse to acknowledge. Indeed, some universities in the South—including Tulane University, my alma mater, as well as Vanderbilt and Emory—were constructed on the sites of former slave plantations.[3]

My positionality and awareness as a postcolonial thinker thus influence my modes of navigating academia: I know that I must remain on my guard to remain whole. I have developed strategies of marronage drawn from my deep cultural roots in the Caribbean that have enabled me to survive in my academic career, including resisting countless forms of microaggression. Although academia has been a hostile and exploitative environment in many ways, these strategies have helped me find powerful, enriching forms of community, find my people and build support through circles of friends, to maintain my cultural and spiritual identity.

As a Black Caribbean woman who wears locks and speaks with an accent, over the course of my experience as a professor and administrator at four different institutions over the past two decades, I have often been challenged to prove my ability and my place in the ivory tower, whether it be in the classroom, as a scholar, or in my capacity as an administrator. Strategies of marronage, which are strategies of both joy and survival, have helped me face these forms of oppression in my academic journey. They have enabled me to gather the courage and strength to use my voice and speak my truth. Silence is not an option for me. As Audre Lorde affirms; "My silences had not protected me. Your silence will not protect you."[4] Being in academia demands emotional and psychological energy. I find solace in marronage, and at the same time, marronage is a weapon providing me strength to confront, struggle with, and liberate myself from the ivory tower, a space designed to exclude, exploit, and perpetuate violence against people who look like me.

Working at public predominantly white institutions (PWIs), I've found that the challenges and overt sexism, racism, and otherism I have faced have not varied much whether I lived on the West Coast, in the Midwest or in the southern United States. In each of these spaces, I remain "other."[5] My otherness in the academy began as early as graduate school in the late 1990s and early 2000s, before terms such as diversity, equity, and inclusion (DEI); diversity, equity, accessibility, and inclusion (DEAI); inclusion, diversity, equity, and access (IDEA); or other variations related to diversity, equity, access/accessibility, inclusion, belonging, and intersectionality were used. I turn again to the words of Audre Lorde: "When I dare to be powerful, to use my strength in the service of my vision, then it becomes less important whether I am afraid or not."[6] I have used this quotation as a reminder of the need to face my fears and my rage head-on. I cannot count the number of times I have repeated these words to myself like a mantra when I have been in position where I knew my voice was not necessarily welcome. Sometimes, my fear is less about being afraid to say something and more about how what I say will be interpreted.

Because the academy is very much conceived in terms of boxes and either/or binaries, when you have several identities, others are not always clear what to do with you and how best to manage you and your opinions. The ivory tower claims it wants diversity but in a very specific and limited manner because many people are uncomfortable with and unable to think in terms of polarity that is both/and; they can think only in binary terms of either/or. As a result, the notion of true diversity and inclusion is scary and problematic for them. Strategies of marronage have enabled me to make my way through this hostile and often unwelcoming world, where microaggression is a common occurrence for me and other people of color. For many colleagues, students, and staff alike, as a person who is Black, Haitian, and a woman with locks, I do not fit the profile of a professor or department chair. Moreover, as LeAnna T. Luney and Cassandra Gonzalez discuss in chapter 14 of this volume, universities may "integrate difference . . . without changing power distribution." Indeed, sometimes even departments such as Ethnic Studies that are intended to create an integrative space may do additional harm to Black people and other people of color by fostering the notion among white liberals that studying people of color is enough and that they do not have to work on their own internalized racism—to question their power, privilege, and positionality.

My hair has become a symbol of the hypervisibility that I experience in the academy. When I first went on the job market back in the early 2000s, many well-meaning people, Black and white, from both my personal and my professional life, asked what I was going to do with my hair. At the time I had twists, and ascribing to the notion that natural hair is not professional, they were convinced that my hairstyle would prevent me from landing a job. Likely despite my hair, I did receive a job offer, but that memory stays with me. Cassandra Gonzalez's description of misogynoir experiences regarding their hair is a classic example of the policing of Black women in academia that I can relate to on many levels. It makes me think of how it is perfectly acceptable for whites to "love" and appreciate Black culture by appropriating braids and locks without any historical, religious, or social context, but when a woman of color chooses to flat-iron their hair, doing so is understood as wanting to "'code-switch away from Blackness.'" The question of whether our hair is acceptable is ingrained in a colonial mindset whereby whiteness and white culture dictates what belonging looks like. As Chimamanda Ngozi Adichie states, "Hair is the perfect metaphor for race in America."[7]

Years later, as a job candidate with locks, I interviewed for a job at a pre-dominantly white institution in the Midwest. I chose to wear my hair up because I did not want people to perceive it as "untidy" and me as unprofessional. In other words, I had to conform to white heteronormative patriarchal society's notion of professionalism, and therefore my interview style was very different from the ways in which I regularly wear my hair. A Puerto Rican colleague who was on the search committee saw me again after I accepted the position and considered me with a mixture of shock, surprise, and confusion. "What happened to your hair?" she asked. Given that she is familiar with women with my type of hairstyle, we had a very real conversation about the change that took place between my self-presentation as a job candidate and my self-presentation as a faculty member.

However, like Ifemelu, the main character in Adichie's novel *Americanah*, who must travel from her home in Princeton, New Jersey, to Trenton to get her hair done, when I was living in the Midwest I had to drive between forty-five minutes to an hour to find a salon where I could have my hair done and find products appropriate to maintaining my hair. The majority of my colleagues did not have to strategically plan to leave town just to get their hair done as I did. This fact alone speaks to the lack of diversity in that college town and to my need to escape so as to find people who looked like me and who could do my hair. Jacqui Alexander notes that "colonization has produced fragmentation and dismemberment at both the material and psychic levels," arguing that "the work of decolonization has to make room for the deep yearning for wholeness, often expressed as a yearning to belong that is both material and existential, both psychic and physical, and which, when satisfied, can subvert and ultimately displace the pain of dismemberment."[8] I felt that yearning to belong, to feel good about myself, and it manifested in part in my desire to search for places where I could get my hair done. My escape to spaces that offered this sense of belonging and the freedom to be myself is an example of a marronage strategy, embodying simultaneously the challenge of flight and the joy of connection.

Marronage for the enslaved was about not only fleeing and going into hiding but also creating something new and powerful. Today in Haiti, people continue to create new strategies to exist despite neoliberal practices that hinder economic development and keep them in a constant state of violence and fear. With limited access to money, they create cooperatives to support one another financially so they can be independent. In Haiti, it had been ingrained in me that respect meant, in part, not looking at others (especially elders) directly in the eyes. When I moved to the United States, I had to unlearn all that. The acting classes I took as an undergraduate in college taught me how to navigate eye contact and how to play the game of paying attention and showing interest. Such skills have been of use in my professional life as well, as I have had to figure out when it is worthwhile to speak and when to use a marronage strategy: listening and not talking much in order not to exhaust my energies.

Marronage for the enslaved was an important method of surviving and creating community. Maroons fled the plantations to leave behind their condition as property and to find their humanity. Part of my marronage has been to actively seek out my people and to build community wherever I go. Even before arriving at my current university, I started looking for my people through various networks. Continuing the legacy of the Maroons who would escape into the mountains or the dense tropical terrains for safety, I would check in with a few colleagues who knew the lay of the land to get advice. When the microaggressions started, I would consult with my people to learn how best to deal with them, including when to remain silent.

Silence can be a powerful form of resistance, and I learned to use it as a strategic pause during meetings, choosing selectively not to engage. My words are my strength, yet silence is my weapon and my treasure in certain circumstances. The more time I have spent in academia, the more I have used silence as marronage. It takes a lot of emotional energy to find ways to help colleagues who really do not want to do the work to make diversity, equity, inclusion, and belonging more than buzzwords, so I have decided to measure my words. In certain meetings and on certain committees, I have strategically chosen to remain silent because I know that in these circumstances, I count as little more than a body that just happens to fit the boxes of "diversity" that are needed:

Racial diversity: I am Black.
Gender diversity: I am a woman.
International/immigration diversity: I have an accent and have lived in various countries.
Linguistic diversity: I speak, read, and write multiple languages.

Even so, as a Black Caribbean woman, my various identities are simultaneously a problem for many in academia because I do not conform easily
to an institution's, or a given individual's, desired or expected notion of
"diversity."

Marronage allows me to see myself not as others see me but as my true
self. It is a constant negotiation. Being conscious is a bitch: once you are
conscious, you cannot become unconscious. As feminist theorist Brittney
Cooper has stated, "The process, of both becoming a feminist and becoming okay with rage as a potential feminist superpower, has been messy as
hell. We need to embrace our messiness more. We need to embrace the
ways we are in process more."[9] Knowing that I am just a body in certain settings, I have learned when to simply fulfill that role. Some well-
meaning colleagues (mainly whites) have said matter-of-factly that I have
the choice to simply say no when I am asked to be on certain committees.
They do not realize how complicated it is to be the only one who qualifies
as "diverse" and to be asked by your chair or dean (who is supposed to
support you) to perform certain services.

Furthermore, I must constantly think about the ramifications of saying no when asked to serve on a committee when its members actually
want to hear different voices and thoughts. When I complained to a white
colleague about that reality, they said that all nontenured faculty must
perform a lot of service. This response blatantly ignores that, in general,
people of color, and especially women of color, do more service than white
people, whether these whites are tenured or untenured. The majority of
PWIs employ very few people of color, and despite all the current buzz
around DEI initiatives, many institutions are not intentional about retaining faculty of color. They want to have a few, but not too many.

Considering my yearly review and witnessing the number of committees on which I have served over a given period is an exhausting endeav-
or that sometimes makes me feel dizzy. By the time I had arrived at my
third university, I had acquired the language of marronage to help me
formulate a diplomatic way to turn down these "invitations" when they
became overwhelming. In her article "An Appeal: Bring the Maroon to
the Foreground in Black Intellectual History," Yannick Marshall argues
that marronage politics are very much rooted in the idea that the institution from which a person is escaping is not likely to change.[10] Marronage
therefore involves finding a space of safety away from racial violence and

microaggressions and is a way to create knowledge and community. What happens to many Black women in academia is that we say yes so much, we spend so much time trying to prove ourselves, that we end up not having time and energy to write or we get burned out. This is one way racism manifests itself. We become distracted as we are trying to prove ourselves. We must therefore learn to be double—to exist in certain places while not being fully present.[11]

Marronage as a strategy of self-preservation and resistance invites the idea of the double. In the Vodou religion, the twin spirits, or *marassas*, represent divine power, justice, truth, and reason. Marronage was a way for the enslaved to find a space in which to exist and be themselves. In the academic world, survival sometimes means being double, for example, by keeping a poker face and not reacting to microaggressions. One of the ways in which my marronage plays out in an academic setting is that I am at once invisible and visible. On the one hand, I may raise my hand and not be acknowledged or say something that is ignored; then someone else (generally a white person) says the same thing and is acknowledged. On the other hand, I am often the only Black person, and sometimes the only person of color, in the room, so if I do not show up somewhere or miss a meeting, people notice. The COVID-19 pandemic facilitated marronage because being on Zoom, Teams, or other similar platforms has enabled me to be myself without having to pretend to respond, for I can have my camera off and minimally be present.

I am now at my fourth university. During the interview process for my current job, two different white women at separate times asked why I had moved around so much. To put this question in perspective, I had spent ten years at one institution and five years at the one from which I was hoping to move, yet I made these women uncomfortable because "it seemed like I had moved around a lot." I'm fairly sure that if I were a white man, my career moves would not have been seen as a reason for suspicion of ungroundedness, unreliability, or perhaps being difficult to work with but as evidence of a healthy ambition.

An older white colleague at my first postgraduate job at a PWI in the Pacific Northwest told me when I was leaving after three years to move back to the South, where I had gone to graduate school: "Do not be loyal to institutions. Be loyal to individuals who you feel deserve your loyalty." These words have remained with me over the past fifteen years; I can still see my colleague's face and the bench outside the university where we were sitting while conversing. This notion of loyalty is complex and often misunderstood. It does not mean that you do not do your job well; it means that you must accept, acknowledge, and understand when it's time to move on.

Jacqui Alexander has pointed out that "inside of all the violence we experience we cannot continue to live fragmented lives—of the kind that was generated as part of that earlier colonization and slavery—yet hope to create holistic institutions. It just cannot happen."[12] One way that I have and continue to attempt to create wholeness (of body, spirit, mind, and soul) is through the formation of a community made up of colleagues from an inner circle as well as nonacademic friends and family members who can help me remain grounded. The self-liberated Maroons strategically formed communities with Indigenous people, and for me it is important to find both colleagues of color and white colleagues who can provide support in the ivory tower. Like the Maroons who felt in constant danger, I have felt and continue to feel in danger of being told not to think a certain way; for example, not long ago, I was chastised by an upper administrator for wanting to speak out against racism vis-à-vis an underrepresented group. As with Maroons, who had to constantly find ways to sustain themselves physically and find food, we must sustain ourselves. These conditions make it hard to create a space to have more faculty of color. For the Maroons, there were threats to their survival: white planters were expanding areas to cultivate food, clearing the parts of the wilderness that the Maroons would use, which caused the displacement and sometimes complete dissolution of communities. Some of us in academia continue to fight to create space to exist holistically and wholly. Yet as Annette Kappert notes in chapter 12 of this volume, "I conclude in reminding you that pain strengthens our experiences of joy, albeit never on a permanent basis, but like the Ancestors, waiting in the wind and surfacing at the very moment you need it."

At the time of this writing, the debate over the banning of critical race theory is still fresh. As planters were afraid of the Maroons because they disrupted their stream of profits by leaving the plantations, many people in positions of power in the United States want to eliminate what they are calling "critical race theory" (really, any mention of the history of slavery and racism in the United States) by politically silencing it on the claim that it is divisive.[13] But many opponents of critical race theory do not really understand what it is and probably could not name a single scholar in the field. Why is critical race theory seen as so threatening? Just as white planters feared that Black people would demand their freedom if they were not systematically oppressed, many whites seem to fear that they will lose their privileges if people start thinking and acting on issues of inclusion, diversity, equity, access, and privilege. Therefore, they simply want to put a stop to the conversation. Faculty of color are enduring the brunt of this attack, feeling even more excluded than before. I wonder how many women of color have left academia or have been pushed out because they didn't have the strength, energy, time, or resources to deploy strategies of marronage.

Marronage has helped me survive in the ivory tower, where I am constantly reminded that I do not belong, because it pushes me to seek community. I cannot survive academia alone. Marronage has enabled me to exist both inside and outside the ivory tower and remain whole. It has also provided tools and resources. In all its complexity, marronage is my superpower: it allows me to have the freedom that I need within my core self to be whole and to continue the work of staying free. It creates a space for me to fight against the epistemological violence that is ingrained in the ivory tower, which manifests in terms of my race and gender, as well as other aspects of my self-presentation. I hope that my colleagues of color entering the academy will feel that it is a context in which they are intentionally, mindfully welcomed and that spaces open for them such that they can contribute all they have to offer while enjoying health and well-being. But I cannot be blind to reality. Although marronage is a survival strategy that responds to oppression, it is not defined by oppression but by the constant renewal of liberty—never taking for granted the necessities of life, central to which is community. There is joy in the continuous, conscious embrace of freedom as a practice.

NOTES

1. See Vásquez and Johnson, "[Taller] Electric Marronage." Vásquez and Johnson write, "Marronage refers to the varying states involved in flight and survival. The name comes from the Spanish cimarron and was originally used of the

cattle which escaped into the hills of the island of Hispaniola. Later the meaning transferred to slaves who escaped into the interior of Hispaniola . . . It all started when: A group of black, brown, queer, writers, artists decided to plot points across their escape matrix. Inspired by the petit marronage of our ancestors we steal away on this electric platform, share our journeys+offer what we find along the way. Electric kin is a collective bound by four rules of fugitivity: escaping+stealing+feeling+whatever. We abscond+reveal. We build [futures] to which we can return."

2. See Ahmed, *Living a Feminist Life*, 9–10. Ahmed writes, "But think of this: those of us who arrive in an academy that was not shaped by or for us bring knowledges, as well as worlds, that otherwise would not be here. Think of this: how we learn about worlds when they do not accommodate us. Think of the kinds of experiences you have when you are not expected to be here. These experiences are a resource to generate knowledge. To bring feminist theory home is to make feminism work in the places we live, the places we work. When we think of feminist theory as homework, the university too becomes something we work on as well as at. We use our particulars to challenge the universal."

3. A number of universities, including the College of William and Mary, Brown University, and Duke University, were built by enslaved people or using profit generated by the practice of slavery. However, some institutions choose to forget the history and culture of enslaved people. For more on this theme, see Wilder, *Ebony and Ivy*.

4. See Lorde, *Sister Outsider*, 41.

5. I cowrote a book chapter with my colleague Anne Dotter relating my experience of being the "other" as a Black immigrant woman administrator. See Dotter and Accilien. "Accented Others, Women, and Immigrants," 188–200.

6. See Lorde, *Cancer Journals*, 13.

7. See Adichie, *Americanah*, esp. chap. 31, which addresses the complexity of Black women's hair. Ifemelu goes through a period in which she stops putting a perm in her hair; after she removed the perm she didn't go to work for a few days because she was ashamed of her hair. She recounts how she is treated differently now that she doesn't have a perm. Later, when she decides to quit her job, a colleague asks her if she was fired because of her hair. Adiche includes some interesting observations about, and perhaps critiques of, the fact that even powerful women like Michelle Obama and Beyoncé do not wear their hair natural; to appear "beautiful" and "professional" in the eyes of society, they have to relax their hair. Though Michelle Obama has started to embrace her natural hair and wearing different hairstyles. The Gonzalez quotation is in chapter 14 of this volume.

8. See Alexander, *Pedagogies of Crossings*, 281.

9. See Cooper, *Eloquent Rage*, 5–6.

10. See Marshall, "An Appeal."
11. See Du Bois, *Souls of Black Folk*, 38. In *The Souls of Black Folk* (1903), W. E. B. Du Bois writes, "It is a peculiar sensation, this double consciousness, this sense of always looking at one's self through the eyes of others, of measuring one's soul by the tape of a world that looks on in amused contempt and pity . . . The history of the American Negro is the history of this strife—this longing to attain self-conscious manhood, to merge his double self into a better and truer self (38)." Du Bois's theory of double consciousness has been expanded to theories such as triple consciousness and intersectionality. For more on triple consciousness, see Flores and Román, "Triple-Consciousness?" For more on intersectionality, see Crenshaw, "Twenty Years of Critical Race Theory."
12. Ulysse, "Groundings on *Rasanblaj* with M. Jacqui Alexander."
13. See Goldberg, "War on Critical Race Theory."

CHAPTER 16

Four Black German Women

On Being Othered, Feeling Anger at Whiteness, Practicing
Joy, and Finding Belonging in Solitude

ANONYMOUS

We, four Black German women, who wish to remain anonymous, felt compelled to reflect on the question of joy and if it will come. We are constantly subjected to spaces in which we experience oppressive and exclusionary tactics within a research field that claims to interdisciplinarily explore our shared history and disparate life experiences. We are at various stages in our careers and are situated within predominantly white higher education institutions and precollegiate entities. We are exhausted and in financially precarious situations that have been exacerbated by the pandemic, which already disproportionately affects the people in our protective circles. We see our contribution as existing within a Black feminist framework where the personal is always already political. We cherish Black feminism's main tenet to center the "lived experience as a criterion of meaning" and see our contribution within a tradition of Black German feminist thought and literature inspired by those who have done it before and alongside us.[1] In our testimonials, we share our diverse experiences with tokenism, identity policing, complex interactions in academia that shape a multitude of intersecting exclusions and marginalizations, and the violence of having to validate our sheer existence and worth. We reflect on intersecting mechanisms of exclusion in white spaces, especially in German studies, in terms of differing Black diasporic experiences and identities, and we confront the impact on our emotional and mental well-being caused by these assaults on our intellectual abilities, identities, and personhood. *When will the joy come?* Our answer focuses on the investment in mentorship among Black women and the ways we heal together, cultivate our own joy, and engage with Black-only and Black, Indigenous, and People of Color safe spaces away from the performative allyship we have seen in the last decade, spaces that are established outside, alongside, and within academia.

BLACK GERMAN WOMAN 1 ON BEING OTHERED

African diaspora studies scholar Michelle M. Wright explores the particularities of experiences in the African diaspora by considering geographies and distinguishing between the Other-from-Within and the Other-from-Without in theorizing the discourses directed at people of African descent in the Western world in her article "Others-from-Within from Without: Afro-German Subject Formation and the Challenge of a Counter-Discourse." In her concept of the "Other-from-Without," the Black German subject originates elsewhere and belongs outside the predominantly white and German borders and as such is misrecognized as African, which Wright connects to the relatively brief German colonial endeavors in Africa.[2] Though Wright addresses a discourse that originated in the early 2000s, my experiences as a German-born Black woman with Ghanaian roots growing up in Germany and later being part of multiple German studies departments in the United States as a student and now as an assistant professor align closely with Wright's theorization. I remember the countless times I have been asked to prove and validate my "Germanness" by explaining that I am not a "military brat," confirming that I had "really and actually" been born in Germany on German soil, and sharing that my "actual blood" immediate family resides in Germany and is Black too. Additionally, initial conversations with white Germans and even white Americans consistently include comments on my "perfect and flawless" German language skills, while also showing a prying interest in learning the specifics of my parents' former refugee status and their journey to Germany to escape the violence following the coup d'état by Jerry John Rawlings in Ghana in 1979. This behavior functions as an attempt to corroborate people's preconceived notions about the impossibility of my "really and actually" being German by blood. African diaspora and ethnic studies scholar Fatima El-Tayeb explains German nationality as operating alongside a myth of a "national essence," an inherently racialized myth that legitimizes white German blood as a requirement for being authentically and ethnically German, in "'Blood Is a Very Special Juice': Racialized

Bodies and Citizenship in Twentieth-Century Germany."[3] These instances contribute to an understanding that places me outside the cultural and physical borders of Germany as well as German studies departments, regardless of my German socialization and citizenship. Furthermore, inquiries about if I can and why I cannot teach any of the West African Ghanaian languages that I speak so as to diversify my teaching portfolio demonstrate my misrecognition as African only from the continent, rather than being part of the African diaspora proper in Germany.

Addressing this very concern, Black studies sociologist Terry Kershaw argues for a nonhegemonic study of people of African descent as a necessary part of Black studies "as an interdisciplinary and multidisciplinary approach to the study of inter and intra group relations." In "Afrocentrism and the Afrocentric Method," Kershaw states that the discipline of Black studies can be liberated only by an Afrocentric framework that allows for a humanizing approach to knowledge production. Drawing on the philosopher and African studies scholar Molefi Asante, Kershaw explains the importance of centering African peoples as subjects and identifies Afrocentricity as accentuating "particular and distinct experiences of people of African descent that have helped shape Black reality and vice versa."[4] Similarly, Black feminist scholar-activist Yaba Blay highlights the diversity of African cultures and peoples and emphasizes the fundamental rootedness "in the cultural and historical *specificity* of the locale" in "All the 'Africans' Are Men, All the 'Sistas' Are 'American,' but Some of Us Resist: Realizing African Feminism(s) as an Africological Research Methodology." While addressing issues of gender within the context of Black studies, Blay rightfully questions from whose center and from whose African diasporic perspective issues are being analyzed and operated on. Blay thematizes Black feminism, womanism, and Africana womanism as exclusively "prioritizing a version of reality that is contextualized by their particular experiences of gender, namely as it is informed by the legacy and experience of being African in America."[5] This prioritization is emblematic of an often-unintentional marginalization of the experiences and contributions of non-American people of African descent who then fall through the cracks. In an attempt to address this concern, panel discussions, webinars, and lecture series under the auspices of Black studies or Africana studies departments claim to try to present a global and transnational perspective of Black social movements such as Black Lives Matter or to touch on the diverse experiences and understandings of Blackness and the

African diaspora, yet they often revert to engagements specific to the American locale. There remains a lack of scholarship focused on and derived from Black Europe. In this regard, even when I am invited to provide academic expertise and commentary on the Black German experience for various panels and webinars, my contributions are either sidelined or ignored.

El-Tayeb discusses in another work how the Black European experience came to be marginalized in larger conversations around the African diaspora. She states that the importance of the Middle Passage in African diasporic understandings and the overarching emergence of the Black Atlantic consciousness result in a marginal position for Black Europeans "due to Europe's supposed irrelevance for the central theme of the African diaspora." Therefore, Black Germans are representative of a Black European population that, for the most part, did not originate in a violent mass removal but instead came to Europe via direct or indirect routes because of colonialism. As El-Tayeb further explains, "It was Black Europe's heterogeneous composition, its ambiguous relationship to constitutive narratives of the African diaspora, and its complicated relationship to and overlap with other communities of color that left Black Europeans at the margin of diaspora discourses."[6]

Through these complex interactions, my experience as a Black German woman in academia is shaped by a multitude of intersecting exclusions and marginalizations. Acknowledging the shared space of Black studies scholarship and the equal importance of experiences such as mine—a Black German immigrant woman with Ghanaian roots who immigrated to the United States from Northern Germany—is what will allow for joint healing through shared coauthorship and storytelling, such as in this very chapter that presents an array of Black German perspectives. To this end, I see my presence as an international and German-born Black woman in the field of German studies as one that challenges notions of belonging, opens up discussions, and thus carves out a space for nontraditional explorations and perspectives within my fields of study, which are often considered homogeneously white and specifically Black in terms of a particular locale in the African diaspora. For me, it is the diverse and shared Black spaces within the academy that will bring about joy. Theorizing and engaging my experiences presents a crucial turning point in claiming and fully capturing diverse and various perspectives of African diasporic experiences at large.

BLACK GERMAN WOMAN 2 ON FEELING ANGER
AT WHITENESS

The only time I feel true joy is when I am in the presence of other Black folk. It has always been that way, and it is the reason I came to the United States. Growing up, there weren't enough Black people in Germany, but I formed long-lasting ties within circles of Black Germans and People of Color. In the United States, at the primarily white institution I attend, I have had to do the same. A white German cohort member once proclaimed how fortunate I was to have found so many friends in grad school compared with her. I explained that it was a coping and survival strategy and that we, the few Black folk on campus, find each other and bond to stay strong. We say that "Black don't crack," but a fellow grad school friend used to add as a cautionary reminder, "but it *do* fissure." Academia has taken a special type of toll on me. I continue to heal still. I found joy and continue to find joy, a purpose for going on, only because of the Black and People of Color women graduate students I found and find myself in the presence of. I met the people who bring me joy at conferences, rallies, and organizing meetings and in the classes I took. To study the Black experience and diaspora in Germany, I most often had to go outside my field of German studies to attend classes in sociology and African American studies to supplement my degree. A decade ago, barring a few courses and panels, not much was offered in the field of German studies that incorporated Black lives. It was in a critical race theory class outside my department that Kant and Hegel were pushed off their pedestals and replaced by Du Bois and C. L. R. James. The course taught me how to practice joy via resistance not only theoretically but also in praxis. That semester, Trayvon Martin was gunned down, and instead of going about our business as usual, the entire class, including the professor, left the room to attend a rally and vigil. We were enraged together, we grieved together, we experienced the beginning of the Black Lives Matter movement together. This was unthinkable in the department I had to go back to after class was over. There, Black lives were rarely, if ever, considered.

Not much changed about that until the summer of 2020, when I was angered and exhausted by the performative allyship I saw following the deaths of George Floyd and Breonna Taylor. The sudden public support for Black Lives Matter in academic departments, the black squares on social media, and all the rhetoric about diversity, equity, and inclusion in higher education was jarring. White colleagues and friends who have been comfortable in their whiteness before and silent around the topic, who have been suspicious or critical of Black Lives Matter since Trayvon Martin's death, almost instantaneously became outspoken allies in solidarity. These topics took over public conversations in Germany as well, but most of the attention was focused on U.S. racism instead of looking inward, where there was plenty to see, like the racist attack in Hanau, Germany, in which eleven people were killed in February 2020, or the rise of neo-Nazis in the German police and military, or the 2005 murder of Oury Jalloh in a German police cell. Black women activists and scholars in the United States and in Germany were called on to explain and re-explain the struggle for racial justice as if they hadn't published or spoken on these topics before. They were often asked to overwork and extend themselves only to feel used up by the end of the year because not much was changing structurally, nor had anything changed since Trayvon Martin was killed.

By then, I was used to the fickle ebbs and flows of how white people around me paid attention to Black lives. If they did try to engage with the topic, they politely danced around terms like "racism," "police brutality," and "white supremacy," as well as their own culpabilities in enabling the realities these terms attempt to encapsulate. In *Hood Feminism*, Mikki Kendall writes about using politeness as a method to control the conversation, noting that politeness "as filtered through fragility and supremacy isn't about manners."[7] It is a method of accessing whiteness via feigned and perhaps sometimes well-intended efforts to be polite, appropriate, and sympathetic. But these moments are often coupled with the not-so-implicit ask or demand to be taught what to think and say. Today, many of the terms white people spent precious minutes stammering over, only to find euphemisms for words that did not need any, are reverberated across the academy at dizzying speeds, including in German studies.

I would be remiss if I left out that important scholarship on diversifying and decolonizing the German studies curriculum has taken place, but very rudimentary debates over, for example, whether one can or cannot say and quote the N-word are still taking place too. There has not been a German studies conference I have attended where the word was not quoted out loud at least once, subjecting those triggered by it to the generational trauma the

word invokes. Although the N-word has been deemed highly discriminatory and Black people in Germany have been advocating for the removal of
it from parliamentary debates, the media, and children's books, many white
Germans (and white Americans studying in Germany) continue to find it
difficult to refrain from its use.[8] They seem to be unaware of how the word
said by a white person creates an immediate fight-or-flight response. The
self-restraint it takes to still these hands of mine "as to not let people catch
them" and to channel that fury into something productive, like writing, is a
strength they will never understand and a strength I never asked for.

Audre Lorde, who played such an important role in the Black German women's movement in Berlin in the 1980s,[9] reminds us that anger
"focused with precision . . . can become a powerful source of energy serving progress and change" and that "you're never really a whole person if
you remain silent, because there's always that one little piece inside you
that wants to be spoken out, and if you keep ignoring it, it gets madder
and madder and hotter and hotter, and if you don't speak it out one day it
will just up and punch you in the mouth from the inside."[10] As an attempt
to duck the punch that Lorde warns us about, I have to say it: It is futile
to build coalitions and bridges with white people, especially in the U.S.
academy, while they are still struggling with the basics of how to walk,
talk, dress, listen, and take a seat in these spaces and how to call in and out
their cousins and colleagues. It is pointless to answer that call unless it is
done strategically and for survival. Gaining a seat at the proverbial table,
eating from the rotten dinner that will be served up before one poisons
oneself from the inside with assumptions that systemic change happens
simply because one of us is at the table, will starve us in the long run. I am
at that table and continue to heal from new wounds that leave me filled
with anger at how slow things are changing. In Peggy Piesche's chapter in
Remapping Black Germany, she argues that someone who is "Black German can't think of Black German studies as a commodity that is fashion-
able right now and then move on to another field when this one seems less
chic" and that "Black German studies' critique of whiteness is resistance."[11]
Resisting whiteness by centering a Black perspective within what Piesche
terms *white German studies* is a necessary survival practice I must continue while finding joy along the way.

BLACK GERMAN WOMAN 3 ON PRACTICING JOY

In the last decade, invitations for work have entered my circles and left me with the impression that my expertise in language acquisition through the Black German lens was highly sought. As an African American German woman who was raised equally in Germany and in the United States, I knew that there would be few other, if any, educators who identified as I did in these exclusive environments. Nevertheless, I hoped for a form of "private regard," which Timo Wandert et al. define in their article "Black German Identities: Validating the Multidimensional Inventory of Black Identity" as a psychological closeness or the extent to which individuals feel positively or negatively toward Black people and their membership in that group. For my yearning for this private regard to be fulfilled, it was necessary for there to be actual other Black persons present and perceivable in my temporary environment to enable the formation of individual bonds.[12] Unfortunately, I encountered such a connection in these exclusive circles only once during my tenure as an educator owing to the lack of Black representation in predominantly white institutional spaces, which cater first and foremost to the majority culture.

Included in these invitations for work were the typical ideas and project goals for all members involved to preplan and bring ideas to the table to produce curricula and assessments for students taking German, enabling the language to compete with more popular options such as Spanish and French. I was under the impression that I could contribute freely on the grounds of trust and respect for my knowledge. But ensuring that every piece of instructional material reflected any and every kind of student who was taught this difficult and stereotyped language, one that seemingly only white students with a connection to German-speaking countries took, was an unrealistic expectation that I later learned to be more of a performance rather than a contribution.

In the beginning, there was a "sense" of joy. I was being compensated for flights out of town, hotel stays, dinners, and, maybe, if an institution's budget allowed, an honorarium between $200 and $500. As a novice educator, all of these "gifts" looked, sounded, and felt like I was valued. This token of appreciation was comparable on a smaller scale to how I had witnessed other professionals in various fields being treated when they were asked to lend their expertise. Preparation for these meetings took copious hours of researching and planning, and it transformed my entire perspective of what it meant to be an educator in the United States. I struggled on numerous occasions to blend in and become one for the purpose of being heard. I began to feel small after numerous instances of being talked over, interrupted, and even blatantly ignored when offering suggestions from a Black German scholarly viewpoint. My perspective was narrowly considered and understood to focus primarily on a diverse student body and thus too little on the mainstream majority culture, without any benefits for the white students.

As time passed, my presence served only the optics of these institutions, allowing them to report diversity, equity, and inclusion data to their membership. The uncertainty of my purpose of being in the room became very real, and I began to seclude my being and decrease my volume. In these moments, I questioned why I was invited and asked to contribute to these projects that would not and overwhelmingly did not include the voices of all the children who would potentially embark on a German studies path. So many emotions began streaming through my head and the rest of my body, hindering me from declining any future requests for fear of being ostracized and overtly alienated. These reactions prompted time with family, with friends, and with myself, for it was at this very moment that I remembered a quote commonly attributed to Zora Neale Hurston: "If you are silent about your pain, they'll kill you and say you enjoyed it."

In fall 2018, a true sense of joy was awakened within me. It came from a source that was unknown to me at the time. A group of students approached me to sponsor a campus club, and I hesitantly, but happily, obliged. I had previously been working in spaces with controlled curricula and few opportunities to make changes to the content or frameworks I was teaching, preventing me from adapting content to be more suitable for Black students and students of color. I wondered how much red tape would be involved in hosting my students and their efforts to bring community to the Black students on our campus. The meetings began, and the faces, the mannerisms, and the language—oh, the love for our language—were painted all over my classroom. Students began to share the experiences they were having in their classrooms and school events. I felt something come over me that I had not felt in a long time. There was a genuine level of happiness that I could not explain, but it felt familiar and like home. I gathered myself and, before we adjourned, invited all of the students to collectively hold hands in a circle. I thanked them for their attendance, engagement, and the individual perspectives they brought to our newly formed group, our Black Student Union. And with joy, I closed the meeting with a call-and-response to complete our union of support that rings clear as a bell to this day. At that very moment, I knew that the joy I had imagined could be readily practiced.

BLACK GERMAN WOMAN 4 ON BELONGING IN SOLITUDE

My personal adoption journey and my scholarship are inseverable. A series of traumatic life events precipitated my return to my alma mater as a nontraditional student after more than a quarter of a century. Beginning in the mid-1990s and over the span of about three years, I learned that I was adopted, left an abusive marriage, became totally and permanently disabled, and met my white German birth mother—in that order. Following an automobile accident, I underwent multiple spinal surgeries over several years while raising two young children on my own. From my recovery bed, I taught myself web design, became certified in computer networking systems, and discovered other Black Germans on the internet. It is within this context of abject isolation, having mastered the art of survival in solitude, that I entered the realm of scholarly activism. The internet provided the interface with which, despite my physical limitations, I was able to both observe and engage with the world.

But even before the accident, the divorce, and learning about my adoption, isolation and I had long been bedfellows. As a socially awkward introvert, an avid reader, and a film enthusiast, I learned from an early age to enjoy my own company. Like many belonging to the adoptive cohort, I grew up during the civil rights era as an only child in an African American military family. We lived like nomads in government housing on newly integrated, performatively color-blind military campuses. When our fathers retired from service, many of us found it difficult to adjust to civilian life. We were acculturated differently and had been afforded advantages that many of our new civilian classmates had not. In contrast, our civilian-raised peers enjoyed the benefits of extended family, community roots, and established social relationships, which we had been deprived of.

For many, this transition exacerbated the sense of isolation and cultural displacement inherent both in transnational adoption and in the military lifestyle.[13] For dual-heritage adoptees who grew up without genetic or cultural mirrors, the typical developmental tasks associated with adolescence were much more complex.

Constructing a positive self-image and locating a sense of home and diasporic belonging are particularly daunting tasks. When members of the postwar generation began searching for their biological kin and bifurcated cultural roots transnationally, they found not only one another but also a multigenerational, multicultural community that was fast becoming the topic du jour in elite academic circles in the United States.[14] This finite cohort is a fairly recent area of interest in two burgeoning interdisciplinary academic realms that developed concomitantly—Black German studies and adoption studies.

Historian Yara-Collette Lemke Muñiz de Faria reintroduced the postwar generation to a German reading audience with her canonical monograph *Zwischen Fürsorge und Ausgrenzung: afrodeutsche "Besatzungskinder" im Nachkriegsdeutschland* (2002) and to an English readership with her articles "Germany's 'Brown Babies' Must Be Helped! Will You?: U.S. Adoption Plans for Afro-German Children, 1950–1955" (2003) and "Black German 'Occupation' Children: Objects of Study in the Continuity of German Race Anthropology" (2005). Until today, no ethnographies and only a few memoirs have been published. In German studies, the discourse almost exclusively focuses on the experiences of Black people living within Germany, and in adoption studies, domestic transracial adoption dominates the conversations involving Black adoptees. Black people living in the United States who still identify as Germans and who still call Germany home are also underrepresented in African American studies and diaspora studies. This multidisciplinary marginalization, I argue emphatically, mirrors a real-life dilemma for many people with dual heritage who feel like they don't fully belong to either society yet think they should feel "at home" in both. I refer to this particular subgroup as Black German Americans.

Identity and belonging are prominent themes in both adoption studies and Black German studies research. Rarely, however, are these concepts explored from an expressly Black German American frame of reference. As the author and activist Noah Sow remarked at a Black German conference in 2011: "If you asked me today who's German, I'd say it depends on your personal history. You can clearly belong to several places, several countries, several families at the same time. You can belong—even if it goes against a whole nation's definition and understanding of itself. To *belong* is a very private thing. Nobody gets to determine where *you belong*."[15] One might also apply Sow's argument to political and cultural affiliation. For instance, not all Black people with a white German parent identify as Black Germans, Afrodeutsch, or Afro-German. Moreover, not everyone who elects to identify as Black German and who resides in the United States is adopted. Furthermore, disrupting the prevailing narrative, not all of the children identified as "mixed race" and who were adopted to the United States in the wake of World War II were the offspring of African American soldiers. Some have African or Puerto Rican fathers. The present-day community of Black Germans in the United States is not insignificant in number and is as culturally and experientially diverse as the one in Germany.

It is from within this social ethos that I envisioned a Black German organization, compelled by my own curiosity about my family of origin, my German heritage, and my cultural roots. The organization creates virtual and physical environments that celebrate our disparate histories, privileging Black German voices as experts of our own knowledge, irrespective of location, occupation, or academic achievement. Within this existential space is where I find joy and belonging in solitude, where I exhale, where my very peculiarity is my strength. As I near the twilight stages of my academic career, it is an exceptional privilege to learn from, exchange ideas with, and live and laugh among so many brilliant and kind young scholars. It is my sincere wish that the organization and the spirit it engenders will live on through them for generations to come long after I'm gone.

CONCLUSION

In our testimonials, we have reflected on our diverse experiences within and alongside the academy. The cultural and historical specificity of the locale is illustrated by these four authors who exemplify unique journeys to Black joy of shared Black coauthorship and storytelling. Thus, Black joy illustrates the multifacetedness of our Blackness and Germanness through various lenses and entry points. In this, Black German Woman 1 centers on the experience of a Black German-born woman with Ghanaian roots by illustrating the infinite and diverse perspectives of Black German encounters, whereas Black German Woman 2 finds joy while healing from the wounds attained during her time in Black German studies, which often showed itself to be more like white German studies. This field is dependent on the survival of Black women scholars who have been inspired by transnational legends such as Lorde, who too found joy in resisting majority discourses by empowering Black women in the 1980s, thus setting in motion the Black German women's movement and a sisterhood that has had a joyous lasting impact that all of us partake in today. It is this resistance and perseverance that Black German Woman 3 draws energy from to create, support, and guide new Black joy in the context of the Black Student Union, another space of long-lasting impact that highlights the importance of Black community and communal spaces that bring about Black joy for us in predominantly white academia. It is in this communal and supportive structure that all of us, despite our different experiences, find joy the most as we are protected and uplifted by our own. Black German Woman 4 takes this task to heart as she beautifully describes how her organization celebrates dissimilar histories that still all represent Black German histories, regardless of "location, occupation, or academic achievement." Each of us brings about joy in different ways, which is emblematic of our heterogeneity of experience.

NOTES

1. Collins, *Black Feminist Thought* (2000), 257.
2. Wright, "Others-from-Within from Without," 297–98.
3. El-Tayeb, "'Blood Is a Very Special Juice,'" 149.
4. Kershaw, "Afrocentrism and the Afrocentric Method," 160, 161.
5. Blay, "All the 'Africans,'" 61, 63.
6. El-Tayeb, "Dimensions of Diaspora," 45, 50.
7. Kendall, *Hood Feminism*, 252.
8. For the 2020 change.org campaign around stopping the N-word led by Black German activist Charlotte Nzimiro, see Greb, "'Always Derogatory'?" Black people in Germany have been advocating for the removal of the word and other racist language in children's books like Pippi Longstocking and *Die Kleine Hexe* (*The Little Witch*) in the past. The white German backlash led to the

Kinderbuchdebatte (children's book debate) in 2013. See Otoo, "'Speaker Is Using the N-Word,'" 291–305.

9. See Ayim, Oguntoye, and Schultz, *Showing Our Colors*; Hügel-Marshall, *Invisible Woman*.

10. Lorde, *Sister Outsider* (2007), 124–33, 42.

11. Lennox, *Remapping Black Germany*, 276–77.

12. Wandert et al., "Black German Identities," 478.

13. Peña, "Stories Matter," 197–221.

14. Peña, "From Both Sides of the Atlantic," 13–20.

15. Sow, "Geteilte Geschichte."

CHAPTER 17

Dreaming of Elsewhere

Black Women Professors Out of Place

ABENA AMPOFOA ASARE

MY STORY

When I was an assistant professor at a large public northeastern university, I was distressed to find that my life as a tenure-track professor felt decidedly unlivable. On paper, all seemed to be going to plan, but the treadmill of research, teaching, grading, writing, mentoring, cleaning, cooking, grocery shopping, birthing children, changing diapers, breastfeeding, publishing, worrying about tenure, fitting in with my colleagues, applying for grants, and succeeding on the tenure track nearly broke my health, wizened my sustaining relationships, and left me decidedly joyless. If this was success, I would quietly muse to myself, what might failure be? During those years I dreamed of other geographies as a potential solution to my malaise. If I had completed my doctoral studies in Makerere, Uganda, would my stomach still be tied up in knots waiting for the next microaggression? If I were teaching at the University of the West Indies, would my colleagues still whisper that my decision to birth children before tenure was poor planning? Perhaps an exit ramp from the furious- paced academic treadmill could be found in Cape Town? Where in the world, I wondered, would this life and labor feel bearable, or perhaps even good?

Throughout graduate school and in my subsequent academic positions, I assumed that the challenge of finding joy while laboring as a Black woman in academia was rooted, at least partially, in the United States' violent past and present. "Within White supremacist capitalist patriarchy," bell hooks claims, "the entire culture works to deny Black women the opportunity to pursue a life of the mind, makes the intellectual realms a place 'off limits.'"[1] If I left the country, I wondered, might I push past this culture with little use for Black women's thriving, let alone joy? "What are the narratives we tell ourselves to keep going, and where do those stories come from?" Shanna Greene Benjamin muses.[2] In this chapter I remember my daydreams of academic work elsewhere as one of these sustaining escape narratives, and I wrestle with the vitality of place for opening and shutting doors to joy for Black women in the professoriate.

Welcome to the "long-suffering, much abused community of black woman academics," quipped historian Nell Painter to a third-year graduate student recounting her experience of misogynoir at a scholarly conference; "we survive by supporting each other and getting together on a regular basis to celebrate our survival."[3] Painter's prescription—support, survival, and celebration—are themes in Black academic women's auto-ethnographic writing. The matter of joy, however, requires plunging into the deeper waters. What level of support enables it? How do we pursue it when struggling to survive? Is it predicated on achievement, or does it stand outside the rubrics of success and striving?

The authors in this third part investigate the enigma and alchemy of joy for the Black woman scholar. What is the formula, where are the ingredients, can we spot the hurdles—public or occult—associated with joyful living? Prisca Anuforo, Elizabeth Locke, Myra Robinson, and Christine Thorpe identify the importance of Black academic women's "backs of steel" and highlight the multiple factors that support our ability to "deconstruct antiquated paradigms and create new standards of excellence" within academia. LeAnna T. Luney and Cassandra Gonzalez's chapter on the persistence of misogynoir in a progressive ethnic studies department explores how obstacles to Black academic women's thriving continue to be institutionalized, even as academia becomes more diverse. Other chapters in this section—in both form and substance—harness history, dreams, and other ways of accounting in order to illuminate the pathways toward joy. An innominate contribution from four Black German women models the healing conversations that may help us find and recognize joy when it comes. Cécile Accilien's incisive meditation on marronage considers the historical and spiritual legacies from which Black women scholars draw as we navigate academia. University life may not be enslavement, but fugitivity, the practice of "stealing away" amid systems of oppression that threaten hegemonic control over one's labor, is surely relevant. Annette Kappert presents a "decolonized" analysis of Black academic women's plight that singes the heart and sings in the ear, reminding us that recognizing our own agency, making a decision to hoist our anchors and "sail fast," is at the foundation of joy.

As a young Black scholar struggling, I would spend inordinate amounts of time thinking about whether my research, teaching, and service might allow me to land in another country. Would Geneva's African communities provide a social anchor? Was comparative work possible with Australia's Aboriginal scholars? How could I find a berth on the African continent? These are the concerns of someone accustomed to free movement, even across oceans and time zones; this is a person supported by the privileges of a United States passport and accustomed to a North American budget. Daydreams like these resonated with my experience as an immigrant child; I often imagined crossing national boundaries and seeking different configurations of home at times when I felt out of place. Now, as an adult facing the pains and privileges of academia, I supposed that leaving the country, finding "elsewhere," might be the way to reconcile it all. Perhaps the problem was not really my work, colleagues, or profession; the problem was the nation!

Scholar Nellie McKay writes that "to be black and female in the academy has its own particular frustration because it was never intended for us to be here. We are in spaces that have been appropriated for us."[4] The *here* McKay refers to is the university, the ivory tower where Black women have faced "ridicule, marginalization, alienation, isolation, and lack of information."[5] But what if Black women academics are not only "out of place" within their particular university but also "out of place" within their town, region, or even country?[6] Ideally, part of the university's work is to acknowledge and wrestle with their local geographies; colleges and universities should dare to ask the "simple questions" about how the U.S. history of racial violence manifests locally and provide "straightforward answers."[7] Often, however, universities struggle to face up to the reality of where they are located, and Black women scholars are expected to absorb the contradictions in our own bodies and minds. Still, we have our feet, and we have the power to use them.

PLACING OURSELVES

The neoliberal academe's claim to objective, universalized knowledge depends on the notion that academic work occurs in a de-territorialized space that hovers above particular national contexts. "Publication and patent counts, citation rates, journal impact factors, and peer rankings": these "dismal devices for making university research output measurable and so auditable," Raewyn Connell explains, depend on the idea of a singular "web of knowledge [that] stretches out smoothly in all directions, embracing all countries and connecting all practitioners in a global, homogenous, tissue."[8] However, our own testimonies disrupt neoliberal academia's insistence that Black women's research, teaching, and creativity occur apart from the geographic places where we live. The violence in our local and national contexts is reflected in our institutions and shapes our work, even as the language of the ivory tower hints that we have been elevated to a world apart. This fiction of elevation and separation from the soil does harm to academic workers who find themselves contending with realities that are decidedly terrestrial.

A Black woman's university experience depends not only on what the institution does (policies) or how she individually navigates the work (practice) but also on where she is. The land we are on profoundly shapes our work and our experience of it. Creating the conditions for our survival requires attending to this land—specifically, considering how the historical geographies through which we move offer resources and liabilities for our thriving, and perhaps even our joy. Unfortunately, conversations about Black women's academic sojourning rarely attend to the question of place; the salience of the land is largely overlooked. Why?

We are disciplined, as U.S. doctoral students and newly minted PhDs, to definitively reject—often publicly—the idea that we should consider geography when charting our academic course. How often do we proclaim to our families and our advisers that *we will go where the job is*, regardless of specific longitude and latitude? Sometimes we must even vocalize this mantra in job interviews. The first and last consideration, we are told, is the institutional package. The prestige, perks, and scholarly potential of the place, including colleagues, scholars, funding, should be the paramount factors in our assessment of when and where to go. Location and geography are expected to be incidental. "The goal," Benjamin writes, reflecting on the directives she received for her academic job search, "was to get the best job you could—something at an Ivy, a large land-grant Research 1, or an elite liberal arts college—someplace highly resourced with minimal teaching."[9] The idea of prioritizing factors extraneous to the institutional package when choosing an academic job is a whispered confession, a risky proposition. But the university is not a world unto itself; our locations matter for how we work and live.

Working in a predominantly white institution may be even more destabilizing when the surrounding "college town" obsessively reminds you that you are out of place. If even the famous Harvard University professor Henry Louis Gates can be arrested at his own Cambridge, Massachusetts, home in a case of mistaken identity, how much more the risk facing junior professors living in decidedly less cosmopolitan communities? Living within and bringing partners and children along to inhospitable geographies is a pedestrian part of academia for Black women professors, but it is a burden. In Stony Brook, New York, a segregated, predominantly white and upper-class village surrounding a large and diverse research university, I was stopped by the police while driving my car multiple times over the course of a few years. There was never any ticket issued, never any speeding violation, never any missing headlight or taillight—I was pulled over, by the police, for no apparent reason. "Was I lost?" "Were my children safely buckled in their car seats?" "Was there a specific address I was seeking?"

I am lucky to have escaped intact, but the hazards of Long Island's racial geography were not incidental. Two sets of large brown eyes in the back seat watched this happen too many times to not notice. Two sets of eyes tracked the fear and exhaustion in my body as it emanated from the front seat to the back seat. They have registered this.

Even though "the prospect of a senior position in the white hinterlands is one that fills many [Black women academics] with dread," we are expected to go to whatever well-funded and prestigious hinterland is offered to us.[10] Academic jobs in a preferred area are hard to come by and even harder to obtain. The advice that we offer to a Black woman is that she must overcome her foreboding using a battery of personal strategies and resources. "One woman chose to change her employment status at the university to 'part-time' and embarked on other forms of employment . . . Several other women draw from their own spirituality and religious backgrounds . . . to provide them with the strength and healing power to cope with the hyper-scrutiny and intensity of the gaze in the marginalized and racialized space which has been carved out for them."[11] Many of the contributors to this volume identify the practices that Black women scholars use to survive; finding a community of like-minded women is mentioned repeatedly. Even this act of community building is not necessarily so easy, depending on where we are located.

In "For Loretta: A Black Woman Literacy Scholar's Journey to Prioritizing Self-Preservation and Black Feminist-Womanist Storytelling," scholar April Baker-Bell describes the loss of a friend, Loretta, during Baker-Bell's first year on the tenure track. Loretta was the author's hair stylist, a woman who stepped into the tradition of the African American beauty salon as a "sacred space" allowing Black women to "briefly escape from a world that oftentimes expected too much of [them]" by providing rituals of community, connection, and comfort. When Loretta succumbed to illness after years of publicly naming her inability to "take care of herself first" amid the stress of work, family, and other personal issues, her repeated warning to Baker-Ball at the biweekly salon visit—"But don't forget to take care of you, Mommy Deluxe!"—was haunting.[12] In response to Loretta's life and death, Baker-Bell shifted her relationship to her university employment. The presence of a Black beauty salon, and the therapeutic relationship it fostered, was a site of transformative wisdom for one sister scholar negotiating academia. However, we cannot take for granted that our jobs will be located near a beauty salon, a Black church, or any other cultural amenities associated with a thriving Black community. On the contrary. In chapter 15 of this volume, Cécile Accilien describes driving miles and "strategically plan[ning] to leave town just to get [her] hair done" as part of her determination to *live* while working in a homogenous college town. Given that in our universities, Black women's bodies are problems to be solved (There are not enough of them!), experiments to be assessed (How will students respond to them?), or tokens to be hoarded (We have one in our possession!), the value of finding spaces where our bodies are legible as unremarkably and fully human is no small matter. Finding community spaces where we can just *be* is critically important.

WHERE ELSE?

Where are the places it might be easier to just *be* a Black woman professor? Clearly, the entanglement of nation, race, culture, and community shape our working conditions. To take seriously my daydreaming of elsewhere, I sought out testimonies of Black academic women in diverse national and geographic locations writing about their experiences of life and labor. However, as I looked across national borders at Black women professors' autoethnography, I felt my heart sinking. Whether South Africa, Ghana, Nigeria, Jamaica, the United Kingdom—I recognized the story. Clearly, North American racism is not the only factor fueling the disrespect, marginalization, overwork, and isolation of Black women professors. Black South African women scholars record being "disillusioned with life in the academy" given that "black women are not taken seriously (or given adequate support) as producers of academic knowledge."[13] In many nations, gender parity within academic positions is rare. A report from Nigeria bluntly explains: "Although universities see themselves as liberal and open-minded, their administrative and decision-making systems remain patriarchal and male-dominated."[14] An article by two women scholars in Botswana describes the difficulty of "juggling" academic labor and "social reproductive roles."[15] Within all these testimonies of adversity, there is a repeating thread: nowhere, it seems, should Black women scholars dare to fulfill multiple roles in the world without being severely taxed for doing so.

Ghanaian women, highly underrepresented in the nation's universities, "cited conflicts in managing their multiple roles as mothers, wives and workers, interrupted careers, impact of family dynamics, lack of mentoring . . . and the power of the 'old boys' network" to contextualize their relative absence from the university's high ranks. Some women's working conditions set at odds, daily, their productive labor as academics and their reproductive labor as mothers. Still, the compromises, choices, and solutions facing women in this struggle "are largely unvoiced at work." This silence is the consequence of policies and practices that shame women (and other people) who undertake mothering, reproductive, or caregiving labor while also working in academia. The shame surrounding women's "childbearing and childbearing roles directly affect[s] their freedom to operate in and articulate issues that affect them in the academy."[16]

This is true not only in Ghana or the United States. Around the world "the gendered nature of work and family introduce[s] many contradictions and conundrums for mothers who work between these domains." A study comparing the experiences of Caribbean-based and United States–based Black women scholars identifies the losses associated with these contradictions. "While working class AfroCaribbean women exercise much power and control in the domestic sphere, those very sources of power that operate within the home become the basis for [women's] curtailment in the public sphere."[17] Universities, across the world it seems, whisper this softly and sometimes loudly: by entering academia, Black women must leave some of our world-work—and thus some of our power—behind. Continuing with social labor, particularly reproductive and caregiving work, requires that we hide these aspects of our lives and assert the primacy of our academic work. We might not all introduce our daughter as a sister, as academic pioneer Nellie McKay did,[18] but many of us keep our children, our partners, our parents, our familial duties, and the time required to maintain and grow these relationships rigorously hidden in our professional self-presentation.

The expectation that Black women be relationless or that we keep our relations hidden is made plain in a single policy: the absence of paid maternal/paternal or caregiving leaves in university settings. I have never worked in an institution that has a clear and reasonable policy for paid maternity/paternity/caregiving leaves for professors. This means that with every pregnancy, I have had to enter a series of negotiations with my employing institution about my body, my family, my time, and my labor. Two pregnancies, two department chairs, two college deans, two different arrangements. "It happens," was what one department chair said to me when I shared news of my pregnancy as part of my effort to cobble together a modicum of paid leave in a public research institution that then lacked a clear and reasonable family leave policy. "These things do happen, and we will all just have to deal with it." "You don't want to go and announce this to the dean" was what another department chair explained to me when I was asking for their support to secure a paid maternity leave, "this dean will not be receptive." The advice was: Do not seek reasonable accommodation. Instead, find some way to fulfill, or at least appear to fulfill, institutional duties. Accordingly, one month into my sought-after maternity period, with a newborn in arms, I was informed that I should start teaching a graduate class immediately so that I might keep up the appearance of uninterrupted labor.

Reading global testimonies of crisis at the corner of academic labor and reproductive labor hits me in the gut: even by crossing borders I would not be able to escape academia's hostility to mothers (and other caregivers). "It is not easy combining [academic life and motherhood]," a Ghanaian interlocutor stated. "I do not think it is easy as a career woman at all. We are managing."[19] Across the ocean, in the United States, theologian and scholar Melva L. Sampson reports, "I am still wading in the murky waters of the academy and I am still exhausted . . . This exhaustion has the potential to leave me mentally spent, spiritually bankrupt, and on the brink of physical crisis. It makes itself most visible in my performance of mothering."[20] "Mothers already find themselves suspect in the academy, their seriousness questioned," because our allegiances appear divided.[21] Our capacity to participate in the rituals of scholarly devotion appears limited by stereotypes about maternal duty.

In this, mothers are not singular. Human beings whose caregiving responsibilities propel them "outside" the neoliberal academy's work culture find themselves similarly "out of place." They, too, are encouraged to hide their relations and the time required to care for them. This paper's focus on mothers is not meant to reify the position of the academic mother. I consider our specificity as a way to expose a destructive trend that extends beyond us. The problem is that caregiving, within a late capitalism that stretches beyond national boundaries, is a dirty secret that individuals, usually women, hide behind their exhausted eyes. Pregnancy is told in a whisper; when confronting the needs of elderly parents, Alzheimer's, cancer, autoimmune disease, the first questions, the real questions, after the murmurs of congratulations or sympathy are: Who will teach the course? Will the tenure clock stop? How will you continue to produce at the pace of a mythical tweed-attired white man in 1950s whose meals, laundry, children, typing, indexing, and sex are taken care of by a wife? This was the curse an older colleague flung in my direction on more than one occasion while staring at my pregnant belly or my baby in arms: "I don't know how you do it! When my kids were small, my wife did everything! All I had to do was write my book and get tenure. I just don't know how you [will] do it!" What does academia look like when you don't have a "wife" capable of managing the mountains of social and domestic labor that are needed to build a life well lived? What does academia look like when you *are* the wife, along with being a teacher, researcher, writer, colleague? Black women are not always wives and not always mothers, but we are always human. "Men are more willing than women to forgo a balanced life and are thus empowered to dominate academia," Christiana Ogbogu writes. "It is, however, not a wise policy decision to have those who forgo a balanced life dominate [the field of universities and knowledge production]."[22]

Caregiving practices are essential to shifting our society's orientation away from exploitation and accumulation and toward survival, regeneration, and restoration. The transnational literature above focuses on mothering, perhaps because that is a social position where notions of value and the needs of the capitalistic economy most clearly clash. However, we need not be mothers to be caregivers. As scholars in disability studies have shown us, there can be no revolution without caretaking. In the soft space between I and thou, we learn what it takes to cultivate freedom; it is a plant to be watered, a story to be told and told again until is passed down. This way of being requires time and intention. Finding freedom, in the shadow of our modern transnational history, requires the mundane and banal work of caregiving.

FUGITIVE FEET

Confronting the global dimensions of a neoliberal academe that sets itself against human and social reproduction requires that we consider where and how we might find our "elsewheres." Crossing national boundaries or swapping institutions often will not transport us beyond these particular restrictions and rigors. Nevertheless, where we are placed and how we locate ourselves are not always the same thing. "Within a White supremacist, capitalist, patriarchal social context," "decolonizing [the] mind" is necessary work for the Black women scholar.[23] Shucking off the values of the slaveholder and the colonialist requires the Black woman scholar to find her elsewhere, even while working within the ivory tower.

My story of pursuing elsewhere from within the ivory tower required that I reorient myself toward caregiving, not as a surreptitious activity but as an

ethic flowing through and within my creative labor. Locating myself elsewhere requires acknowledging all the different communities that have claim
on my creativity and labor and, in turn, decentering the primacy of the university as the site for my intellectual work. I start by acknowledge that I work
and walk on Setalcott Nation and Unkechaug Nation lands. Beyond a verbal formula, recognizing my place within a local history of Indigenous land
is a relational claim that requires time and attention. In Sewanhackey/Long
Island, supporting Indigenous sovereignty is an urgent task with implications
not only for the region's political and social trajectory but also for our collective ecological survival. As a Black woman scholar, my creativity and time
cannot be rationed out only to my classroom, graduate students, professional
readers, or my colleagues. There are schoolchildren coming up and elders
looking on who ground me firmly in a reality where my labor is a shared
resource that holds value beyond the tenure file or the academic curriculum
vitae. As a Black woman professor, the imperative to care for my mind, body,
and spirit—in a world that continues to make Black women's capacity to be
exploited and productive the nexus of our worth—is more than an individual or incidental goal. Freedom must be visible in our lives and our living; it is
a tragedy when Black women scholars, with our relative generational privileges, remain caught in ways of work that feel far from freedom. Taking care,
understanding care, seeking care, prioritizing care is a compass pointing to
an elsewhere that exists within and without the ivory tower.

In this way, finding geographies where we might live joyfully requires
travel of a different sort. Annette Kappert's chapter in this volume offers
an exuberant image of the analytic and spiritual journeying that Black
women scholars must take on if they are to be free. Kappert encourages us
to "sail fast," through the allegory of the Annette 2, a cargo ship that finally
"simply decided to sling her hook; she gave five short blasts, hoisted her
sails, and hit the open waters. And in her wake, I am told, you could hear
the gentle voices of the Ancestors whispering in the wind."

*This is my joyful dream: one clear blue day I walk out of my university hall,
and I do not turn back. As I exit, the building shrinks down, and I am still
as big and heavy as ever. The earth outside the hall has been transformed.
Now warm and loamy, the ground molds and forms itself into shifting
shapes around my feet. Each step is a revelation; multiple forms rise and
fall away; the ground is alive with possibility. Suddenly I realize that there*

are generations here. I can hear singing and groaning; there is whistling and wailing. I can hear what I cannot see; I can feel what lies underneath. "There are many missions," they whisper to me, "but only one of them is for you. There are many ways to go, but only one direction is home."

NOTES

1. hooks, "Black Women Intellectuals," 153.
2. Benjamin, *Half in Shadow*, xiv.
3. Painter quoted in Feimster, "Not So Ivory," 283.
4. Guy-Sheftall, *Words of Fire* (2011), 451.
5. Jones, Hwang, and Bustamante, "African American Female Professors' Strategies," 133.
6. Wright, Thompson, and Channer, "Out of Place," 145–62.
7. Simmons and Bogues, "'A Simple Question.'"
8. Connell, "Using Southern Theory," 211.
9. Benjamin, *Half in Shadow*, 164.
10. Wright, Thompson, and Channer, "Out of Place," 158.
11. Wright, Thompson, and Channer, 145–62.
12. Baker-Bell, 528, 527, 528.
13. Mabokela and Magubane, *Hear Our Voices*, 84.
14. Ogbogu, "Gender Inequality in Academia," 6.
15. Maundeni and Mookodi, "Experiences of Two Female Academics," 75.
16. Adusah-Karikari, "Experiences of Women in Higher Education," 5, 42, 67.
17. Esnard and Cobb-Roberts, *Black Women, Academe*, 237.
18. Benjamin, *Half in Shadow*, xi.
19. Adusah-Karikari, "Experiences of Women in Higher Education," 96.
20. Sampson "I'm Exhausted."
21. Leonard and Malina, "Caught between Two Worlds," 30.
22. Ogbogu, "Gender Inequality in Academia," 1.
23. hooks, "Black Women Intellectuals," 160.

BIBLIOGRAPHY

Acker, Sandra, and Eve Haque. "The Struggle to Make Sense of Doctoral Study." *Higher Education Research and Development* 34, no. 2 (October 2015): 229–41. https://doi.org.10.1080/07294360.2014.9 56699.

Adiche, Chimimanda Ngozie. *Americanah.* New York: Alfred A. Knopf, 2013.

Adusah-Karikari, Augustina. "Experiences of Women in Higher Education: A Study of Women Faculty and Administrators in Selected Public Universities in Ghana." PhD diss., College of Education of Ohio University, 2008.

Ahmed, Sara. *Complaint!* Durham, NC: Duke University Press, 2021.

———. *Living a Feminist Life.* Durham, NC: Duke University Press, 2017.

———. *On Being Included: Racism and Diversity in Institutional Life.* Durham, NC: Duke University Press, 2012.

Aidoo, Ama Ata. *Our Sister Killjoy: Or Reflections from a Black-Eyed Squint.* London: Longman, 1977.

Alexander, M. Jacqui. *Pedagogies of Crossings: Meditations on Feminism, Sexual Politics, Memory, and the Sacred.* Durham: Duke University Press, 2005.

Alexander, Karen. "Julie Dash: 'Daughters of the Dust' and a Black Aesthetic." In *Women and Film: A Sight and Sound Reader*, edited by Pam Cook and Philip Doss, 224–31. Philadelphia: Temple University Press, 1993.

Allen, Antija M., and Justin T. Stewart, eds. *We're Not OK: Black Faculty Experiences and Higher Education Strategies.* Cambridge: Cambridge University Press, 2017.

Allen, Evette L., and Nicole M. Joseph. "The Sistah Network: Enhancing the Educational and Social Experiences of Black Women in the Academy." *NASPA Journal about Women in Higher Education* 11, no. 2 (April 2018): 151–70. https://doi.org.10.1080/19407882.2017.14 09638.

Allen, Walter R., Edgar G. Epps, Elizabeth A. Guillory, Susan A. Suh, and Marguerite Bonous-Hammarth. "The Black Academic: Faculty Status among African Americans in U.S. Higher Education." *Journal of Negro Education* 69, no. 1/2 (Winter–Spring 2000): 112–27. https://www.jstor.org/stable/2696268.

Ampaw, Frim D., and Audrey J Jaeger. "Completing the Three Stages of Doctoral Education: An Event History Analysis." *Research in Higher Education* 53, no. 6 (September 2012): 640–60.

Andrei, Petre. *Filosofia Valorii* [The philosophy of values]. Bucharest: Fundatia Regele Mihai I, 1945. https://upload.wikimedia.org /wikipedia/commons/b/b9/Petre_Andrei_-_Filosofia_valorii.pdf.

Anonymous. "Vital Signs: Statistics That Measure the State of Racial Inequality." *Journal of Blacks in Higher Education*, no. 49 (Autumn 2005). https://www.proquest.com/scholarly-journals /vital-signs-statistics-that-measure-state-racial/docview/1955323 76/se-2.

Antony, James Soto. "Reexamining Doctoral Student Socialization and Professional Development: Moving beyond the Congruence and Assimilation Orientation." In *Higher Education: Handbook of Theory and Research*, edited by John C. Smart, 349–80. Dordrecht: Springer, 2002.

Antony, James Soto, and Tamara Lynn Schaps. "The More Things Change, the More They Stay the Same: The Persistence, and Impact, of the Congruence and Assimilation Orientation in Doctoral Student Socialization and Professional Development." *Higher Education: Handbook of Theory and Research* 36 (2021): 383–417.

Arday, Jason, and Heidi Safia Mirza, eds. *Dismantling Race in Higher Education: Racism, Whiteness and Decolonizing the Academy*. London: Palgrave Macmillan, 2018.

Asmelash, Leah. "Nikole Hannah-Jones Declines UNC Tenure Position and Will Join Howard University." CNN, July 6, 2021. https:// www.cnn.com/2021/07/06/us/howard-university-nikole -hannah-jones-ta-nehisi-coates/index.html.

Aurélia, Dominique. "Crossing Troubled Seas: The Metaphor of Flight in Caribbean Literature." Paper presented at the Conference at King's College in London, 2007.

Ayim, May, Katharina Oguntoye, and Dagmar Schultz. *Showing Our Colors: Afro-German Women Speak Out.* Amherst: University of Massachusetts Press, 1992.

Bacchus, Denise N. A. "Coping with Work-Related Stress: A Study of the Use of Coping Resources among Professional Black Women," *Journal of Ethnic & Cultural Diversity in Social Work* 17, no. 1 (October 2008): 60–81.

Bailey, Moya. *Misogynoir Transformed: Black Women's Digital Resistance.* New York: New York University Press, 2021.

———. "They Aren't Talking about Me . . ." Crunk Feminist Collective, March 4, 2010. Accessed July 2, 2021. http://www.crunkfeminist collective.com/2010/03/14/they-arent-talking-about-me/.

Bailey, Moya, and Trudy. "On Misogynoir: Citation, Erasure, and Plagiarism." *Feminist Media Studies* 18, no. 4 (March 2018): 762–68.

Baker-Bell, April. "For Loretta: A Black Woman Literacy Scholar's Journey to Prioritizing Self-Preservation and Black Feminist–Womanist Storytelling." *Journal of Literacy Research* 49, no. 4 (December 1, 2017): 526–43. https://doi.org/10.1177/1086296X 17733092.

Baldwin, James. *James Baldwin: Early Novels and Stories,* edited by Toni Morrison. New York: Library of America, 1998. Volume 97 of DE-601)374069697: Library of America series.

Bandyopadhyay, Ranjan. "Volunteer Tourism and 'the White Man's Burden': Globalization of Suffering, White Savior Complex, Religion and Modernity." *Journal of Sustainable Tourism* 27, no. 3 (March 2019): 327–43.

Bannerji, Himani, Linda Carty, Kari Delhi, Susan Herald, and Kate McKenna. *Unsettling Relations: The University as a Site of Feminist Struggles.* Toronto: Women's Press, 1991.

Barker, Robert L. *The Social Work Dictionary.* 6th ed. Washington, D.C.: NASW Press, 1995.

Barkley Brown, Elsa. "Bodies of History." In White, *Telling Histories,* 215–27.

Barnes, Benita J., and Jennifer Randall. "Doctoral Student Satisfaction: An Examination of Disciplinary, Enrollment, and Institutional Differences." *Research in Higher Education* 53, no. 1 (February 2012): 47–75.

Barsh, Joanna, and Lareina Yee. "Special Report: Unlocking the Full Potential of Women in the U.S. Economy." McKinsey & Company, August 20, 2012. https://www.mckinsey.com/careers/our _people_and_values/diversity_and_inclusion_networks/mckin

sey_women/~/media/mckinsey/dotcom/client_service/organiza
tion/2012_may_women_matter/unlocking_the_full_potential_of
_women_at_work.ashx.

Beauboeuf-Lafontant, Tamara. *Behind the Mask of the Strong Black
Woman: Voice and the Embodiment of a Costly Performance.*
Philadelphia: Temple University Press, 2009.

Bell, Ella Louise. "The Bicultural Life Experience of Career-Oriented
Black Women." *Journal of Organizational Behavior* 11, no. 6
(November 1990): 459–77.

Bell, Kanika. "Sister on Sisters: Inner Peace from the Black Woman
Mental Health Professional." In *Black Women's Mental Health:
Balancing Strength and Vulnerability*, edited by Stephanie Y.
Evans, Kanika Bell, and Nsenga K. Burton, 23–41. Albany: State
University of New York Press, 2017.

Benjamin, Shanna Greene. *Half in Shadow: The Life and Legacy of Nellie
Y. McKay.* Chapel Hill: University of North Carolina Press, 2021.

Bennett, Louise. "Colonization in Reverse." In *Writing Black Britain,
1948–1998: An Interdisciplinary Anthology*, edited by James
Proctor, 16. Manchester: Manchester University Press, 2000.

Berkowitz, Alexandra, and Irene Padavic. "Getting a Man or Getting
Ahead: A Comparison of White and Black Sororities." *Journal of
Contemporary Ethnography* 27, no. 4 (January 1999): 530–57.

Bhopal, Kalwant. *White Privilege: The Myth of a Post-Racial Society.*
Bristol: Bristol University Press, 2018.

Bhopal, Kalwant, and June Jackson. "The Experiences of Black and
Minority Ethnic Academics: Multiple Identities and Career
Progression." Southampton: University of Southampton, 2013.
https://eprints.soton.ac.uk/350967/1/__soton.ac.uk_ude_person
alfiles_users_kb4_mydocuments_Diversity%2520research_Final
%2520report%2520April%25202013_Final%2520Report%25208
July%25202013_Research%2520Report%2520The%2520Experien
ces%2520of%2520Black%2520and%2520Minority%2520Ethnic%
2520Academics.pdf.

Biakolo, Kovie. "Black Women Are More than Their Strength." *Thought
Catalog*, January 22, 2016.

Black Scholars Collective. "Constitution." Indiana University, Bloomington, Indiana, July 2006.

Blay, Yaba Amgborale. "All the 'Africans' Are Men, All the 'Sistas' are
'American,' but Some of Us Resist: Realizing African
Feminism(s) as an Africological Research Methodology."
Journal of Pan African Studies 2, no. 2 (March 2008): 58–73.

Bourdieu, Pierre. "The Forms of Capital." In *Handbook of Theory and Research for the Sociology of Education*, edited by J. E. Richardson, 241–58. Westport, CT: Greenwood, 1986.

Bowen, Deidre M. "Visibly Invisible: The Burden of Race and Gender for Female Students of Color Striving for an Academic Career in the Sciences." In *Presumed Incompetent: The Intersections of Race and Class for Women in Academia*, edited by Gabriella Gutiérrez y Muhs, Yolanda Flores Niemann, Carmen G. González, and Angela P. Harris, 116–32. Boulder: University of Colorado Press, 2012.

Boylorn, Robin M., and Mark P. Orbe. "Critical Autoethnography: Implications and Future Directions." In *Critical Autoethnography: Intersecting Cultural Identities in Everyday Life*, edited by Robin M. Boylorn and Mark P. Orbe, 234–38. Oakland, CA: Left Coast Press, 2014.

Broman, Clifford L. "Race-Related Factors and Life Satisfaction among African Americans." *Journal of Black Psychology* 23, no. 1 (February 1997): 36–49.

Brown, Brené. *I Thought It Was Just Me (but It Isn't): Making the Journey from "What Will People Think?" to "I Am Enough."* New York: Avery, an imprint of Penguin Random House, 2007.

Brown, Jayna. *Babylon Girls: Black Women Performers and the Shaping of the Modern.* Durham, NC: Duke University Press, 2008.

Brown, Leslie. "How a Hundred Years of History Tracked Me Down." In White, *Telling Histories*, 252–69.

Browning, Michelle. "Self-Leadership: Why It Matters." *International Journal of Business and Social Science* 9, no. 2 (February 2018): 14–18.

Burton, Valorie. *Get Unstuck, Be Unstoppable: Step into the Amazing Life God Imagined for You.* Eugene, OR: Harvest House Publishers, 2014.

Busia, Abena P. A. "What Is Your Nation? Reconnecting Africa and Her Diaspora through Paule Marshall's Praise Song for the Widow." In *Changing Our Own Words: Essays on Criticism, Theory, and Writing by Black Women*, edited by Cheryl A. Wall, 196–211. New Brunswick, NJ: Rutgers University Press, 1991.

Campbell, Joseph. *The Hero's Journey.* Princeton, NJ: Princeton University Press, 2004.

Campbell, Kendall M., Michaela M. Braxton, Dmitry Tumin, and José E. Rodríguez. "Reverse Mentoring between Minority Students and Faculty." *Journal of Best Practices in Health Professions Diversity* 13, no. 2 (Fall 2020): 184–88.

Campbell-Stephens, Rosemary M. *Educational Leadership and the Global Majority: Decolonising Narratives*. Cham, Switzerland: Springer International, 2021.

Campus Policies. "Discrimination and Harassment Policy." University of Colorado–Boulder. Accessed July 2, 2021. https://colorado.edu /policies/discrimination-harassment-policy.

Carby, Hazel Z. "White Woman Listen! Black Feminism and the Boundaries of Sisterhood." In *Materialist Feminism: A Reader in Class, Difference, and Women's Lives*, edited by Rosemary Hennessy and Chrys Ingraham, 110–28. New York: Routledge, 1982.

Carter, Prudence L. "'Black' Cultural Capital, Status Positioning, and Schooling Conflicts for Low-Income African American Youth." *Social Problems* 50, no. 1 (February 2003): 136–55.

Carty, Linda. "Black Women in Academia: A Statement from the Periphery." In *Unsettling Relations: The University as a Site of Feminist Struggles*, edited by Himani Bannerji, Linda Carty, Kari Dehli, Susan Heald, and Kate McKenna, 13–44. Toronto: Women's Press, 1991.

Cavill, Sarah. "The Growth of Ethnic Studies Programs in Higher Education," Digital Media Solutions. Accessed July 2, 2021.

Chapdelaine, Robin P. "Black Votes Matter. Black Votes REALLY Matter." *Huffington Post*, December 13, 2017. https://www.huffpost.com /entry/black-votes-matter-black-votes-really-matter_b_5a3168 6de4b0b73dde46a973.

———. "Celebrating Breast Cancer Awareness Month amidst a War against Women's Bodily Autonomy." *Huffington Post*, October 12, 2017. https://www.huffpost.com/entry/celebrating-breast-cancer-awareness-month-amidsta_b_59de968ce4b069e5b833b221.

Chapman, Gary D. *The 5 Love Languages: The Secret That Will Revolutionize Your Relationships*. Chicago: Northfield, 2017.

Chatterjee, Piya, and Sunaina Maira, eds. *The Imperial University: Academic Repression and Scholarly Dissent*. Minneapolis: University of Minnesota Press, 2014.

Chavez, Alicia Fedelina. "Women and Minorities Encouraged to Apply: Challenges and Opportunities of Critical Cultural Feminist Leadership in Academe." In *Tedious Journeys: Autoethnography by Women of Color in Academe*, edited by Pauline Clardy and Cynthia Cole Robinson, 177–99. New York: Peter Lang, 2010.

Chemaly, Soraya. *Rage Becomes Her: The Power of Women's Anger*. New York: Atria, 2018.

Clance, Pauline Rose, and Suzanne Imes. "The Imposter Phenomenon in High-Achieving Women: Dynamics and Therapeutic Intervention." *Psychotherapy: Theory, Research and Practice* 15, no. 3 (Fall 1978): 241–47.

Clary, Mike. "Faulkner Takes Her Place as a Citadel Knob." *Washington Post*, August 13, 1995. https://www.washingtonpost.com/archive/politics/1995/08/13/faulkner-takes-her-place-as-a-citadel-knob/9b49dbeb-d41a-4fc4-ae4b-53de02f7f681/.

Cochran, Kathryn, James A. De Ruiter, and Richard A. King. "Pedagogical Content Knowing: An Integrative Model for Teacher Preparation." *Journal of Teacher Education* 44 (September–October 1993): 263–72.

Collins, Patricia Hill. *Black Feminist Thought: Knowledge, Consciousness, and the Politics of Empowerment*. New York: Routledge, 1990.

———. *Black Feminist Thought: Knowledge, Consciousness, and the Politics of Empowerment*. New York: Routledge, 2000.

———. *Black Feminist Thought: Knowledge, Consciousness, and the Politics of Empowerment*. New York: Routledge, 2009.

———. "Learning from the Outsider Within: The Sociological Significance of Black Feminist Thought." *Social Problems* 33, no. 6 (December 1986): 13–42.

———. "The Social Construction of Black Feminist Thought." *Signs* 14, no. 4 (Summer 1989): 745–73.

Connell, Raewyn. "Using Southern Theory: Decolonizing Social Thought in Theory, Research and Application." *Planning Theory* 13, no. 2 (May 2014): 210–23.

Cooper, Brittney. *Eloquent Rage: A Black Feminist Discovers Her Superpower*. New York: St. Martin's, 2018.

Cordóva, Teresa. "Knowledge and Power: Colonialism in the Academy." In *Living Chicana Theory*, edited by Carla Trujillo, 17–45. Berkeley: Third Woman Press, 1998.

Covington-Ward, Yolanda. "Fighting Phantoms: Mammy, Matriarch, and Other Ghosts Haunting Black Mothers in the Academy." In *Laboring Positions: Black Women, Mothering, and the Academy*, edited by Sekile Nzinga-Johnson, 236–56. Bradford, ON: Demeter Press, 2013.

Craighead, W. Edward, and Charles B. Nemeroff, eds. *The Concise Corsini Encyclopedia of Psychology and Behavioral Science*. Hoboken, NJ: Wiley, 2004.

Crenshaw, Kimberlé. "Demarginalizing the Intersection of Race and Sex: A Black Feminist Critique of Antidiscrimination Doctrine,

Feminist Theory and Antiracist Politics." *University of Chicago Legal Forum*, no. 1 (1989): 139–67.

———. "Twenty Years of Critical Race Theory: Looking Back to Move Forward Commentary." *Connecticut Law Review* 43, no. 5 (July 2011): 1253–1353.

Creswell, John, and Cheryl Poth. *Qualitative Inquiry and Research Design: Choosing among Five Approaches*. 4th ed. Thousand Oaks: Sage, 2017.

Cunningham, Phillip Lamarr. "'There's Nothing Really New under the Sun': The Fallacy of the Neo-Soul Genre." *Journal of Popular Music Studies* 22 (September 2010): 240–58.

Dalla Costa, Mariarosa, and Selma James. "Women and the Subversion of the Community (1972)." In *Materialist Feminism: A Reader in Class, Difference, and Women's Lives*, edited by Rosemary Hennessy and Chrys Ingraham, 40–53. New York: Routledge, 1982.

Dancy, T. Elon, Kristen T. Edwards, and James Earl Davis. "Historically White Universities and Plantation Politics: Anti-Blackness and Higher Education in the Black Lives Matter Era." *Urban Education* 53, no. 2 (February 2018): 176–95.

Danticat, Edwidge. *The Farming of Bones*. New York: Soho Press, 1998.

Davis, Angela Y.. "Black Women and the Academy." *Callaloo* 17, no. 2 (1994): 422–31. https://doi.org/10.2307/2931740.

———. "Women and Capitalism: Dialectics of Oppression and Liberation." In *The Black Feminist Reader*, edited by Joy James, and T. Denean Sharpley-Whiting. Oxford: Blackwell Publishers, 2000.

Davis, Danielle Joy. "Mentorship and the Socialization of Underrepresented Minorities into the Professoriate: Examining Varied Influences." *Mentoring & Tutoring: Partnership in Learning* 16, no. 3 (August 2008): 278–93.

DeSouza, Flavia, Carmen Black Parker, E. Vanessa Spearman-McCarthy, Gina Newsome Duncan, and Reverend Maria Myers Black. "Coping with Racism: A Perspective of COVID-19 Church Closures on the Mental Health of African Americans." *Journal of Racial and Ethnic Health Disparities* 8, no. 1 (February 2021): 7–11.

de la Luz Reyes, María, and John J. Halcón. "Racism in Academia: The Old Wolf Revisited." *Harvard Educational Review* 58, no. 3 (1988): 299–314.

de Valero, Yaritza Ferrer. "Departmental Factors Affecting Time-to-Degree and Completion Rates of Doctoral Students at One

Land-Grant Research Institution." *Journal of Higher Education* 72, no. 3 (2001): 341–67.

Dewey, J. *How We Think: A Restatement of the Relation of Reflective Thinking to the Educative Process.* Boston: D. C. Heath, 1933.

Donohue, Dana K. "Religiosity and Multicultural Experiences Predict Cultural Values in College Students." *Current Psychology*, nos. 1–10 (2020): 539–48.

Dotter, Anne, and Cécile Accilien, "Accented Others, Women, and Immigrants: A Conversation about Institutional Stalling and Dismissal." In *Confronting Equity and Inclusion Incidents on Campus: Lessons Learned and Emerging Practices,* edited by Hannah Oliha-Donaldson, 188–200. New York: Routledge, 2020.

Du Bois, W. E. B. *The Souls of Black Folk.* Chicago: A. C. McClurg, 1903.

Durant, Thomas J., and J. David Knottnerus. *Plantation Society and Race Relations: The Origins of Inequality.* Westport, CT: Greenwood, 1999.

Durham, Aisha S. *Home with Hip Hop Feminism: Performances in Communication and Culture.* New York: Peter Lang, 2014.

Elbaz, Freema. "Hope, Attentiveness, and Caring for Difference: The Moral Voice in Teaching." *Teaching and Teacher Education* 8, nos. 5–6 (October–December 1992): 421–32.

El-Tayeb, Fatima. "'Blood Is a Very Special Juice': Racialized Bodies and Citizenship in Twentieth Century Germany." *International Review of Social History* 44, no. 7 (1999): 149–69.

———. "Dimensions of Diaspora: Women of Color Feminism, Black Europe, and Queer Memory Discourses." In *European Others: Queering Ethnicity in Postnational Europe,* 48–80. Minneapolis: University of Minnesota Press, 2011.

Elias, Ana Sofia, Rosalind Gill, and Christina Scharff. *Aesthetic Labour: Rethinking Beauty Politics in Neoliberalism.* London: Palgrave Macmillan, 2017.

Elk, Ronit, Linda Emanuel, Joshua Hauser, Marie Bakitas, and Sue Levkoff. "Developing and Testing the Feasibility of a Culturally Based Tele-palliative Care Consult Based on the Cultural Values and Preferences of Southern, Rural African American and White Community Members: A Program by and for the Community." *Health Equity* 4, no. 1 (March 2020): 52–83.

Ellis, Carolyn, Tony E. Adams, and Arthur P. Bochner. "Autoethnography: An Overview." *Historical Social Research/Historische*

Sozialforschung 36, no. 4 (2011): 273–90. http://www.jstor.org /stable/23032294.

Ellis, Evelynn M. "The Impact of Race and Gender on Graduate School Socialization, Satisfaction with Doctoral Study, and Commitment to Degree Completion." *Western Journal of Black Studies* 25, no. 1 (Spring 2001): 30–45.

El-Tayeb, Fatima. "'Blood Is a Very Special Juice': Racialized Bodies and Citizenship in Twentieth-Century Germany." *International Review of Social History* 44, no. 7 (1999): 149–69.

Esnard, Talia, and Deirdre Cobb-Roberts. *Black Women, Academe, and the Tenure Process in the United States and the Caribbean.* London: Palgrave Macmillan, 2018.

Etter-Lewis, Gwendolyn. "Black Women in Academe: Teaching/Administrating inside the Sacred Grove." In *Black Women in the Academy: Promises and Perils,* edited by Lois Benjamin, 81–90. Gainesville: University Press of Florida, 1997.

Evans, Stephanie Y. *Black Women in the Ivory Tower, 1850–1954: An Intellectual History.* Gainesville: University Press of Florida, 2007.

Feimster, Crystal N. "Not So Ivory: African American Women Historians Creating Academic Communities." In White, *Telling Histories,* 270–84. https://doi.org/10.5149/9780807889121_white.22.

Ferguson, Roderick A. *The Reorder of Things: The University and Its Pedagogies of Minority Difference.* Minneapolis: University of Minnesota Press, 2012.

Flaherty, Colleen. "Barely Getting By: New Report on Adjuncts Says Many Make Less than $3,500 Per Course and $25,000 Per Year." Inside Higher Ed, April 20, 2020. https:// www.insidehighered. com/news/2020/04/20/new-report-says-many-adjuncts -make-less-3500-course-and-25000-year.

Fleetwood, Nicole R. *Troubling Vision: Performance, Visuality, and Blackness.* Chicago: University of Chicago Press, 2011.

Flores, Juan, and Miriam Román. "Triple-Consciousness? Approaches to Afro-Latino Culture in the United States." *Latin American and Caribbean Ethnic Studies* 4 (2009): 319–28.

Fluker, Elayne. *Get Over "I Got It": How to Stop Playing Superwoman, Get Support, and Remember That Having It All Doesn't Mean Doing It All Alone.* New York: HarperCollins Leadership, 2021.

Fordham, Signithia, and John U. Ogbu. "Black Students' School Success: Coping with the Burden of 'Acting White.'" *Urban Review* 18 (September 1986): 176–206. https://doi.org/10.1007/BF01112192.

Fournillier, Janice B. "Plus ça change, plus c'est la même chose: An Afro Caribbean Scholar on the Higher Education Plantation." *Creative Approaches to Research* 3, no. 2 (December 2010): 52–62.

Gaertner, Samuel L., and John F. Dovidio. "Understanding and Addressing Contemporary Racism: From Aversive Racism to the Common Ingroup Identity Model." *Journal of Social Issues* 61, no. 3 (August 2005): 615–39.

Gilkes, Cheryl Townsend. "Going Up for the Oppressed: The Career Mobility of Black Women Community Workers." *Journal of Social Issues* 39, no. 3 (October 1983): 115–39.

Glover, M. H. "Existing Pathways: A Historical Overview of Black Women in Higher Education Administration." In *Pathways to Higher Education Administration for African American Women*, edited by Tamara Bertrand Jones, LeKita Scott Dawkins, Melanie Hayden Glover, and Marguerite M. McClinton, 4–17. Sterling, VA: Stylus Publishing, 2012.

Goldberg, David Theo. "The War on Critical Race Theory." *Boston Review*, accessed July 25, 2021. http://bostonreview.net/race -politics/david-theo-goldberg-war-critical-race-theory.

González, Deena J. Introduction to section 5, "Tenure and Promotion." In Gutiérrez y Muhs et al., *Presumed Incompetent*, 333–35.

Grant, Cosette M., and Juanita Cleaver Simmons. "Narratives on Experiences of African-American Women in the Academy: Conceptualizing Effective Mentoring Relationships of Doctoral Student and Faculty." *International Journal of Qualitative Studies in Education* 21, no. 5 (September 2008): 501–17. https:// www.tandfonline.com/doi/abs/10.1080/09518390802297789.

Gravley-Stack, Kara, Chris M. Ray, and Claudette M. Peterson. "Understanding the Subjective Experiences of the Chief Diversity Officer: AQ Method Study." *Journal of Diversity in Higher Education* 9, no. 2 (June 2016): 95–112.

Greb, Verena. "'Always Derogatory'? Germany Battles over the N-word," *Deutsche Welle*, February 2, 2020. https://p.dw.com/p/3XYrA.

Grey, ThedaMarie Gibbs, and Bonnie Williams-Farrier. "#Sippingtea: Two Black Female Literacy Scholars Sharing Counter-Stories to Redefine Our Roles in the Academy." *Journal of Literacy Research* 49, no. 4 (December 2017): 503–25.

Guillaume, Rene O., and Elizabeth C. Apodaca. "Early Career Faculty of Color and Promotion and Tenure: The Intersection of

Advancement in the Academy and Cultural Taxation." *Race Ethnicity and Education* 25, no. 4 (January 2020): 1–18.

Gururaj, Suchitra, Julian Vasquez Heilig, and Patricia Somers. "Graduate Student Persistence: Evidence from Three Decades." *Journal of Student Financial Aid* 40, no. 1 (January 2010): 31–46.

Gutiérrez y Muhs, Gabriella, Yolanda Flores Niemann, Carmen G. González, and Angela P. Harris, eds. *Presumed Incompetent: The Intersections of Race and Class for Women in Academia.* Boulder: University of Colorado Press, 2012.

Guy-Sheftall, Beverly. *Words of Fire: An Anthology of African American Feminist Thought.* New York: New Press, 1995.

———. *Words of Fire: An Anthology of African American Feminist Thought.* New York: New Press, 2011.

Hall, Stuart, and Paul Du Gay, eds. *Questions of Cultural Identity.* London: Sage Publications, 1996.

Hannah-Jones, Nikole. "Nikole Hannah-Jones Issues Statement on Decision to Decline Tenure Offer at University of North Carolina-Chapel Hill and to Accept Knight Chair Appointment at Howard University." *LDF,* July 6, 2021.

Hanson, Katherine, Vivian Guilfoy, and Sarita Pillai. *More than Title IX: How Equity in Education Has Shaped the Nation.* Lanham: Rowman & Littlefield, 2009.

Hardt, Michael, and Antonio Negri. *Empire.* Cambridge, MA: Harvard University Press, 2000.

Harnois, Catherine. "Race, Gender, and the Black Women's Standpoint." *Sociological Forum* 25, no. 1 (March 2010): 68–85.

Harris, Adam. "The Death of an Adjunct." *Atlantic,* April 8, 2019.

Harris, Angela P., and Carmen G. González. Introduction to Gutiérrez y Muhs et al., *Presumed Incompetent,* 1–14. Boulder: University of Colorado Press, 2012.

Harris-Perry, Melissa V. *Sister Citizen: Shame, Stereotypes, and Black Women in America.* New Haven, CT: Yale University Press, 2011.

Harrison, Rashida L. "Building a Canon, Creating Dialogue: An Interview with Cheryl A. Wall." In *Written/Unwritten: Diversity and the Hidden Truths of Tenure,* edited by Patricia A. Matthew, 46–64. Chapel Hill: University of North Carolina Press, 2016.

Harley, Debra A. "Maids of Academe: African American Women Faculty at Predominately White Institutions." *Journal of African American Studies* 12, no. 1 (March 2008): 19–36.

Hartman, Saidiya. "The Territory between Us: A Report on 'Black Women in the Academy: Defending Our Name: 1894–1994.'"

Callaloo 17, no. 2 (1994): 439–49. https://www.jstor.org/stable
/2931742?seq=1#page_scan_tab_contents.

———. *Wayward Lives, Beautiful Experiments: Intimate Histories of
Riotous Black Girls, Troublesome Women, and Queer Radicals.*
New York: W. W. Norton, 2019.

Harvey, William B. "Chief Diversity Officers and the Wonderful World of
Academe." *Journal of Diversity in Higher Education* 7, no. 2 (June
2014): 92–100.

Hendricks, Wanda A. "On the Margins: Creating a Space and Place in
the Academy." In White, *Telling Histories*, 146–57.

Hernandez, Kathy-Ann, Faith Wambura Ngunjiri, and Heewon Chang.
"Exploiting the Margins in Higher Education: A Collaborative
Autoethnography of Three Foreign-Born Female Faculty of
Color." *International Journal of Qualitative Studies in Education*
28, no. 5 (2014): 533–51.

Hill, Lauryn. *MTV Unplugged No. 2.0.* Columbia, 2002, Spotify.

Hirshfield, Laura E., and Tiffany D. Joseph, "'We Need a Woman, We
Need a Black Woman': Gender, Race, and Identity Taxation
in the Academy." *Gender and Education* 24, no. 2 (2012):
213–27.

hooks, bell. "Black Women Intellectuals." In *Breaking Bread: Insurgent
Black Intellectual Life,* edited by bell hooks and Cornell West,
147–65. Boston: South End Press, 1991.

———. *Talking Back: Thinking Feminist, Thinking Black.* London: Taylor &
Francis Group, 2014.

———. *Yearning: Race, Gender, and Cultural Politics.* Boston: South End,
1990.

House, Jeremy. "How Faculty of Color Hurt Their Careers Helping
Universities with Diversity." *Diverse: Issues in Higher Education,*
November 27, 2017. http://diverseeducation.com/article/105525/?
fbclid=IwARopxGY8OG3jGd-k7zidWw65Ws7iaUHN9n-LM38
-vt-3yYT6zQ3lf9uLBwU.

Huddleston-Mattai, Barbara. "The Black Female Academician and the
'Superwoman Syndrome.'" *Race, Gender & Class* 3, no. 1 (Fall
1995): 49–64.

Hügel-Marshall, Ika. *Invisible Woman: Growing up Black in Germany,*
trans. Elizabeth Gaffney. New York: Continuum, 2001.

Hurston, Zora Neale. *Their Eyes Were Watching God.* Champaign:
University of Illinois Press, 1978.

———. *Their Eyes Were Watching God: A Novel.* London: Virago, 1986.

———. *Their Eyes Were Watching God.* New York: HarperCollins, 1998.

———. *Their Eyes Were Watching God*. New York: Harper Collins, 2000.

Indiana University–Bloomington. Division of Student Affairs, Student Advocates Office. "We Listen. We Connect. We Advocate." https://studentaffairs.indiana.edu/student-support/advocates/index.html.

INSIGHT Staff. "An INSIGHT Investigation: Accounting for Just 0.5% of Higher Education's Budgets, Even Minimal Diversity Funding Supports Their Bottom Line." INSIGHT Into Diversity, October 16, 2019. https://www.insightintodiversity.com/an-insight-invest igation-accounting-for-just-0-5-of-higher-educations-budgets-even-minimal-diversity-funding-supports-their-bottom-line/.

Jackson, Kellie Carter. "I Am a Black Woman in Academia. Nikole Hannah-Jones's Tenure Saga Isn't Unique." WBUR, July 9, 2021. https://www.wbur.org/cognoscenti/2021/07/09/nikole-hannah -jones-unc-howard-black-women-in-academia-kellie-carter-jackson?fbclid=IwAR3GhcY9tLdVPUJ-lt7i3HKWtZqoC4MHx LfVKPYqiXEOF_2VHqIIbmSjsTQ.

Jacobs, Harriet. *Incidents in the Life of a Slave Girl*. Unabridged ed. 1861; Mineola: Dover, 2001.

Jaschik, Scott. "Next Generation President." Inside Higher Ed, February 7, 2008. https://www.insidehighered.com/news/2008/02/07 /next-generation-president#.Y82vou36RgA.link.

Jimenez y West, Ilda, Gokce Gokalp, Edlyn Vallejo Pena, Linda Fischer, and Jarrett Gupton. "Exploring Effective Support Practices for Doctoral Students' Degree Completion." *College Student Journal* 45, no. 2 (June 2011): 310–23.

Jones, Brandolyn, Eunjin Hwang, and Rebecca M. Bustamante. "African American Female Professors' Strategies for Successful Attainment of Tenure and Promotion at Predominately White Institutions: It Can Happen." *Education, Citizenship and Social Justice* 10, no. 2 (July 1, 2015): 133–51. https://doi.org/10.1177/17461979155 83934.

Jordan, Mary. "Citadel Ordered to Admit Woman." *Washington Post*, July 23, 1994. https://www.washingtonpost.com/archive/politics /1994/07/23/citadel-ordered-to-admit-woman/5c699301-ac47 -457f-898f-6c4a584d3cf2/.

Joseph, Gloria. "The Incompatible Menage à Trois: Marxism, Feminism, and Racism (1981)." In *Materialist Feminism: A Reader in Class, Difference, and Women's Lives*, edited by Rosemary Ingraham and Chrys Hennessy, 107–9. New York: Routledge, 1982.

June, Aubrey Williams, and Brian O'Leary. "How Many Black Women Have Tenure on Your Campus?" *Chronicle of Higher Education*, May 27, 2021. https://www.chronicle.com/.

Kappert, Annette. "Professional and Personal Experiences as Leverage for Learning." *Frontiers in Education* 5 (July 21, 2020): 98. https://doi.org/10.3389/feduc.2020.00098.

Kelsky, Karen. *The Professor Is In: The Essential Guide to Turning Your Ph.D. into a Job*. New York: Three Rivers Press, 2015.

Kendall, Mikki. *Hood Feminism: Notes from the Women That a Movement Forgot*. New York: Viking, 2020.

Kershaw, Terry. "Afrocentrism and the Afrocentric Method." *Western Journal of Black Studies* 16, no. 3 (Fall 1992): 160–68.

Kilomba, Grada. *Plantation Memories: Episodes of Everyday Racism*. Münster, Germany: Unrast-Verlag, 2008.

King, Martin Luther. "Letter from a Birmingham Jail" (1963). https://www.africa.upenn.edu/Articles_Gen/Letter_Birmingham.html.

Kovel, Joel. *White Racism: A Psychohistory*. New York: Pantheon, 1970.

Kramer, Andie. "Recognizing Workplace Challenges Faced by Black Women Leaders." *Forbes*, January 7, 2020. https://www.forbes.com/sites/andiekramer/2020/01/07/recognizing-workplace-challenges-faced-by-black-women-leaders/?sh=514c24cf53e3.

Kroeber, Alfred L., and Talcott Parsons. "The Concepts of Culture and of Social System." *American Sociological Review* 23, no. 5 (1958): 582–83.

Kupenda, Angela M. "Facing Down the Spooks." In *Presumed Incompetent: The Intersections of Race and Class for Women in Academia*, edited by Gabriella Gutiérrez y Muhs, Yolanda Flores Niemann, Carmen G. González, and Angela P. Harris, 20–28. Boulder: University of Colorado Press, 2012.

Kuykendall, J., S. Johnson, Thomas F. Nelson Laird, Ted N. Ingram, and Amanda Suniti Niskode. "Finding Time: An Examination of Faculty of Color Workload and Non-Instructional Activities by Rank." Paper presented at the annual meeting of the Association for the Study of Higher Education, Anaheim, CA, November 2–4, 2006. Microsoft Word - 2006 ASHE Workload Paper.doc (iu.edu).

Kwhali, J. "The Accidental Academic." In *Inside the Ivory Tower: Narratives of Women of Colour Surviving and Thriving in British Academia*, edited by D. Gabriel and S. Tate, 5–22. London: Trentham Books, 2017.

LeanIn.Org and McKinsey & Company. "The State of Black Women in Corporate America." 2020. https://media.sgff.io/sgff_r1eHet bDYb/2020-08-13/1597343917539/Lean_In_-_State_of_Black _Women_in_Corporate_America_Report_1.pdf.

Lee, Cynthia. "Surviving a Difficult Tenure Process." In *Presumed Incompetent II: Race, Class, Power, and Resistance of Women in Academia*, edited by Yolanda Flores Niemann, Gabriella Gutiérrez y Muhs, and Carmen G. González, 48–58. Logan: Utah State University Press, an imprint of University Press of Colorado, 2020.

Lee, Michael Y., Melissa Mazmanian, and Leslie Perlow. "Fostering Positive Relational Dynamics: The Power of Spaces and Interaction Scripts." *Academy of Management Journal* 63, no. 1 (February 2020): 96–123.

Lennox, Sara, ed. *Remapping Black Germany: New Perspectives on Afro-German History, Politics, and Culture.* Amherst: University of Massachusetts Press, 2016.

Leonard, Pauline, and Danusia Malina. "Caught between Two Worlds: Mothers as Academics." In *Changing the Subject: Women in Higher Education*, ed. Sue Davies, Cathy Lubelska, and Jocey Quinn. Abingdon, England: Taylor & Francis, 1994.

Lewis, John (@repjohnlewis). Twitter, June 27, 2018, 8:15a.m. https:// twitter.com/repjohnlewis/status/1011991303599607808?lang=en.

Lewis-Flenaugh, Jamie, Sharee L. Myricks, and Eboni N. Turnbow. "When Intersections Collide: Young Black Women Combat Sexism, Racism, and Ageism in Higher Education." In *Black Women and Social Justice Education: Legacies and Lessons*, edited by Andrea D. Domingue, Stephanie Y. Evans, and Tania D. Mitchell, 55–66. Albany: State University of New York Press, 2019.

Library Journal Reviews. "Literary Afrofuturism, Black Art Renaissance, End of the Middle Passage, and More in African History." *Academic Best Sellers. Library Journal*, September 22, 2021. https://www.libraryjournal.com/?detailStory=literary-afrofutur ism-black-art-renaissance-end-of-the-middle-passage-african -history-academic-best-sellers.

Lomax, Tamura. "Black Women's Lives Don't Matter in Academia Either, or Why I Quit Academic Spaces that Don't Value Black Women's Life and Labor." *Feminist Wire*, May 18, 2015. https://thefeminist wire.com/2015/05/black-womens-lives-dont-matter-in-aca demia-either-or-why-i-quit-academic-spaces-that-dont-value -black-womens-life/.

Lorde, Audre. *The Cancer Journals*. San Francisco: Aunt Lute, 1997.

———. "Eye to Eye: Black Women, Hatred, and Anger." In *Sister Outsider* (2007).

———. "The Master's Tools Will Never Dismantle the Master's House." In *Sister Outsider* (1984), 110–13.

———. "Poetry Is Not a Luxury." In *Sister Outsider* (Berkeley: Crossing Press, 1984), 36–39.

———. *Sister Outsider. Essays and Speeches.* Trumansburg, NY: Crossing Press, 1984.

———. *Sister Outsider. Essays and Speeches by Audre Lorde.* Berkeley: Crossing Press, 1984.

———. *Sister Outsider. Essays and Speeches.* Berkeley: Crossing Press, 2007.

———. "Uses of Anger: Women Responding to Racism." In *The Master's Tools Will Never Dismantle the Master's House.* London: Penguin Random House UK, 2017. Originally given as a keynote presentation at the National Women's Studies Association Conference, Storrs, CT, 1981.

———. "The Uses of Anger: Women Responding to Racism." *Women's Studies Quarterly* 9, no. 3 (Fall 1981): 7–10.

———. "The Uses of the Erotic: The Erotic as Power." https://uk.sagepub. com/sites/default/files/upm-binaries/11881_Chapter_5.pdf.

Love, Barbara J., and Valerie D. Jiggetts. "Foreword: Black Women Rising: Jumping Double-Dutch with a Liberatory Consciousness." In *Black Women and Social Justice Education: Legacies and Lessons*, edited by Stephanie Y. Evans, Andrea D. Domingue, and Tania D. Mitchell, xi–xx. Albany: State University of New York Press, 2019.

Love, Bettina L., and Sarah Abdelaziz. "We Got a Lot to Be Mad About: A Seat at Solange's Table." In *Black Women and Social Justice Education: Legacies and Lessons*, edited by Stephanie Y. Evans, Andrea D. Domingue, and Tania D. Mitchell, 165–80. Albany: State University of New York Press, 2019.

Luney, LeAnna T. "Coping to Survive the 'Wild West': Black College Womxn and Femmes Enduring Anti-Black Gendered Racism in a University of the American West." PhD diss., University of Colorado–Boulder, 2021.

Mabokela, Reitumetse Obakeng, and Zine Magubane. *Hear Our Voices: Race, Gender, and the State of Black South African Women in the Academy.* Pretoria: University of South Africa Press, 2004.

Macaulay, Alexander. *Marching in Step: Masculinity, Citizenship, and the Citadel in Post–World War II America*. Athens: University of Georgia Press, 2009.

Madyum, Na'im, Sheneka M. Williams, Ebony O. McGee, and H. Richard Milner IV. "On the Importance of African-American Faculty in Higher Education: Implications and Recommendations." *Educational Foundations* 27, nos. 3–4 (2013): 65–84.

Manz, Charles. "Self-Leadership: Toward an Expanded Theory of Self-Influence Processes in Organizations." *Academy of Management Review* 11, no. 3 (1986): 585–600.

Marshall, Yannick. "An Appeal: Bring the Maroon to the Foreground in Black Intellectual History." *Black Perspectives*, June 19, 2020. https://www.aaihs.org/an-appeal-bring-the-maroon-to-the-foreground-in-black-intellectual-history/.

Matias, Cheryl E. "'I Ain't Your Doc Student': The Overwhelming Presence of Whiteness and Pain at the Academic Neoplantation." In *Racial Battle Fatigue in Higher Education: Exposing the Myth of Post-Racial America*, edited by Kenneth J. Fasching-Varner, Katrice A. Albert, Roland W. Mitchell, and Chaunda Allen, 59–68. Lanham: Rowman & Littlefield, 2015.

Matthew, Patricia A. "What Is Faculty Diversity Worth to a University?" *Atlantic*, November 23, 2016. https://www.theatlantic.com/education/archive/2016/11/what-is-faculty-diversity-worth-to-a-university/508334/.

Maundeni, Tapologo, and Godisang Mookodi. "The Experiences of Two Female Academics at the University of Botswana." *Asian Women* 22, no. 3 (2006): 63–80.

McGee, Ebony O. "Ready to be an Ally for Black Academics? Here's a Start." *Chronicle of Higher Education*, November 11, 2020. https://www.chronicle.com/article/ready-to-be-an-ally-for-black-academics-heres-a-start.

McKay, Nellie. "Black Woman Professor—White University." In "Women in Academe." Special issue, *Women's Studies International Forum* 6, no. 2 (January 1, 1983): 143–47. https://doi.org/10.1016/027753 95(83)90004-3.

Meat Loaf. "Two Out of Three Ain't Bad." *Bat Out of Hell*. Cleveland International, 1977, album.

Mihalyfy, David. "When Is Criticism Bullying?" Inside Higher Ed, May 11, 2021. https://www.insidehighered.com/advice/2021/05/11/four-ways-determine-when-criticism-has-become-bullying-academe-opinion.

Mikaelian, Allen. "The 2013 Jobs Report: Number of AHA Ads Dip, New Experiment Offers Expanded View." Perspectives on History, January 1, 2014. https://www.historians.org/publications-and-direct ories/perspectives-on-history/january-2014/the-2013-jobs-report -number-of-aha-ads-dip-new-experiment-offers-expanded-view.

Minnett, Jari L., ArCasia D. James-Gallaway, and Devean R. Owens. "Help A Sista Out: Black Women Doctoral Students' Use of Peer Mentorship as an Act of Resistance." *Mid-Western Educational Researcher* 31, no. 2 (2019): 210–38.

Mirza, Heidi Safia. "Postcolonial Subjects, Black Feminism and the Intersectionality of Race and Gender in Higher Education." *Counterpoints* 369 (2009): 233–48.

Mitchell, Koritha. *From Slave Cabins to the White House: Homemade Citizenship in African American Culture*. Champaign: University of Illinois Press, 2020.

Moll, L. "Reflections and Possibilities." In *Funds of Knowledge: Theorizing Practices in Households, Communities, and Classrooms*, edited by Norma Gonzalez, Luis C. Moll, and Cathy Amanti, 275–88. Mahwah, NJ: Lawrence Erlbaum, 2005.

Monroe, Kristen, Saba Ozyurt, Ted Wrigley, and Amy Alexander. "Gender Equality in Academia: Bad News from the Trenches, and Some Possible Solutions." *Perspectives on Politics* 6, no. 2 (June 2008): 215–33.

Moore, James L., III, and Marjorie C. Shavers. "The Double-Edged Sword: Coping and Resiliency Strategies of African American Women Enrolled in Doctoral Programs at Predominately White Institutions." *Frontiers: A Journal of Women Studies* 35, no. 3 (September 2014): 15–38.

Morrison, Toni. *Song of Solomon*. New York: Knopf, 1977.

Motro, Daphna, Jonathan Evans, Aleksander P. J. Ellis, and Lehman Benson. "Race and Reactions to Negative Feedback: Examining the Effects of the 'Angry Black Woman' Stereotype." *Academy of Management Proceedings*, no. 1 (August 2019).

National Center for Education Statistics. "Characteristics of Postsecondary Faculty," May 2020. https://nces.ed.gov/programs/coe/indica tor/csc.

Neck, Christopher, Charles Manz, and Jeffrey Houghton. *Self-Leadership: The Definitive Guide to Personal Excellence*. 2nd ed. Thousand Oaks: Sage, 2019.

Ngunjiri, Faith Wambura, and Kathy-Ann Hernandez. "Problematizing Authentic Leadership: A Collaborative Autoethnography of

Immigrant Women of Color Leaders in Higher Education." *Advances in Developing Human Resources* 19, no. 4 (October 2017): 394–406.

Niemann, Yolanda Flores. "Lessons from the Experiences of Women of Color Working in Academia." In *Presumed Incompetent: The Intersections of Race and Class for Women in Academia,* edited by Gabriella Gutiérrez y Muhs, Yolanda Flores Niemann, Carmen G. González, and Angela P. Harris, 446–500. Boulder: University of Colorado Press, 2012.

———. "The Making of a Token: A Case Study of Stereotype Threat, Stigma, Racism, and Tokenism in Academe." In Gutiérrez y Muhs et al., *Presumed Incompetent,* 336–55.

Niemann, Yolanda Flores, Gabriella Gutiérrez y Muhs, and Carmen G. González. *Presumed Incompetent II: Race, Class, Power, and Resistance of Women in Academia.* Logan: Utah State University Press, an imprint of the University Press of Colorado, 2020.

Nixon, Monica L. "Experiences of Women of Color University Chief Diversity Officers." *Journal of Diversity in Higher Education* 10, no. 4 (December 2017): 301–17.

Nzinga, Sekile M. *Lean Semesters: How Higher Education Reproduces Inequity.* Baltimore, MD: Johns Hopkins University Press, 2020.

Ogbogu, Christiana O., "Gender Inequality in Academia: Evidences from Nigeria." *Contemporary Issues in Education Research* 4, no. 9 (September 2011): 1–8.

Oksala, Johanna. "Affective Labor and Feminist Politics." *Signs: Journal of Women in Culture and Society* 41, no. 2 (2016): 281–303.

Otoo, Sharon Dodua. "'The Speaker Is Using the N-Word': A Transnational Comparison (Germany-Great Britain) of Resistance to Racism in Everyday Language." In *Rassismuskritik und Widerstandsformen,* edited by Meral El and Karim Fereidooni, 291–305. Wiesbaden: Springer, 2017.

Pace, Cindy. "How Women of Color Get to Senior Management." *Harvard Business Review,* August 31, 2018.

Patton, Lori D., and Chayla Haynes. "Hidden in Plain Sight: The Black Women's Blueprint for Institutional Transformation in Higher Education." *Teachers College Record* 120, 14 (2018).

Peña, Rosemarie. "From Both Sides of the Atlantic: Black German Adoptee Searches in William Gage's Geborener Deutscher (Born German)." *Genealogy* 2, no. 4 (October 2018): 13–20.

———. "Stories Matter: Contextualizing Black German American Adoptee Experience(s)." In *International Adoption in North American Literature and Culture: Transnational, Transracial and Transcultural Narratives*, edited by Mark Shackleton, 197–221. London: Palgrave-Macmillian, 2017.

Perlow, Olivia N., Durene I. Wheeler, Sharon L. Bethea, and Barbara M. Scott. *Black Women's Liberatory Pedagogies: Resistance, Transformation, and Healing Within and Beyond the Academy*. Cham, Switzerland: Palgrave Macmillan, 2018.

Peterson, Carla L. "Foreword: Eccentric Bodies." In *Bodies in Dissent: Spectacular Performances of Race and Freedom, 1850–1910*, edited by Daphne A. Brooks, x–xi. Durham, NC: Duke University Press, 2004.

Piepzna-Samarasinha, Leah Lakshmi. *Care Work: Dreaming Disability Justice*. Vancouver: Arsenal Pulp Press, 2018.

Pillay, Daisy, Inanathan Naicker, and Kathleen Pithouse-Morgan. *Academic Autoethnographies: Inside Teaching in Higher Education*. Rotterdam: Sense Publishers, 2016.

Pittman, Chavella T. "Race and Gender Oppression in the Classroom: The Experiences of Women Faculty of Color with White Male Students." *Teaching Sociology* 38, no. 3 (July 2010).

———. "Racial Microaggressions: The Narratives of African American Faculty at a Predominantly White University." *Journal of Negro Education* 81, no. 1 (Winter 2012): 82–92.

Pitts, Britney. "'Uneasy Lies the Head That Wears a Crown': A Critical Analysis of the CROWN ACT." *Journal of Black Studies* 52, no. 7 (June 2021): 716–35.

Porter, Christa J., Candace M. Moore, Ginny J. Boss, Tiffany J. Davis, and Dave A. Louis. "To Be Black Women and Contingent Faculty: Four Scholarly Personal Narratives." *Journal of Higher Education* 91, no. 5 (2020): 674–97.

Prempeh, Prince D. GYE W'ANI: A Symbol of Enjoyment, Celebration. Akindrabrand, October 18, 2020. https://www.adinkrabrand.com/blogs/portfolio/gye-w-ani-enjoy-yourself.

President's Council on Inclusive Excellence 12th Annual Report. Indiana State University, July 23, 2020. https://www.indstate.edu/sites/default/files/media/equal-opportunity/inclusive-excellence-12th-report-final4.pdf.

Puwar, Nirmal. "Thinking about Making a Difference." *British Journal of Politics and International Relations* 6, no. 1 (February 2004): 65–80.

Pyke, Karen D. "Service and Gender Inequity among Faculty." *PS: Political Science and Politics* 44, no. 1 (January 2010): 85–87.

Quash, Tiffany Monique. "Academic Hazing Is Abuse—WOC Guest Post." *The Professor Is In* (blog), ed. Karen Kelsky, August 22, 2019. https://theprofessorisin.com/2019/08/22/academic-hazing-is-abuse-woc-guest-post/.

"The Racial Insult Built into the National Merit Scholarship Program." *Journal of Blacks in Higher Education*, no. 32 (Summer 2001): 30–32. https://doi.org/10.2307/2678755.

Rankine, Claudia. *Citizen: An American Lyric*. Minneapolis: Graywolf, 2014.

Ransby, Barbara. "Dancing on the Edge of History, but Never Dancing Alone." In White, *Telling Histories*, 240–51.

Roach, Shoniqua. Black Respectable Currency: Reading Black Feminism and Sexuality in Contemporary Performance. *Journal of American Culture* 42 (2019): 10–20.

Rockquemore, Kerry Ann, and Tracey A. Laszloffy. *The Black Academic's Guide to Winning Tenure—Without Losing Your Soul*. Boulder, Utah: Lynne Reiner, 2008.

Rojas, Fabio. *From Black Power to Black Studies: How a Radical Social Movement Became an Academic Discipline*. Baltimore, MD: Johns Hopkins University Press, 2007.

Rollock, Nicola, David Gillborn, Carol Vincent, and Stephen Ball. *The Colour of Class: The Educational Strategies of the Black Middle Classes*. Abingdon, England: Routledge, 2014.

Rosette, Ashleigh Shelby, and Robert W. Livingston. "Failure Is Not an Option for Black Women: Effects of Organizational Performance on Leaders with Single Versus Dual-Subordinate Identities." *Journal of Experimental Social Psychology* 48, no. 5 (September 2012): 1162–67.

Roy, Arundhati. "The Pandemic Is a Portal." *Financial Times*, April 3, 2020.

Rushin, Donna Kate. "The Bridge Poem." In *This Bridge Called My Back: Writing by Radical Women of Color*, edited by Cherrie Moraga and Gloria Anzaldua, lvii–lviii. New York: Kitchen Table: Women of Color Press, 1983.

Saint-Exupéry, Antoine de. "Citadelle." In *Oeuvres*, sec. 75. (1948; repr., Paris: Gallimard, 1959).

Sampson, Melva L. "I'm Exhausted but I Do Want to Be Well: Raising Womanish Girls, the Performance of Mothering and Wading in Murky Waters." Feminist Wire, October 12, 2012. https://the feministwire.com/2012/10/im-exhausted-but-i-do-want-to-be

-well-raising-womanish-girls-the-performance-of-mothering
-and-wading-in-murky-waters/.

Santos, Joana Dos. "Who Are These Diversity Officers?" *Higher Education Today* (blog), May 20, 2020. https://www.higheredtoday.
org/2020/05/20/who-are-these-diversity-officers/.

Schnall, Marianne. "When Black Women Lead, We All Win: 10 Inspiring
Leaders Show Us the Way." *Forbes*, August 17, 2020. https://www
.forbes.com/sites/marianneschnall/2020/08/17/when-black-
women-lead-we-all-win/?sh=86e2ab74513d.

See, Sarita Echavez. "Talking Tenure Don't Be Safe: Because There Is No
Safety There Anyway." In *Written/Unwritten: Diversity and the
Hidden Truths of Tenure*, edited by Patricia A. Matthew, 148–62.
Chapel Hill: University of North Carolina Press, 2016.

Shapin, Steven. The Ivory Tower: The History of a Figure of Speech and
Its Cultural Uses. *British Society for the History of Science* 45, no.
1 (March 2012): 1–27.

Sharpe, Christina Elizabeth. *In the Wake: On Blackness and Being.*
Durham, NC: Duke University Press, 2016.

Shung-King, Maylene, Lucy Gilson, Chinyere Mbachu, Sassy Molyneux,
Kelly W. Muraya, Nkoli Uguru, and Veloshnee Govender.
"Leadership Experiences and Practices of South African Health
Managers: What Is the Influence of Gender? A Qualitative,
Exploratory Study." *International Journal for Equity in Health* 17,
no. 1 (September 2018): 148–60.

Simmons, Ruth J., and Anthony Bogues. "'A Simple Questions Needed to
be Met with a Straightforward Answer': An Interview with
Brown University President Emerita Dr. Ruth J. Simmons."
January 11, 2021. https://slaveryandjusticereport.brown.edu
/essays/simmons-bogues/.

Simone, Nina. "Mississippi Goddam." Track 7 on *Nine Simone in Concert.*
Philips, 1964.

Smith, Barbara. "Where's the Revolution? (1993)." In *Materialist Feminism: A Reader in Class, Difference, and Women's Lives*, edited by
Rosemary Hennessy and Chrys Ingraham, 248–52. New York:
Routledge, 1997.

Smith, Carolyn, and Bonnie E. Carlson. "Stress, Coping, and Resilience
in Children and Youth." *Social Service Review* 71, no. 2 (June
1997): 231–56.

Smith, Linda. *Decolonizing Methodologies.* London: Zed Books, 1999.

Smith, William. "Black Faculty Coping with Racial Battle Fatigue: The
Campus Racial Climate in a Post-Civil Rights Era." In *A Long*

Way to Go: Conversations about Race by African American Faculty and Graduate Students, edited by Darrell Cleveland, 171–90. New York: Peter Lang, 2004.

Social Sciences Feminist Network Research Interest Group. "The Burden of Invisible Work in Academia: Social Inequalities and Time Use in Five University Departments." In "Diversity and Social Justice in Higher Education," edited by Joshua Smith and Meredith Conover-Williams, 228–45. Special issue, *Humboldt Journal of Social Relations* 39 (May 2017).

Sow, Noah. "Geteilte Geschichte: Inaugural Conference Report." In *Black German Heritage and Research Association*. Washington, D.C.: German Historical Institute-DC, 2011.

Squire, Dian D., and Kristin McCann. "Women of Color with Critical Worldviews Constructing Spaces of Resistance in Education Doctoral Programs." *Journal of College Student Development* 59, no. 4 (July 2018): 404–20.

Squire, Dian D., Bianca Williams, and Frank Tuitt. "Plantation Politics and Neoliberal Racism in Higher Education: A Framework for Reconstructing Anti-Racist Institutions." *Teachers College Record* 120, no. 14 (April 2018): 1–2.

Stanley, Christine A. "Coloring the Academic Landscape: Faculty of Color Breaking the Silence in Predominantly White Colleges and Universities." *American Educational Research Journal* 43, no. 4 (Winter 2006): 701–36.

Stansell, Kaitlin. "Citadel Cadets Will Change Companies after Freshmen Year Starting in 2020." Live 5 WCSC, February 14, 2019. https://www.live5news.com/2019/02/14/citadel-cadets-will-change-companies-after-freshmen-year-starting/.

Stewart, Lindsey. *The Politics of Black Joy: Zora Neale Hurston and Neo-Abolitionism* Chicago: University of Chicago Press, 2021.

Sue, Derald Wing, Christina M. Capodilupo, Gina C. Torino, Jennifer M. Bucceri, Aisha M. B. Holder , Kevin L. Nadal, and Marta Esquilin. "Racial Microaggressions in Everyday Life: Implications for Clinical Practice." *American Psychologist* 62, no. 4 (2007): 271–86. https://doi.org/10.1037/0003-066X.62.4.271.

Sverdlik, Anna, Nathan C. Hall, Lynn McAlpine, and Kyle Hubbard. "The PhD Experience: A Review of the Factors Influencing Doctoral Students' Completion, Achievement, and Well-Being." *International Journal of Doctoral Studies* 13, no. 1 (2018): 362–88.

Tate, Shirley Ann, and Deborah Gabriel, eds. *Inside the Ivory Tower: Narratives of Women of Colour Surviving and Thriving in Academia*. London: UCL Institute of Education Press, 2017.

Taylor, Ula. "The Death of Dry Tears." In White, *Telling Histories*, 172–81.

Tevis, Tenisha, Marcia Hernandez, and Rhonda Bryant. "Reclaiming Our Time: An Autoethnographic Exploration of Black Women Higher Education Administrators." *Journal of Negro Education* 89, no. 3 (Summer 2020): 282–97.

Thomas, Gloria D., and Carol Hollenshead. "Resisting from the Margins: The Coping Strategies of Black Women and Other Women of Color Faculty Members at a Research University." *Journal of Negro Education* 70 (July 2001): 166–75.

Thompson, Lisa B. *Beyond the Black Lady: Sexuality and the New African American Middle Class*. Champaign: University of Illinois Press, 2012.

Ulysse, Gina Athena. "Groundings on *Rasanblaj* with M. Jacqui Alexander." Accessed July 25, 2021. https://hemisphericinstitute.org/en/emisferica-121-caribbean-rasanblaj/12-1-essays/e-121-essay-alexander-interview-with-gina.html.

U.S. Department of Education. National Center for Education Statistics. Integrated Postsecondary Education Data System (IPEDS), IPEDS Spring 2021, Human Resources component, Fall Staff section. See Digest of Education Statistics 2021, table 315.20." http://nces.ed.gov/programs/coe/indicator/csc#3.

Vásquez, Yomaira Figueroa, and Jessica Marie Johnson. "[Taller] Electric Marronage." Updated July 25, 2021. https://www.electricmarronage.com/.

Võ, Linda Trinh. "Navigating the Academic Terrain: The Racial and Gender Politics of Elusive Belonging." *Presumed Incompetent: The Intersections of Race and Class for Women in Academia*, edited by Gabriella Gutiérrez y Muhs, Yolanda Flores Niemann, Carmen G. González, and Angela P. Harris, 93–109. Boulder: University of Colorado Press, 2012.

Walker-Barnes, Chanequa. "When the Bough Breaks: The StrongBlackWoman and the Embodiment of Stress." In *Black Women's Mental Health: Balancing Strength and Vulnerability*, edited by Stephanie Y. Evans, Kanika Bell, and Nsenga K. Burton, 43–55. Albany: State University of New York Press, 2017.

Walkington, Lori. "How Far Have We Really Come? Black Women Faculty and Graduate Experiences in Higher Education." In

"Diversity and Social Justice in Higher Education," edited by Joshua Smith and Meredith Conover-Williams, 51–65. Special issue, *Humboldt Journal of Social Relations* 39 (May 2017).

Wallace, Jennifer. "From Foster to the Future." *The Citadel: The Magazine of the Military College of South Carolina* (2019). https://magazine.citadel.edu/2019/from-foster-to-the-future/.

Wallace, Michele. *Black Macho and the Myth of the Superwoman.* New York: Dial Press, 1999.

Wallace, Sherri L., Sharon E. Moore, and Carla M. Curtis. "Black Women as Scholars and Social Agents: Standing in the Gap." *Negro Educational Review* 65, nos. 1–4 (2014): 44–62.

Wallace, Sherri L., Sharon E. Moore, Linda L. Wilson, and Brenda G. Hart. "African American Women in the Academy: Quelling the Myth of Presumed Incompetence." In *Presumed Incompetent: The Intersections of Race and Class for Women in Academia,* edited by Gabriella Gutiérrez y Muhs, Yolanda Flores Niemann, Carmen G. González, and Angela P. Harris, 421–38. Boulder: University of Colorado Press, 2012.

Wandert, Timo, Randolph Ochsmann, Peary Brug, Aneta Chybicka, Marie-Françoise Lacassine, and Maykel Verkuyten. "Black German Identities: Validating the Multidimensional Inventory of Black Identity." *Journal of Black Psychology* 35, no. 4 (January 2009): 456–84.

Washburn, Jennifer. *University Inc.: The Corporate Corruption of American Higher Education.* Cambridge, MA: Perseus Books Group, 2005.

Watkins, Tionne. *Thoughts.* New York: HarperCollins, 1999.

Wehnert, Kathleen. *Passing: An Exploration of African Americans on Their Journey for Identity along the Colour Line.* Hamberg: DiplomicaVerlag GmbH, 2010.

West, I. J., Gokce Gokalp, Edlyn Vallejo Pena, Linda Fischer, and Jarrett Gupton. "Exploring Effective Support Practices for Doctoral Students' Degree Completion." *College Student Journal* 45, no. 2 (June 2011): 310–23.

White, Deborah Gray. "Introduction: A Telling History." In *Telling Histories,* 1–27.

———, ed. *Telling Histories: Black Women Historians in the Ivory Tower.* Chapel Hill: University of North Carolina Press, 2008.

White, Gillian B. "The Recession's Racial Slant." *Atlantic,* June 24, 2015. https://www.theatlantic.com/business/archive/2015/06/black-recession-housing-race/396725/.

Whitehead, Karsonya Wise. "Commentary: HBCU Graduates: We Just See the World Differently." Afro News: The Black Media Authority, May 21, 2022. https://afro.com/commentary-hbcu-gradu ates-we-just-see-the-world-differently/.

———. "5 Women Who Influenced Me: Karsonya Wise Whitehead." *Maryland Daily Record*, February 18, 2021. https://thedaily record.com/2021/02/18/5-women-who-influenced-me-karso nya-wise-whitehead/.

Wilder, Craig Steven. *Ebony and Ivy: Race, Slavery, and the Troubled History of America's Universities*. New York: Bloomsbury, 2013.

Wilson, Sherrée. "They Forgot Mammy Had a Brain." In *Presumed Incompetent: The Intersections of Race and Class for Women in Academia*, edited by Gabriella Gutiérrez y Muhs, Yolanda Flores Niemann, Carmen G. González, and Angela P. Harris, 65–77. Boulder: University of Colorado Press, 2012.

Wilson, Valerie, and William Rogers III. "Black-White Wage Gaps Expand with Rising Wage Inequality." Economic Policy Institute, September 20, 2016. https://www.epi.org/publication /black-white-wage-gaps-expand-with-rising-wage-inequality/.

Wingfield, Aida Harvey. "Women are Advancing in the Workplace, but Women of Color Still Lag Behind." Brookings, October 2020. https://www.brookings.edu/essay/women-are-advancing-in -the-workplace-but-women-of-color-still-lag-behind/.

Wrench, John, and Edgar Hassan. *Ambition and Marginalisation: A Qualitative Study of Underachieving Young Men of Afro-Caribbean Origin*, DfEE Research Series no. 31. London, DfEE, 1996.

Wright, Cecile, Sonia Thompson, and Yvonne Channer. "Out of Place: Black Women Academics in British Universities." *Women's History Review* 16, no. 2 (June 2007): 145–62, https://doi.org/10 .1080/09612020601048704.

Wright, Michelle. "Others-from-Within from Without: Afro-German Subject Formation and the Challenge of a Counter-Discourse." *Callaloo* 26, no. 2 (January 2003): 296–305.

Yep, Gust A. "My Three Cultures: Navigating the Multicultural Identity Landscape." In *Intercultural Communication: Experiences and Contexts*, edited by Judith N. Martin, Lisa A. Flores, and Thomas K. Nakayama. Boston: McGraw-Hill, 2002.

Young, Jemimah Li, and Dorothy E. Hines. "Promotion while Pregnant and Black." In *Presumed Incompetent II: Race, Class, Power, and*

Resistance of Women in Academia, edited by Yolanda Flores
Niemann, Gabriella Gutiérrez y Muhs, and Carmen G.
González, 73–80. Boulder: University of Colorado Press, 2020.

Zambrana, Ruth E. *Toxic Ivory Towers: The Consequences of Work Stress
on Underrepresented Minority Faculty*. New Brunswick, NJ:
Rutgers University Press, 2018.

CONTRIBUTORS

ANONYMOUS—The anonymous authors are four Black women who were born in Germany and wish to remain anonymous. Because they are at various stages in their careers and are situated within predominantly white higher education institutions and precollegiate entities, writing their truths puts them in precarious positions. They have published their research and presented their work via various journals, publishers, and professional associations.

CÉCILE ACCILIEN is professor of African and African diaspora studies and former chair of the Interdisciplinary Studies Department at Kennesaw State University in Kennesaw, Georgia. She is the author of *Rethinking Marriage in Francophone African and Caribbean Literatures*. She has also coedited and contributed to various collections of essays, including *Revolutionary Freedoms: A History of Survival, Strength, and Imagination in Haiti*, and *Just Below South: Intercultural Performance in the Caribbean and the U.S. South*. She has published articles in the *Journal of Haitian Studies*; *Women, Gender, and Families of Color*; *Revue française*; *Southern Quarterly*; and *Diaspora in Caribbean Art*. She recently coedited *Teaching Haiti: Creating New* and has a forthcoming monograph *Bay lodyans: Haitian Popular Film Culture* (SUNY Press). She is chair of the Editorial Board of the journal *Women, Gender and Families of Color* and president elect of the Haitian Studies Association.

ABENA AMPOFOA ASARE is associate professor of Africana studies and history at Stony Brook University. Her research and writing span questions of human rights, citizenship, and transformative justice in Africa and the African diaspora. She is the author of *Truth without Reconciliation: A Human Rights History of Ghana*.

PRISCA ANUFORO, DNP, RN, is the executive director of the School of Nursing at Kean University. She received her BSN and MSN in Transcultural Nursing Administration from Kean University and her DNP in Nursing Leadership from Fairleigh Dickinson University. She is nationally certified as a Transcultural Nurse Leader (CTN-A). Engaged in nursing practice and education for over thirty years, Dr. Anuforo has taught students at all levels of education. Her research interests include holistic nursing education and practice, women's rights and health issues, widowhood, transcultural nursing, and interprofessional education and practice. She is a member of the New Jersey State Nurses Association, Nigerian Nurses Association in North America, Transcultural Nursing Society, and Sigma Theta Tau International, Lambda Iota Chapter.

LITTISHA A. BATES is the inaugural associate dean for Inclusive Excellence and Community Partnership in the College of Arts and Sciences at the University of Cincinnati and faculty in the Department of Sociology with an affiliation in the Department of Africana Studies. She received both her MA and PhD in sociology from Arizona State University. Her research focuses on the intersection of race/ethnicity and poverty on educational outcomes. She is also interested in how family processes impact educational outcomes. As associate dean, Dr. Bates oversees human resources for the college and is responsible for leading the college to be a more inclusive, equitable, socially just space through programming, initiatives, and policies. She currently serves as president of the Association of Black Sociologist.

ROBIN PHYLISIA CHAPDELAINE is associate professor and director of undergraduate studies in the History Department at Duquesne University and author of *The Persistence of Slavery: An Economic History of Child Trafficking in Nigeria*. Dr. Chapdelaine holds a PhD in women's and gender history and African history from Rutgers University, and her research addresses the history of child labor, global slavery, marriage practices, and adoption. She is currently working on a human trafficking textbook and her second monograph, which promises to offer a gendered and religious analysis of labor migration from Nigeria to the former Spanish colony Fernando Pó during the twentieth century.

ASHLEY D. CLEMONS is assistant professor of African American literature at California Polytechnic State University in San Luis Obispo, California. Ashley earned her PhD in English from the University of Florida. Her research interests include contemporary African American literature, Black women writers, Black Midwest literature, Afrofuturism, and Black labor stories. Ashley conducts archival research in the University of

Virginia Library's Mary & David Harrison Institute for American History, Literature, and Culture. Her current book project is "Keepin' It 313: A Women's History of Contemporary Black Music and Art in Detroit."

KRISTIAN CONTRERAS, PhD, is a Black feminist dreamer, educator, and recent alumna of Syracuse University's School of Education. Her dissertation (#NotYourMammyStudy) explored the ways Black women are expected to embody the colonial Mammy trope while learning in and laboring for White Serving Institutions in American higher education. Her work focuses on honoring the ways in which Black women survive, create, love, learn, and resist despite the presumed deficits associated with our sociopolitical identities. Kristian's experiences as a first-generation Afro-Dominican-Guyanese daughter of Caribbean immigrants and Scholastics Book Fair afficionado form the foundation of an ever-present curiosity: Who holds the power in telling our stories? Her research merges social justice education, Black feminist fire, ancestral lullabies and blueprints of refusal, a love for art as activism, and critical race theory's power of storytelling to transform her curious daydreams into liberatory realities.

SAYAM DAVIS, using a pseudonym that pays homage to the incredible women in her family, is a tenured professor at an R1 institution. She has published extensively on race and language. She spends much of her time and energy trying to make her institution, her field, and her surrounding environment a better place for those with the fewest resources and the least amount of power.

JESSICA A. FRIPP is associate dean of the College of Behavioral Health and Sciences at Austin Peay State University. Prior to becoming a counselor educator, Dr. Fripp served as a mental health counselor for ten years, where her primary population included low-income communities, where engagement with treatment was lacking. Her training, development, and scholarship efforts include strategies to increase counseling engagement through identifying cultural factors that prevent Black people from seeking services.

WHITNEY GASKINS is the assistant dean of inclusive excellence and community engagement in the University of Cincinnati College of Engineering and Applied Science, the only African American female currently teaching in the College of Engineering faculty. She earned her PhD in biomedical engineering/engineering education. As assistant dean, Dr. Gaskins has revamped the summer bridge program to increase student support and retention and developed and strengthened partnerships with local area school districts to aid in the pathway to college. She currently serves as the DEI co-lead for the Ohio Department of Higher Education's transfer credit program.

EVA M. GIBSON is assistant professor at Austin Peay State University in the Department of Psychological Science and Counseling. Prior to becoming a counselor educator, she served eleven years in the public school system as a licensed school counselor. Her research areas include school counseling, social justice, and advocacy.

CASSANDRA GONZALEZ is assistant professor in the Department of Criminal Justice and Criminology at Sam Houston State University. She researches Black women's and girls' experiences with sex trafficking and gendered violence and their navigation of the criminal legal system. She has published on the necessity of love in research and the courtroom experiences of Black women and girl survivors of sex trafficking.

NYASHA M. GURAMATUNHUCOOPER, PhD, is an award-winning leadership educator, consultant, and speaker whose body of work reflects a commitment to helping individuals and organizations discover and use their leadership capacity to create and nurture shared spaces where members can thrive as leaders, learners, and innovators. She works with individuals, organizations across industries, and community partners to facilitate leadership development rooted in cultural humility, global mindset, and a comprehensive understanding of diversity, equity, and inclusion as leadership work. With extensive experience in global learning in higher education, Nyasha has served as associate professor of leadership studies at Our Lady of the Lake University and as assistant and associate professor of leadership studies at Kennesaw State University.

ANNETTE KAPPERT focuses on educational leadership and policy— equity and social diversity. Her research examines historical and postcolonial narratives of educational inequality, with particular reference to the impact of personal and professional experiences on learning and teaching in higher education. Autoethnographic by nature, she draws on Black female educators' experiences to critique "inclusive policies," educator development, equity, and the influence of epistemological beliefs on persistent achievement gaps. She is particularly interested in further developing ideas about Black cultural capital, ways of knowing, autoethnographic encounters, and the diversification of leadership.

FELICE FERGUSON KNIGHT is assistant professor of history at The Citadel: The Military College of South Carolina. She received a PhD in African

American History from the Ohio State University. Her publications include academic book reviews and contributions to a five-volume oral history anthology entitled *Champions of Civil and Human Rights in South Carolina*. She serves as chair of The Citadel's Universities Studying Slavery Committee. Her previous roles include codirector of The Citadel's Truth, Racial Healing and Transformation Center and chair of the history and culture subcommittee of the City of Charleston Special Commission on Equity, Inclusion, and Racial Conciliation.

ELIZABETH LOCKE, PhD, is executive director and associate professor of physical therapy in the School of Physical Therapy within the College of Health Professions and Human Services at Kean University. She was the first African American appointed to a full-time core physical therapy faculty position in the School of Rehabilitation Sciences at Old Dominion University and served as its director of clinical education for twenty-six years. She received the University Designation of Faculty Emerita of Rehabilitation Sciences by the Old Dominion University Board of Visitors in 2020. Dr. Locke earned her PhD in health services research from Old Dominion University. She is a national NEDIC commissioner for the American Council of Academic Physical Therapy and is listed in Who's Who in America, Who's Who in Health Sciences Education, and Who's Who among Students in American Universities and Colleges.

LEANNA T. LUNEY is a visiting assistant professor of African and African American studies at Berea College. Her research and scholarship centralize Black girls', womxn's, and femmes' lived experiences in educational institutions using theoretical and praxis-driven frameworks of Black feminism and decolonization. Dr. Luney specifically focuses on Black girls', womxn's, and femmes' practices of coping and care using intersectional ethnographic research methodologies to create and implement equitable policy in P-20 educational systems. Her work has been published in the *Journal of Diversity in Higher Education, The Griot: The Journal of African American Studies, Research Issues in Contemporary Education*, and book volumes.

TIFFANY MONIQUE QUASH is the qualitative/survey research methodologist for American University in the Center for Teaching, Research & Learning. She earned her PhD from Indiana University–Bloomington in leisure behavior with a minor in higher education. Dr. Quash's research interests include the intentional use of de/colonizing language when addressing aquatic accomplishments and barriers centered on the experiences of Black Womxn.

MYRA ROBINSON holds a PhD in social work from Yeshiva University. She has worked over thirty-eight years in social work practice, has a clinical social work license (LCSW), a clinical social work supervisor license, and is a certified clinical professional. Her practice has been in the fields of child and adult services. Dr. Robinson is a full-time faculty member in the clinical specialization area at Kean University and served as the director of the Graduate Social Work Program. She has also worked for the East Orange School District and as a social worker with the Veterans Medical Center in the psychiatry and substance abuse units. She is a certified clinical trauma professional (CCTP) and has worked extensively with individuals experiencing PTSD and has conducted numerous workshops on the topics of trauma and her work with urban clients.

HEATHER I. SCOTT, PhD, is the assistant dean for inclusive leadership curriculum and cocurriculum, SUMMIT, at Agnes Scott College. She has been awarded numerous fellowships to advance research in the areas of inclusive excellence and leadership and has been named as associate faculty for Kennesaw State University's Center for Africana Studies, a Summit Fellow at Agnes Scott College, and a Division of Inclusive Excellence and Diversity Faculty Fellow at Kennesaw State University. Her research focuses on women and leadership, with lines of inquiry in higher education administration, Black women in the professoriate, global education equity, and leadership identity development of girls and women.

KIMBERLY M. STANLEY is assistant professor of ethnic studies in the School of Cultural and Critical Studies at Bowling Green State University. She is currently working on her manuscript, "Pulling Down the House and Tearing Up the Yard, which examines the discursive constructions of Black masculinity within the Black press, 1920s–60s. She received her PhD from Indiana University–Bloomington in 2015 with dual degrees in history and American studies. Dr. Stanley is the caretaker of her daughter as well as a four-year old grandson.

MICHELLE DIONNE THOMPSON, JD, PhD, is a historian and taught at City College of New York in New York City. She teaches survey courses about Caribbean history and seminars about the African diaspora and women in the African diaspora. She is currently writing her monograph entitled "Jamaica's Accompong Maroons, 1838–1905: Retooled Resistance for Continued Existence." She also coaches women in law and academia to reach personal and professional goals sanely. You can find out more at https://resistantvision.com.

CHRISTINE THORPE is a certified wellness coach and health education specialist with over twenty-two years of experience in higher education and the health and human services field. Her interests and research publications focus on women's health, health disparities, historical traumas, holistic nutrition, patient navigation, motivational interviewing, health literacy, and enterprising family wellness. Dr. Thorpe is founder of Stronger Tomorrow LLC, a workplace wellness company that serves to influence and reshape wellness in organizations through the lens of diversity, equity, and inclusion, and the codirector of Navigating Health Services (NHS), an organization that represents a movement to transform the health sector and to positively impact the lives of the medically underserved in Jamaica and across the Caribbean region through education, advocacy, and support. Dr. Thorpe is the author of *Living beyond the Façade: Inside the Health and Wealth Practices of Americans of African Descent* and holds a doctor of education in health education from Teachers College, Columbia University.

PAULA W. WHITE is assistant professor at Austin Peay State University in the Department of Languages and Literature and coordinator of women's and gender studies in the College of Arts and Letters. She specializes in African American literature and Black women's studies. Her research focuses on twentieth-century Black women writers within Black, Southern, and Queer genres.

INDEX

academic writing and publication: Academic Writers' Meetup, 87; affinity groups in academia as support for, 135; Black women's writing, legacy of, 29–30; legacy of Black women's writing, 29–30; publishing without tenure, 86–89; "publish or perish" mantra, 34; requirements and revision, 107–9. *See also* transnational lens for Black women's writing

Accilien, Cécile, 44, 49, 53n6, 78, 219, 223

Adichie, Chimamanda Ngozi, 196, 202n7

adjunct positions: business ownership in conjunction with, 11, 83–90; invisibility of Black faculty, 95; working in, vs. tenure-track, 31–39

administrative work, tenure work in tandem with, 11–12, 91–103. *See also* diversity, equity, and inclusion

adoption studies, on identity and belonging, 213–15

affinity groups: and AAEC, 131, 139–41; Black Student Union formation and practicing joy, 211–13, 216; for "communities of resistance," 12, 131–32;

and imbalance of service requirements between white and Black faculty, 130–31; individual perspectives on, 132–37; and invisibility vs. visibility, 138; and marronage as survival technique, 196–97, 200, 201; peer-to-peer counseling, 85–86, 105–6, 112–13; and performativity, 138; and representation, 138–39; "sister girls"/"Sistah Network" for backs of steel, 166, 174–75. *See also* backs of steel

African American Employee Council (AAEC), 131, 139–41

"Afrocentrism and the Afrocentric Method" (Kershaw), 206

agency and resistance: "All the 'Africans' Are Men, All the 'Sistas' Are 'American,' but Some of Us Resist: Realizing African Feminism(s) as an Africological Research Methodology," 206; "communities of resistance," 12, 131–32; marronage as refusing additional work, 44, 49, 53n6, 198–200; for post-tenure career progression, 12, 107, 110, 114, 116; prioritization for agency, 84,